BIBLE GEMS
from
JERUSALEM

History and Theology in the Feasts of Israel

Lesley Ann Richardson

WESTBOW
P R E S S®
A DIVISION OF THOMAS NELSON
& ZONDERVAN

Scripture taken from the New King James Version®. Copyright © 1982 by Thomas Nelson. Used by permission. All rights reserved.

WestBow Press books may be ordered through booksellers or by contacting:

WestBow Press
A Division of Thomas Nelson & Zondervan
1663 Liberty Drive
Bloomington, IN 47403
www.westbowpress.com
1 (866) 928-1240

Back cover photograph by Lyle Stafford, *Victoria Times Colonist*

ISBN: 978-1-5127-6872-5 (sc)
ISBN: 978-1-5127-6873-2 (hc)
ISBN: 978-1-5127-6871-8 (e)

Library of Congress Control Number: 2016920872

Print information available on the last page.

WestBow Press rev. date: 01/04/2017

This book is dedicated to my mother
Marie
With much love

Table of Contents

Foreword

Lesley Richardson is a great communicator simply because she's first and foremost a great lover. This can only be said for writers and teachers that are truly in love with both their subjects and their audiences. Lesley's profound insights into the Jewish Feasts are conveyed with simple clarity, always straight from the heart. This masterful style of communication reflects her own life-long pursuit of the Living God, as well as her inexhaustible fascination with Israel and the Jewish people. Despite her keen intellect, we are never bogged down with dry minutiae. Instead, Lesley makes the Bible come alive through her personal passion and warm first-hand experiences with both The Book and the People of the Book. Her warm and very human approach creates sparkling gems of revelation that shine through on every page. Most Christians are aware of our need for God and the importance of seeking after Him. Through Lesley's revelations on the biblical Feasts of Israel we will encounter an even more astounding truth. As it turns out, the Wonderful God of the Bible, the Holy One of Israel, deeply longs to fellowship and meet with us as well!

Pastor David N. Decker
Jerusalem, Israel

Preface

This series of articles was written over the course of a year spent in Jerusalem, where my husband and I have resided for the past decade. They examine different aspects of the feasts of Israel and the church, blending together history, theology, geography and biblical narrative. While each piece is self-contained and may stand on its own, certain themes may also be detected weaving their way through the text. The articles do assume some knowledge of scripture of both Testaments, but should also appeal to any thinking person who is interested in the foundational text of our western civilization - the Bible. This is the compendium of books containing prophecy and history, gospel and law, narrative and poetry, which more than any other sounds the deep notes of human existence and ascends the heights of revelation.

The articles are also written from the point of view of a Christian who has been "grafted in" to the fruitful olive tree of Israel, and with the intention of stirring the reader to a fresh awareness of the richness of the spiritual heritage bequeathed to us through our Jewish brethren. The feasts of Israel provide the prophetic template for the festivals of the church year, and offer a wealth of meaning to the Christian who delves into their symbolism. They also unfold vast resources for understanding the Jewish Messiah, who said to the Woman of Samaria, "Salvation is of the Jews" (John 4:22). Yet although Jesus was a Hebrew of the Hebrews, at the same time He cannot be confined to any particular time or place, but is the true universal man whose message speaks to the hearts of every tribe, tongue, nation and people.

From earliest times the church has also confessed the inseparable unity of the Old Testament (Tanach) and the New, as formulated in the well known axiom: "In the Old Testament the New is concealed, in the New the Old is revealed" (Augustine). The Bible is one indivisible whole, with each and every part pointing to Christ, a fact which more than anything else bears evidence of its divine authorship. So it is that, although I have tried to ensure that the writings are precise in their scholarship, I have avoided questions related to historical criticism of the biblical text, and accept the scriptures as they have come down to us at the present day. Ultimately each of the writings is intended to set forth some new facet of the truth given in the Messiah, Jesus.

In the articles I have also attempted to evoke an awareness of the singular interest and beauty of the land of Israel. I have had the privilege of traveling through the length and breadth of the country - over the rugged Judean mountains, across stony deserts and down to the lowest valley on earth where the Jordan slips softly into the Dead Sea. We have made our way through the heartland of Samaria where the hills are covered with vines and groves of olives, their leaves silver in the breeze, gazed with wonder across the vast flat plain of Megiddo, the scene of so many battles, and floated over the gentle waves of the Sea of Galilee. To the west, the wooded slopes of Carmel have provided challenges for climbing; we have also noted where the long mountain ridge thrusts like the prow of a ship into the ocean, there on the long coastline lapped by the everlasting blue waters of the Mediterranean.

However, it is not so much the physical allure of these scenes which strikes the onlooker who is well versed in the scriptures. Rather, the eye everywhere meets with places which bring to mind biblical memories, so that, gazing over the sundrenched beauty of the landscape there rises up visions of the illustrious events and stirring deeds of the past, which reverberate down through the ages into our present time and forged the world in which we live. Here it is that the patriarchs walked, the prophets declaimed, kings and armies clashed; but, above all, this is the landscape which served as a background to the Messiah's presence and miracles. And thus in travelling through the land it is as if we were reading the immortal pages of a great book in which these episodes are recounted.

But it is the sacred city of Jerusalem, arched by the blue dome of heaven, her stones golden in the sunlight, where the rabbis believe God is closest, where His presence lingers in the air. The idea of the City of Gold - *Yerushalayim Shel Zahav* - at the heart of the earth is of divine origin: "'This is what the Sovereign Lord says: 'This is Jerusalem: I have set her in the midst of the nations and the countries all around her'" (Ezekiel 5:5). The city is a dazzling mix of ancient and new, of a hi-tech society and followers of ancient customs who remain true to the ways of their forefathers, the patriarchs of the nation, Moses and David. Today, almost a million Jews, Arabs, Christians and expatriates make their home in the city, while every year new immigrants from Africa, Europe and the ends of the earth are drawn to join the native Jerusalemites. On the narrow streets of the Old City, or in the modern shopping malls, religious and secular rub shoulders; they also mingle at the *shuk* on Friday mornings to buy fresh produce then rush home before the siren sounds for Shabbat at sundown.

At the same time, Jerusalem remains a continual focus of world attention, for this city, set like a jewel in her mountain fastness, continues to engage the nations with her magnetic appeal. The three Abrahamic faiths – Judaism, Christianity and Islam – all consider the city sacred. For Christians, Jerusalem is the place where Jesus walked, preached and healed, where He shed His blood and rose from the dead. For the Jews, this is where David and his descendants established a great kingdom and built two holy Temples - the irreplaceable centerpoint of their history and faith. According to the Bible, Jerusalem also holds a special place in the heart of God, who identified Jerusalem as the city He had chosen for Himself and desired as His dwelling place, where His presence would rest forever (Psalm 132:13-14).

According to Jewish tradition Jerusalem has more than 70 names, which include: *Zion, City of our Solemnities, Perfection of Beauty, Faithful City*, and *Sought After*. But the most common and favored interpretation of her Hebrew name is that it comes from a conjunction of two words: *ir*, which means city, and *shalem*, which means peace, so that *Yerushalayim*, Jerusalem, is thus the City of Peace. Perhaps the most beautiful accolade comes from the modern Israeli poet Naomi Shemer, who writes that the name Jerusalem "scorches the lips like a seraph's kiss". All these names are also prophecies of the Jerusalem that is yet to come and the biblical writings indicate that the prominence of the holy city set on a hill will only continue to increase.

As this is not primarily intended as an academic work I have avoided the use of footnotes; however, I have included further notes on each chapter at the end of the book, giving information on sources. I must here also acknowledge my indebtedness to three outstanding writers of the Christian tradition: the two great Hebrew Christians, Alfred Edersheim and Adolph Saphir, and the English preacher Alexander MacLaren, whose biblical exegesis is incomparable. Their influence will be evident throughout the text, but I have also had my thinking and theological understanding enhanced by numerous other authors, both Jewish and Christian, from the days of the early church to the present. So it is that I have tried to play the part of that wise scribe whom Jesus commended: bringing treasures new and old from his storehouse (Matthew 13:52).

Jerusalem is a city which is endlessly fascinating, and it is my hope and prayer that the reader will be as enriched in reading these small articles as I have been in composing them. It has been more than anything else an attempt to express my own love song to Jerusalem, on her lonely heights, straddling the nation. As David requested: *"Pray for the peace of Jerusalem: May they prosper who love you."*

Lesley Ann Richardson
Rosh Hashanah, October 2016/5777

PASSOVER AND EASTER

The Song of the Exiles

●●●

The young man in a dark suit, with a face which might have been carved on the walls of an ancient palace, stands beneath the bridal canopy and lifts his foot. The guests at the wedding hold their collective breath - and crash! The bridegroom's heel comes down and the crystal is shattered - then bride and groom step out from the *chuppah* and the joyful mood reasserts itself. This ritual recalling the destruction of the Temple in Jerusalem has been repeated at countless Jewish weddings over the centuries. At this crowning moment of his life, on the night in which the bridegroom makes the most heartfelt of vows, there is one which transcends it and to which he gives solemn utterance as he breaks the glass:

"If I forget thee, O Jerusalem, may my right hand forget its cunning.
If I do not remember thee, let my tongue cleave to the roof of my mouth;
if I do not set Jerusalem above my highest joy" (Psalm 137:5,6)

What has caused Zion to become so powerful an image in a whole people's collective mind and imagination? According to the Hebrew Scriptures, God identified Jerusalem as the city He desired as His dwelling place, and entrusted it to a people He had chosen for Himself from among the nations. The story of the children of Israel is inseparably woven into the story of Jerusalem, and the Bible introduces the father of the Jewish people as well as the Holy City in its first book, Genesis. In the mists of time, some 4,000 years ago, God called a man named Abraham from Ur of the Chaldees, pledging to lead him to a land which would be given to his descendants as an everlasting possession (Genesis

3

13:14-17). After his long journey to Canaan the patriarch was met and blessed by a priest of the Most High God, Melchizedek, who was king of Salem, the City of Peace which later would be called Jerusalem. In the same region lay the mountain called Moriah, where Abraham made his mournful journey from Hebron to offer up his only son, Isaac, before his upraised hand was stayed by the angel.

The shepherd tribes descending from Abraham experienced many vicissitudes before settling in the land the patriarch had trodden: years of slavery under a foreign power, decades of wandering in the desert, struggles for possession of the promised land. The country through which the Hebrews drove their herds and flocks was at first less developed than the highly civilized empires to north and south; during the chaotic period of the judges the tribes of Israel also experienced centuries of wars against their smaller neighbors. Then, around 1000 BC, a young shepherd king set his sights on a small city ensconced in the central hill region. Capturing it from the Jebusites, David established Jerusalem as the capital of a united Hebrew kingdom and there led a procession in song and dance to bring the Ark of the Covenant, central symbol of God's presence in Israel, to reside in the Tabernacle. David's son Solomon later realized his father's dream of building a house to God in the midst of Jerusalem. Once the Temple was constructed on Mount Moriah, and lavishly adorned, the Golden Age of Hebrew life and literature at the time of the great kings began.

During this period, a religious liturgy and a culture was created in Israel which, although it drew from surrounding influences, yet far surpassed them. The music of the Temple owed its origin to David, the "sweet psalmist of Israel", who was not only a poet and composer but also made musical instruments *to be used when he gave thanks to God, saying, 'His love endures forever'"* (2 Chronicles 7:6). David established an orchestra and chorus for performing sacred music during the sacrificial rites, choosing 4,000 Levites as singers. At the dedication of Solomon's Temple, when the priests and the congregation of Israel assembled before the Ark and the musical service began, *"the house of the Lord was filled with a cloud; so that the priests could not continue ministering because of the cloud: for the glory of the Lord filled the house of God"* (2 Chronicles 5:13,14).

The psalms which were so central a feature of the praise offering in the Temple have been sung and recited in countless settings since that time, and bequeathed a loftiness of thought and spiritual aspiration to succeeding generations. The legendary splendor of King Solomon's Temple has also been retold throughout the ages - but its glory was not, alas, to endure. After the death of Solomon, the 12 tribes were divided into two kingdoms. Two of the southern tribes, Judah and Benjamin, remained loyal to the House of David centered in Jerusalem, while the ten northern tribes, retaining the name of Israel, were ruled by a succession of dynasties. However, in the eight century BC the Assyrians swept through the northern kingdom and the peoples were taken into captivity. Judah managed to resist the Assyrian threat, but her turn came in the sixth century BC when the Babylonian armies under King Nebuchadnezzar breached the walls of Jerusalem and burned the Temple, destroyed the city and sent the leading citizens into exile in Babylon. It was there that the captives' sentiments of yearning for their homeland were transmuted into a psalm, the 137th of the Psalter, and one of the most poignant elegies ever written.

"By the rivers of Babylon, there we sat down; there we wept when we remembered Zion ...". These famous opening words suggest the contrast between their new home and the city they had left behind, and the painful impression this produced upon the hearts and minds of the exiles. The great metropolis of Babylon, located on the broad flat plain of Shinar with the sinuous Euphrates flowing through its midst, differed so greatly from Jerusalem in her rugged mountain fastness. In their native land the olives and vines growing in the hills and valleys provided shelter from the burning noonday sun; here a torpid heat favored the cultivation of luxurious formal gardens and terraces. How alien appeared

to them also the colossal ziggurat and temple of the Babylonian deity Marduk, with its seven stories seeming to aspire to heaven! And so it was that as the captives sat down beside one of Babylon's many streams, the flow of the waters seemed to be in sympathy with their tears. It was only now, in their exile, that the understanding of all they had lost was inexorably borne in upon them, the remembrance of their city adorned with its beautiful Temple where they participated in the solemn feasts and daily sacrifices, where they had seen the tribes of Israel come up - but which now lay in ruins.

Over the abundant streams the willows bent low and trailed their long slender branches, seeming to accentuate the captives' mood of melancholy and drawing forth the most plaintive line in all literature: "*We hanged our harps upon the willows in the midst thereof*". The song of the Levites in the Temple was renowned – so much so that when they arrived as exiles the Babylonians asked them to *"Sing for us one of the songs of Zion"*. But the request evoked a wondering response from the Hebrews: *" How,"* they asked, *"can we sing the Lord's song in a strange land?"* - how could they raise their voices in one of their sacred melodies for an audience which could never comprehend the deep springs of their music? The very thought led the exiles to a fresh access of resolution and the utterance of personal vows of great intensity in verses 5 and 6: that it were better far to lose all skill in lyre and harp, all divine gift of song, than to forget Jerusalem, the memory of which was to be treasured above all.

Thus this very psalm in which the question is asked, "How can we sing?," itself becomes a song, an opaline thing built up of tears and the quintessential expression of exile. Yet the poet who wrote with such heart-melting pathos could also smite sternly with his pen: Babylon, that ruthless empire which stood for everything opposed to God and His kingdom, was itself to be destroyed - a prophecy which was literally fulfilled. The conqueror of Babylon was the Persian king Cyrus, who permitted the people of Judah to return and rebuild Jerusalem and its

Temple after their 70-year captivity. Yet for many centuries Jerusalem continued to languish under foreign domination, despite a glorious period of independence under the Maccabees, until in the first century BC the city came under the yoke of the expanding Roman Empire and received from her new masters the client-king who came to be known as Herod the Great.

The Jerusalem to which came Jesus of Nazareth in the first century of the present era had achieved a splendor which rivaled the other great cities of the Roman world, due in no small measure to the extensive building programs undertaken by the Idumean king. Crowning her mountain heights lay the city built "compact together", with crowded streets, squares and markets, and adorned with cedar palaces. But high above all rose the Temple, surrounded by its vast platform and encircled by stately pillars, a magnificent edifice of marble and gold which sparkled in the sunlight, the apotheosis of earthly glory or so it seemed to the many thousands who assembled at the great feasts. For the Christian, however, it is the presence of Jesus which more than all has cast a hallowed light about the city and the House of God. The New Testament depicts Him attending the festivals, teaching, preaching and healing in the streets and Temple porches, withdrawing at times to the cool shade of Gethsemane. But still further, for His followers, this is the city where He laid down His life for all humanity, and as such Jerusalem has become a name which is precious beyond all others.

Some forty years after that great Personality came to Jerusalem with His message of love and ushered in a new era of history, Jerusalem and the Temple fell under the blow of the Romans; the Jews were then dispersed among the nations of the globe and subjected to oppression and persecution for two millennia. Scattered across different worlds and cultures from that point onward - Greco–Roman, Spanish, Renaissance, Russian and Central European - the Jewish people continued to look toward Jerusalem with ardent longing. The concentration of all thought and liturgy upon the Holy City and its glorious Temple provided them with the moral power to resist assimilation, so that the years of separation actually strengthened the bond between the Jewish people and Zion. The oft-repeated pledge "Next year in Jerusalem!" expressed the hopes which burned ever brighter as the weary centuries stretched out through Crusades, pogroms, and expulsions, until the culminating experience of the Holocaust.

In an historical development which reads more strangely than fiction, this second exile ended for the Jews with the miraculous rebirth of Israel in 1948. Despite inestimable losses and unimaginable suffering, the Jewish people were back in their land and one year later Israel's government declared Jerusalem the capital of the new nation. As her first prime minister, David Ben-Gurion, explained to the UN: "Twice in the history of our nation were we driven out of Jerusalem" ... yet during 2,500 years of wandering among the nations, the Jewish people "faithfully adhered to the vow made by the first exiles by the waters of Babylon not to forget Jerusalem." The sound of the harp floats again in the air of Jerusalem, songs are heard in the cities of Judah and the voice of bridegroom and bride, just as the prophet foretold; while during the festivals in Jerusalem the nations gather and the choir and orchestra raise their voices to the Lord. In the Knesset building, the seat of the Government of Israel in Jerusalem, a large wall mosaic by the Jewish artist Marc Chagall depicts Psalm 137; the scene is dominated by a large lighted menorah, a symbol of the harps that once hung in the willows, but now the golden flames flicker with light and hope.

Thousands of years after its composition, Psalm 137 has also remained one of the church's melodies and during Lent is added to the liturgy in the Orthodox Church as a song which crystallizes the spiritual condition of humanity - for the story of the exile of the Jews in Babylon is the story of all people writ large. The longing for Zion symbolizes the aspiration for a larger realm of truth and freedom, all the goodness intended for humans at the beginning, the gift of heaven bestowed by a love beyond conception. But the psalm also evokes a sense of loss and fragmentation as it awakens an apprehension of the vast preciousness we have forfeited; therefore its music haunts us and we cannot push it aside. And the willows on which the harps are hanged symbolize the tears and longing of all generations, which sound in the moan of ocean waves, the wind through the trees, the call of the dove. Then God listens to our lament and makes a way back through the impossible wilderness, a stern journey, but one which has springs and fountains gushing in the desolate places. The psalm is for the whole of our lives, accompanies us all our days and draws us back continually to the deep center and source of our being, even as it brings an echo of eternity washing translucent in our ears.

But the yearning for the heavenly Zion does not negate the earthly Jerusalem which stands forever as sign and symbol - her towers, bulwarks and palaces, about which we can walk, with prayer on our lips and blessing in our hearts. Around her are encircling mountains, and she stands fast on her heights, this city built for love and unity, where we may catch a glimpse of a vision of peace that is so strong, steadfast and true that it can never more be shaken - this city of peace drenched in so much blood and fire and yet rising again, where David's God-inspired vision of worship and *shalom* shall yet come to pass.

The King Comes to His City

From earliest times Jerusalem has possessed an allure, not only for pilgrims, but for the many dignitaries and heads of state who have come to her over the centuries. During the biblical era, stories of kings and rulers who were drawn to the city were also recounted in the scriptures. Some came on missions of peace, attracted by tales heard in their own lands of the splendor of the house of David or Israel's lofty monotheism; in this way came the Queen of Sheba to visit Solomon, and departed so overwhelmed by the glory of his reign that "there was no spirit left in her" (1 Kings 10:5). But many others who came to Jerusalem were bound on conquest.

The city David took from the Jebusites around 1000 BC was not an obvious choice for the new capital of a united Israel. Lifted high above sea level in the central hill country of Judea, and far from major trade routes, it did not appear to be a strategic location. However the rugged terrain of the city was a definite military advantage, especially important when, throughout the course of her long history, Jerusalem became a desirable prize over which some of the world's most famous empires fought. The city was surrounded on the west, south, and east by deep ravines and beyond these were mountains and desert - but she was not impregnable. To the north the narrow table-land of Judea continues for a number of miles before breaking into the tumbled landscape of Samaria, and the prophet Isaiah describes how easily a foreign army could advance by this open route to come and "shake his fist at the mount of the daughter of Zion" (Isaiah 10:32).

This was probably the way taken by Nebuchadnezzar and the armies of Babylon when they came thundering in their chariots to conquer and destroy the city in the sixth century BC. The Syrian generals with their vast cavalries and elephants of war came from this direction also in 160 BC, before the Jewish people were delivered through the inspiring military exploits of the Maccabees. In 64 Pompey marched from the north to the gates of Zion and commenced the long Roman subjugation of the area; he was followed in 37 BC by Herod the Great, who then commenced his momentous reign over Jerusalem. After the time of Jesus, Roman general Titus led his legions along the same route to the great siege which laid Jerusalem waste for the second time in 70 AD; later also came the forces of Islam and the Crusaders. The city whose name means "peace" has experienced perhaps more war, bloodshed and devastation in her 4000 year history than any other in the globe.

For the Christian, the visit to Jerusalem which surpasses all others was that of Jesus when He rode into the city on the back of a donkey just before the Feast of Passover in the early decades of the present era - the so-called Triumphal Entry, and one of the comparatively few events recorded in all four Gospels. His arrival at Jerusalem was in marked contrast to those of the conquerors who came before and after Him - but He came nevertheless with as full an assumption of His rights to rulership of the city.

The Nazarene Rabbi and his disciples had traveled to Jerusalem from Galilee for the Passover feast like many thousands of other pilgrims who came from all over the Mediterranean world. The city was unable to hold them and they overflowed to the surrounding villages; Jesus Himself would stay in Bethany, located on the southeast side of the Mount of Olives. On the Sunday before the Feast commenced, in preparation for His entry, Jesus sent His disciples Peter and John into the nearby village of Bethphage. With a hint of supernatural knowledge He informed them that they would find tied by the side of the road an ass with a colt on which no man had ever sat, and these they were to loose and bring to Him. If any objection was raised, they were to answer, "The Lord has need of him", just as emissaries of a king would assert the royal prerogatives of their master. And as they carried out this commission the disciples discovered that all was as they had been told. They reached Bethphage and saw the colt with its mother by a doorway where two roads met; then as they loosed the animals some of those standing by asked their purpose, and when they answered as directed no further protest was made.

In this small incident was evidenced a remarkable feature of Jesus' ministry as set forth in the New Testament, emblematic of His whole life as lived among His people: the blending of kingly authority with absolute dependence. The Gospels paint Jesus as a Sovereign who owned all things and was heir of all the worlds, but who nevertheless subjected Himself to the goodwill of His subjects and was reliant on them for the supply of His needs. In His hands, however, the small gifts He received were transformed into sources of divine life and blessing. A Galilean boy offered Him five loaves and two fishes and with these He fed the multitudes; the boat from which He preached to the crowds gathered by the seashore was borrowed from local fisherfolk, but then across the waves were carried the words that would never pass away. He had nowhere to lay His head apart from the place provided for Him by loving friends, yet brought the power of resurrection into those homes; even in death He had "no friendly tomb, but what a stranger gave" - but arose from it having conquered the grave. This inseparable mingling of Lordship and humility was the whole, paradoxical manner of Jesus' life upon earth - and now with this small donkey He was to provide a picture that would forever afterwards impact the imagination of the world.

The disciples brought the colt to Jesus, spread their garments over the animal and set Him on it. The festal procession set out on a bright spring day, travelling on the well-known road from Jericho to Jerusalem and passing the villages of Bethany and Bethphage along the way. A large crowd went with Jesus, spreading their cloaks before Him to form a carpet; meanwhile news of the approach of the prophet from Nazareth had also reached the city so that a great multitude went forth to meet Him, waving palm branches and crying "Hosanna". Gradually the long procession, those who went before and those that came after, swept up over the top of the Mount of Olives where began the descent towards Jerusalem. Across the Kidron Valley the many-towered Holy City lay before them, dazzling in the sunlight, and dominating all the great Temple, lavishly rebuilt and adorned by King Herod. As the vista of Jerusalem broke upon their gaze, the whole multitude was swept up into ecstatic praise as if summoning the city to welcome its King: " Blessed is he that comes in the Name of the Lord" (Psalm 118:26).

Luke's Gospel also records words of acclaim from the crowd that echoed the angels' song at Bethlehem on the night Christ was born: *"Peace in heaven and glory in the highest"* (Luke 19:38). It was at this point in Jesus' ministry, then, that the purpose of His Incarnation was to be unfolded, the goal to which all had been directed from the beginning. Jesus' present advent to the city signaled, for those with eyes to see, that now was commencing the train of events leading to the great act of redeeming love which would win reconciliation between heaven and earth, just as the scriptures had foretold. The prophetic praise of the multitudes was unconscious, however, for they were welcoming Jesus as a political Messiah, one who would deliver them from the oppression of their Roman overlords. They dreamed of an earthly kingdom, He of one eternal; they envisioned a throne, He a cross.

Hearing this praise, some of the Pharisees who had mingled with the crowd called to Jesus that He should rebuke His disciples. At that He broke His silence and pointed to the rocks and stones which lay about His pathway, saying that, if the people held their peace, the very stones would cry out. This remarkable response may have contained a reference to the warning given by the prophet Habakkuk that "the stone would cry out from the wall" against those who give "shameful counsel" to their house (Habakkuk 2:10,11). However, one thing was made very clear in Jesus' words: this was a very singular moment in the history of Israel, the long-awaited fulfillment of one of the great Messianic prophecies of the Hebrew Scriptures and manifestly an occasion calling for praise. In his Gospel, Matthew blended the words of Isaiah 62:11 and Zechariah 9:9 to show that it had long ago been predicted that the King of Israel would enter the Holy City in humble fashion and with lowly demeanor:

"Tell the daughter of Zion,
Behold, your King is coming to you,
Lowly, and sitting on a donkey,
A colt, the foal of a donkey" (Matthew 21:5)

When Jesus thus entered the city on this slow-pacing colt, He presented Himself as One who had come in fulfillment of this ancient prophecy, and who moreover was the subject of all the divine promises which had been made to Israel from the beginning. As those that went before and those that followed after Jesus cried Hosanna, or "Save now", it was a symbolic presentation of the fact that the very centerpoint of the ages had been reached; all previous time and history converged upon that regal Figure seated on the gentle animal with the exultant crowd surging about Him, and flowed from Him again.

And yet this was a course of action strangely unlike the rest of Christ's recorded life. During His ministry to that point He had seemed to shun publicity and continually, sternly even, damped down Messianic expectations and fervor; and when the crowds in Galilee who had received the multiplied loaves and fishes wished to make Him king He had withdrawn to the solitude of the hills. Yet now He appeared to suddenly reverse His whole previous mode of conduct, and took a step which was like flinging a lighted spark into a cauldron. At a time when the crowds were gathered in Jerusalem for the Passover and when popular enthusiasm ran highest, He consciously adorned Himself in the robes of prophecy, and planned to fulfill in minute detail the well-known scripture from Zechariah. What was the reason for this marked contrast?

Jesus knew His work of teaching and preaching was drawing to its appointed close and the final great consummation of His ministry lay ahead; there was no further danger that His "hour" would arrive in premature fashion. He felt that the moment had come that He should present Himself solemnly and publicly before the assembled nation as the King and Messiah for whom they waited, and thus compel the issue of their acceptance or rejection of His claim - even though He knew that this would precipitate the end for which He had come. In His heart was also the fervent desire to make one last plea to those who had so consistently refused the evidence of His presence and miracles among them. He had experienced much disappointment and opposition in His mission, but this open declaration reflected the longsuffering in the heart of the Father, who never ceased to plead with His wayward people to turn again to Him. Perhaps with this final appeal they would have their eyes opened to recognize the One of whom their scriptures had borne such minute witness, who was coming to them in such gentleness and humility.

When Jesus came riding into Jerusalem on that singular Palm Sunday, it was more than all else a striking revelation of the character of this King and the nature of His kingdom. The way in which the ancient world conceived of monarchs is clearly to be read in the monuments they have left behind - the sculptured reliefs and paintings of the palaces of Egypt and Assyria, triumphant warriors enthroned in their chariots, loosing their arrows into the heart of their foes and boasting of their victories. But the Gospels sound celestial notes of beatific harmony and peace in describing the coming of this new kind of king, who sent His disciples to find the gentle animal on which He would ride and was set upon it by their loving hands. This is One who came not mounted on a warhorse but on the emblem of meekness and patience, while those who attended

Him were not warriors bearing spears but men and women waving palm branches. The contrast of this kingdom with such a dominion as that of Rome, or of such rulers as the Herods, could not be greater.

Yet here was the true King of Israel, entering His city with love burning in His heart, even while knowing that the shouts of acclamation would soon die away, enthroned as the Prince of Peace according to the picture given by the prophet, its dim outline now fleshed out in living reality. The world had not dreamed of such a gentle Monarch, whose short-lived reign was thus inaugurated, One who only days later would bow His head in the meekness of suffering love and yield up His life for the people who rejected Him.

But the kingdom that is established in humility, rules in gentleness and has for its only weapon the power of love is the kingdom which shall last forever. When the last scroll of history is unrolled by a mighty, irresistible Hand, the omnipotence of meekness and sacrificial love shall be finally vindicated. Throughout the annals of the unfolding ages it has ever been so: the unexpected, surprising victories of the powerless, the inexplicable reversals of the mighty and puissant. Just forty years after Jesus' death, the corrupt house built by the religious leaders in Jerusalem was destroyed - but the Kingdom of God which Jesus proclaimed has spread to every corner of the globe. It is a victory shall be yet more manifest and complete. The prophecy in Zechariah which shows the way of the Messiah as one of lowliness and obedience continues, indicating that His voluntary humiliation would ultimately be translated into universal dominion, "*from the River to the ends of the earth*".

The Runners to the King

· ·

Each year around Passover, the streets of Jerusalem are closed to traffic as runners from near and far descend upon the city to take part in the annual marathon. First held in 2011 under Jerusalem's current mayor, the entrepreneurial Nir Barkat, this has since become a significant international event and drawn a number of elite athletes, for Jerusalem's historical and cultural significance combined with her challenging terrain provide it with a unique attraction. The religious and ethnic diversity of the runners who participate suggest it may be the most cosmopolitan such race in the world.

The route of the marathon is intended to take in important landmarks of the city, both ancient and modern, which visually illuminate Jerusalem's long and eventful past. Starting point for the runners is the Israeli Parliament building, the Knesset; they then continue through various neighborhoods including the Valley of the Cross, Ammunition Hill and the Hebrew University on Mount Scopus before heading toward the majestic walls of the Old City. Entering through Jaffa Gate, they then pound along the narrow cobblestoned streets of the Armenian and Jewish Quarters, where they are granted a glimpse of the Western Wall, the holiest site of Judaism, then pass out through the Zion Gate on to the broad promontory from which may be viewed a sweeping panorama of the mountains cradling the city. Further significant locales are traversed, including the spectacular archaeological park which is the City of David, while hundreds of spectators line the streets to cheer on the runners who have stayed the distance. But it is certain that all who participate are granted moments of special beauty, glimpses of the timeless charm of Jerusalem.

The Road Leading through the Valley of the Cross

Watching the marathon taking place in present-day, twenty-first-century Jerusalem, it's also easy to have one's thoughts turn to biblical stories of running. Many Old Testament figures were superb athletes, such as Asahel, one of King David's mighty men, who was "fleet of foot as a wild gazelle". One particular scriptural passage which deals with the theme of running is especially rich in detail. This is the story found in 2 Samuel 18, relating the way in which news of the death of Absalom, King David's son, is revealed to his father. It comes as the culmination of a long dramatic sequence, full of emotional tension and described with superb aesthetic skill.

Following David's liaison with the beautiful Bathsheba the prophet Nathan informed the king that, as a consequence of his adultery and despite his subsequent repentance, the sword would never leave his house. In rapid succession Tamar, Absalom's lovely sister, was raped by her half-brother Amnon; Absalom then killed Amnon in revenge and finally, in an ultimate act of betrayal, staged a rebellion against his father. David fled from Jerusalem over the Jordan while Absalom entered the city, and a final battle was then waged in the mountains of Ephraim between the king's men and followers of the usurper. David was persuaded to stay behind in his base of Mahanaim during the conflict and as his loyal fighters left the city he entreated the commanders to deal gently with the young man Absalom for his sake. It was a scenario ripe for tragedy.

Absalom was famed throughout Israel for his beauty, in particular for the long thick locks which crowned his head. As the battle turned against his troops in the dense forests of Ephraim, he was riding his mule through the trees and his hair became entangled in the branches of an oak. There he was left hanging, suspended between heaven and earth. David's general Joab, in contravention of the king's orders, swiftly thrust three darts through Absalom's heart. So the battle had been won – but the king's son was dead. How would David receive the news?

The biblical storyteller then, with consummate artistry, focused his dramatic lens on two different locations. In Mahanaim, David was seated "between two gates", anxiously awaiting intelligence concerning the battle; above him on the walls the lookout was posted to descry the first messengers returning from the front. Back at the scene of battle, Joab was giving instructions that the news of victory should be swiftly carried to Mahanaim. One of the young men, Ahimaaz, the son of Zadok, David's priest, was longing to run to the king with the tidings – but Joab was reluctant that he should do so. He judged that a foreigner with no emotional ties to the king was better suited to deliver this equivocal good news and so commanded a Cushite (from Ethiopia) to take the information. But Ahimaaz persisted in his request and Joab finally granted his permission.

And so the race, carrying the momentous news, began. The Cushite had started first, but Ahimaaz took a different route by the plain and approached close to the king's location before his rival. At Mahanaim, the watchman at the gate, scanning the distance intently, perceived the first runner approaching. He called and told the king who expressed his hope that he bore "*good news*". Then the watchman saw the second runner drawing closer; again the king was told, and repeated that it must be "*good news*". Finally, as the first messenger came near, the watchman informed the monarch that his running was "like the running of Ahimaaz, the son of Zadok". The king, upon hearing this, proclaimed his hope for the third time: "This is a good man, and comes with *good news*".

Ahimaaz, winning the race, flung himself on the ground before David. Uttering the word "*Shalom*", or "All is well", he delivered news of the victory in battle. The king, perhaps heartened by this word *shalom* which resonated with his son's name, asked immediately for news of Absalom. Ahimaaz was unable to bring himself to tell what had occurred and equivocated: "I saw a great tumult," he said, "but did not know what it was". The king then asked him to turn aside and the second runner arrived, again declaring he had come with "good news" – the battle has been won. But the driven king burst out with his most pressing question: "Is it well (*shalom*) with the young man Absalom?" And the Cushite finally imparted the news to David – that his son had perished.

What transpired now is one of the most poignant scenes in the biblical narrative – the impact of this terrible "good news".

"Then the king was deeply moved and went up to the chamber over the gate and wept. And as he went he said thus, 'O my son Absalom, my son, my son Absalom - if only I had died in your place! O Absalom, my son, my son!'" (2 Samuel 18:33)

It is David's ultimate and most heart-rending lament. Moreover, it is impossible to reduce this story to a simple matter of reflections on correct behavior in admittedly difficult situations. Admonitions concerning the importance of delivering a message effectively (in relation to the failure of Ahimaaz to inform the king of his son's death) or on the duties of kings to put matters of state above personal feelings of grief (in relation to Joab's subsequent rebuke of the king) fail to do justice to the text. Rather, each word seems freighted with a significance which carries the reader far beyond the present occurrence. The drama of this passage is centered around the bringing of "news/tidings". This word, a translation of the Hebrew verb *basar* meaning "to bear news, publish, preach and show forth", appears in it a number of times. It also forms the subject of one of the most exalted visions of the prophet Isaiah:

"How beautiful upon the mountains are the feet of him who brings good news, who proclaims peace, who brings glad tidings of good things, who proclaims salvation, who says to Zion, 'Your God reigns!'. Your watchmen shall lift up their voices, with their voices they shall sing together, for they shall see eye to eye when the Lord brings back Zion" (Isaiah 52:7-8)

This is not the only thematic connection between the two passages. The verses in Isaiah in the Hebrew speak of the "herald" who is bringing "good news" – and the latter phrase is repeated four times in the Second Samuel episode. The feet of this herald are also specifically mentioned, a focus echoed in the words of David's watchman, who recognizes the stride of the first runner as that of Ahimaaz, then asserts that the second runner "is also a herald". The Isaiah herald is one "announcing peace" – and the first word which Ahimaaz calls out to the waiting king is *"Shalom"*. There is further similarity between the Isaiah watchmen who lift up their voices, and David's lookout who "called out" concerning the runners as they approached. Finally, just as David's lookout "raised his eyes and looked", so in the Isaiah passage it is said that "with their own eyes they [the watchmen] will see that the Lord returns to Zion".

The events occurring in 2 Samuel thus become a kind of prophetic anticipation of the vision of Isaiah, which in turn is a foreshadowing of the greatest "good news" of all. Both passages may be seen as looking forward to the "glad tidings" of the resurrection of Jesus Christ. And then, in their turn, the events of the Gospels provide the key to unlocking the full significance of the story of "The Runners to the King" in 2 Samuel 18 – an incredibly rich vein of exploration. Thus does the Lord shed His amazing light over His word!

The Runners to the Tomb

Each year, Christian pilgrims come to visit Jerusalem in the spring, around Passover/Easter, to remember and celebrate the resurrection of Jesus Christ on that singular morning nearly 2000 years ago. For many of them, a highlight of their experience is attending the sunrise service at the Garden Tomb on Easter Sunday. This beautifully maintained garden enclosure, situated just north of the Old City walls, is an oasis of tranquility in the midst of the hustle and bustle of downtown Jerusalem. To enter within its high walls is to discover a leafy sanctuary, in which winding paths lead to arbors adorned with flowering native plants and trees, where the wings of birds flutter in the coolness of the shade. But the stony walkways all eventually lead to the center of the garden where the rock-cut tomb itself is located. And this, if studied carefully with a copy of the Gospels in hand, can be recognized as being of a singular construction and design which fits all the requirements of the Gospel narratives.

It is certainly a rich man's tomb such as Joseph of Arimathea might have built; according to all four Gospels it was this wealthy nobleman who provided a tomb for the body of Jesus and the early church was unanimous in seeing this as a fulfillment of the prophecy in Isaiah concerning God's Suffering Servant who "made his grave .. with the rich at his death" (Isaiah 53:9). The tomb was originally set within a garden area, just as it is today, as evidenced by the discovery of a large cistern and wine press within the precincts. This accords with the statement in John's Gospel: "Now in the place where He was crucified there was a garden, and in the garden a new tomb in which no one had yet been laid" (John 19:41). At the entrance to the grave is a groove for a large rolling stone, similar to the one mentioned by the Evangelists which provided such a source of perplexity to the women who came to anoint the body ("Who will roll away the stone for us?" they asked one another as they went).

The inner part of the tomb also conforms to the Gospel accounts. The entrance leads first to a large "weeping chamber" and to the right is a single burial place (loculus) that was prepared for a body. Two other loculi were unfinished, suggesting that it was a new tomb which may never have been completed after a body was placed there. If mourners entered the tomb, as did the disciples on the resurrection morning, it would have been possible to view the whole length of the burial place, which also provided extra space at both ends. This would have permitted Mary Magdalene to see "two angels in white sitting, one at the head and the other at the feet, where the body of Jesus had lain" (John 20:12). It is remarkable that, out of over 300 ancient tombs in and around Jerusalem which have been examined, not one other than the Garden Tomb fits the biblical description of Jesus' grave.

Another noticeable feature of the Garden Tomb is a small window cut into the upper right hand area of the rock face as a part of the original construction, and too narrow to be intended as another entrance. This was a *nephesh* (literally "soul" hole), through which by Jewish tradition the spirit of the dead departed after three days in the tomb. In this case it is located directly above the completed loculus where the body would have lain. This latter feature particularly draws attention to one of the events related as having taken place on the resurrection morning. According to John's Gospel, Mary Magdalene, early in the morning on the first day of the week, *ran* to Peter and John to tell them that someone had removed the Lord's body from the tomb. In response, they themselves *ran* to the tomb:

"Peter therefore went out, and the other disciple (John), and were going to the tomb. So they both ran together, and the other disciple outran Peter and came to the tomb first. And he, stooping down and looking in, saw the linen cloths lying there; yet he did not go in. Then Simon Peter came, following him, and went into the tomb; and he saw the linen cloths lying there and the handkerchief that had been around His head, not lying with the linen cloths, but folded together in a place by itself" (John 20:3-7).

Because this activity was taking place very early in the morning (John 20:1), what therefore made it possible for the two disciples to see clearly all these details, first as John peered into the tomb from outside and then as they entered the mourning chamber? The *nephesh* hole may have enabled the dawning light to shine directly into the tomb so that Peter and John could see into what otherwise would have been darkness. Then, as they entered the tomb and looked to the right, they could have seen where the body of Christ had lain, gazed upon His grave clothes lying by themselves where His body had been, but otherwise could perceive that the tomb was empty.

This compelling account of the runners to the tomb catches the reader up in the emotion and perplexity of the protagonists as the undreamed-of good news begins to break in upon their understanding. The story's effect is further heightened by consideration of the parallels with the story of those earlier runners, found in 2 Samuel 18. The way in which Ahimaaz and the Cushite brought the news of victory to King David following the defeat and death of his rebellious son Absalom shows many striking correspondences with the actions of the later set of runners. Just as in the earlier story Ahimaaz outran the Cushite, so in the Gospel account John ("the other disciple") outran Peter; and just as Ahimaaz "turned aside" at the direction of the King, John also stood aside, mirroring exactly the action of the son of Zadok, so that Peter, arriving after him, entered the tomb first. There are therefore very strong links tying the New Testament "Runners to the Tomb" to the Old Testament "Runners to the King". And in turn, as already noted, this latter story lays a strong claim to be a prophetic enactment of the vision announced by Isaiah:

"How beautiful upon the mountains are the feet of him who brings good news, who proclaims peace, who brings glad tidings of good things ..." (Isaiah 52:7)

Moreover, just as the emphasis of both passages in the Hebrew Scriptures was very much upon the watchmen who were "looking for" and anxiously awaiting the good news which is to be proclaimed, so it proves in the Gospel story as well. When the Evangelist describes how Peter and John entered the empty tomb to examine more closely what they had observed from the outside, he draws upon every possible Greek verb for "looking" and "seeing" to provide a further concatenation of images. He relates how John, who arrived at the tomb before Peter, was *looking in* (the Greek word *blepo* meaning "to clearly see a material object") and saw the grave clothes still in the tomb. Peter then also arriving, and entering before John, *saw* (*theoreo* meaning "to contemplate, observe, scrutinize") that the wrappings were lying in a fashion which was orderly and seemingly undisturbed. After Peter entered the tomb John followed, and at that point he *saw* (*eido* meaning, "to understand, to perceive the significance of") the manner in which the grave clothes were still lying in the rocky grave. And thus the climax of the Gospel story is reached – for John *sees* and also *believes*. The linen wrappings were still lying there, as a witness that Jesus had passed through them and left them behind as He rose from the dead.

The Garden Tomb in Jerusalem

This, then, is the "glad tidings" to which the Isaiah passage ultimately points, the impossible good news that the Love that is stronger than death has overcome the grave. According to orthodox Christian belief, the death and resurrection of Jesus Christ is the central event of the ages, when He also "destroyed the works of the Evil One" (1 John 3:8). All the powers that had so grievously burdened the lives of men and women were routed by Him in a complete and assured victory, the effects of which are still being worked out in history. The nature of that conquest is reflected in the words of Ahimaaz the son of Zadok when he requested that he might bear news to King David concerning the victory that had been won: *"How that the Lord has avenged him from the hand of all his enemies"* (2 Samuel 18:19).

And following that singular resurrection morning, both men and women were among those who hastened out bearing the "good news" – "He is risen from the dead!" Joyful were their voices raised in proclamation, lovely their feet upon the mountains of Moriah, Olivet, and Zion. Their voices have gone out to the ends of the world and the glad tidings yet resounds with the greatest message of the aeons – "Jesus saves, Jesus saves …"

The Heart of the Father

··

During Passover and Christian Holy Week, which fall close together or sometimes even coincide, Jerusalem displays her most beautiful face. This is the time when "the rains are over and gone", the skies have been washed to an intense shade of blue, and the atmosphere possesses a sparkling clarity. Standing on the great plaza outside Jaffa Gate, or wandering within the walls of the Old City, it is impossible not to be struck by the immense throngs of people, seemingly from every corner of the globe, who have arrived there to remember, celebrate and worship.

One of the most memorable services of Holy Week, for the Christian visitor, takes place on the evening of Maundy Thursday. This is traditionally held to be the night of the Last Supper, when Jesus gave His farewell address to His disciples before leading them out across the Kidron Valley to the Garden of Gethsemane where His betrayal and arrest took place. In commemoration of these events large groups of worshippers gather at various churches to take part in a meditative walk from the Old City to Gethsemane. Those who gather at Christ Church, the oldest Protestant church in the Middle East located just inside Jaffa Gate, make their way in quiet procession through the narrow streets of the Armenian Quarter, out through Zion Gate, to pass by the Room of the Last Supper and then continue down towards the Kidron Valley.

It is surely one of the great walks of the world. The pilgrims follow the line of the Old City walls, the massive contours of which are softened by lighting which reflects the golden coloring of their stones. High in the heavens a full and glowing Passover moon pours a luminous radiance upon the scene, highlighting the Temple Mount area, the dark gulf of the valley into which the walkers are descending, and the gentle outlines of the Mount of Olives rising on the eastern side of the city. Very soon the pilgrims find themselves in the depths of the ravine; here a breathless hush descends and a chill wind invariably blows as they make their way along the stony path through scattered trees. Finally they come within sight of their destination – the exquisite façade of the Church of All Nations marking the site of the massed olive grove of the Garden of Gethsemane.

Along their way, the pilgrims passed an impressive structure located in the deepest part of the Kidron Valley. The Tomb of Absalom (*Yad Avshalom*) is an ancient monument carved out of the natural rock, 47 feet in height and elegant in design: the lower part of the monument is a square base and on top of this a three-meter drum built of ashlar stones, while the top section is a concave cone engraved with a lotus flower. The tomb has traditionally been identified as the monument of Absalom, King David's son, based on 2 Samuel 18:18, which states that

"Absalom in his lifetime had taken and reared up for himself a pillar, which is in the king's dale: for he said, I have no son to keep my name in remembrance; and he called the monument after his own name".

However, the monument is an example of Egyptian-Hellenistic architecture and archaeologists have now dated it to about a thousand years after Absalom's death, to the 1st century AD; it existed in the days of the Jewish historian Josephus and was referred to in his *Antiquities.* This leaves open the question: did the monument exist in the days of Jesus, and would He have seen it as He traversed the Kidron Valley on numerous occasions with His disciples? And did He perhaps give Absalom, the rebellious son of King David, a fleeting thought as He trod that familiar path on the last night of His earthly life?

As noted, there are many links between the narratives of the death of Absalom and the death and resurrection of Jesus Christ. Most particularly, the story of "The Runners to the King" in 2 Samuel 18 has provided an interpretive lens through which the tale of "The Runners to the Tomb" recorded in John 20 may be viewed. In turn, it is the Gospel narratives which provide a key to unlock the inner significance of the story of King David and his son Absalom. This intricately woven narrative is a masterpiece of the storyteller's art.

After his son Absalom stole the hearts of the people David fled Jerusalem over the Jordan with his loyal followers. While the battle raged between his men and those of Absalom, he was persuaded to stay in his base at Mahanaim (the "Double Camp"), for, the people said, "You are worth ten thousand of us now" (2 Samuel 18:3). It was there, the same place in which the patriarch Jacob had wrestled with the Angel while on his way back to the promised land, that David positioned himself between two gates and with much trepidation awaited news from the front. While he longed for victory, he also passionately desired that no harm should come to Absalom, but the end of his vigil brought him heartbreak. And when David learned that his son had perished, his outburst of sorrow was unparalleled in its intensity:

My son, Absalom, my son, my son Absalom,
Would I had died instead of you,
O Absalom, my son, my son (2 Samuel 18:33)

David's poignant cry is simple and elemental, dense with pathos. It is made up mostly of nouns, linked with only one verb. The first and last lines have but two words: *beni*, "my son", and *Absalom*, "father of peace", while the five-fold repetition, "my son", through its very understatement, becomes laden with a weight of sorrow. The centerpiece of David's lament is his impossible wish to have taken the place of his son; in fact, it is precisely because his son has died that his kingdom is secured. And in the grief-stricken utterance of the king, do we not gain a further insight into the heart of the Greater Father as His own Son was suffering?

It is a remarkable fact that, when the New Testament is turned to and the accounts of the death of Jesus are studied, the reader is drawn into the narrative from many points of view save that of the One with the deepest, most intimate concern of all. The Gospels are utterly silent when it comes to delineating God's personal emotional involvement throughout the whole intense drama of Jesus' betrayal, arrest, trial and crucifixion. The anguish which surely resided within the heart of the Father as He saw His Son fulfilling the prophecies that He should be "a man of sorrows and acquainted with grief" is not in any way disclosed, nor the manner in which He endured to see the terrors which gripped Jesus' soul in those final hours, when the powers of hell were unleashed, as the whole weight of sin was placed upon Him, and as He listened to that agonized cry, *"Eloi, Eloi, lama sabachthani: My God, My God, why hast Thou forsaken Me?"*

Nevertheless, in this picture given of King David, as he was seated between two gates and anxiously awaiting news of his son, it is possible to see a reflection of the face of the Greater Father above - straitened as it were between heaven and earth, with His face turned away from His Son but yearning after Him with an infinite measure of paternal love. In the lament of David when he learned that his son had perished in the battle is granted a momentary glimpse of the sorrow that pierced the heart of God as He witnessed the "dearly beloved of his soul" suffer and die. It is noteworthy also that it was here in Mahanaim, where Jacob wrestled with the Angel all night long, the place he named Peniel for, he said, *"I have seen God face to face"* – that the Face of the Father was revealed once again – a Face displaying the very features and lineaments of heartbreak.

Perhaps this is a revelation upon which the church should meditate during the Easter season: the suffering in the heavenly realms as the earth was mantled in darkness, the ground quaked and the skies were rent, when death and hell were defeated through the oblation of the Son. The Father who gave His Only-Begotten for the life of the world does not display his anguish openly but nevertheless allows a small shaft of light to pierce into otherwise impenetrable depths. In this way, a fresh understanding may be granted to those who wait at the foot of the cross, concerning the unimaginable cost of the immeasurable Sacrifice. And those who stand thus, speechless and worshiping, may be drawn in this way into a deeper sharing, a new dimension, of the love between the Father and the Son.

Pharaoh's Hard Heart and
the Mystery of Free Will

. . . .

While Christians take part in the Easter rites and remembrances, the Jewish people are celebrating Pesach (Passover), the great epic of the deliverance of the Children of Israel from slavery in Egypt. On the first night of the holiday, after all the intense preparation, families gather together around the table laden with the symbolic foods of the feast. All the homes in Jerusalem seem filled with light and warmth, song and laughter, and in every dwelling the solemn question is being asked: "Why is this night different from all other nights?"

The story of Passover actually begins somewhat earlier: at the burning bush in the desert of Midian, when God revealed to Moses that He had heard the cry of His enslaved people in Egypt. After Joseph had risen to a position of great power in this nation, second only to Pharaoh himself, the descendants of Jacob had gone down to Egypt to dwell. But after that generation died a new king arose who "did not know Joseph". As the children of Israel multiplied, their lives were made bitter with hard bondage, in mortar, brick and service in the field, for weary generations. But now God was commissioning Moses with the great task of leading them out of Egypt, out of the house of bondage (Exodus 3:7-10).

After Moses returned to Egypt God revealed further details of His plan of deliverance to His prophet-in-the-making: that He, as their faithful, covenant-keeping God, would rescue His people from slavery "with an outstretched arm and with great judgments," to take them to Himself for a people, and be to them a God (Exodus 6:1-8). These promises introduced the predominant theme of Exodus - the making known of Yahweh as the one true God to both Israel and the nations. In Genesis, Yahweh was known personally only to a few individuals, nor was Joseph ever pictured as revealing to the Egyptians the name of the Deity at work in his life. In Exodus, however, Yahweh's presence was manifested to both the Children of Israel and the Egyptians, and through His mighty judgments evidenced that He possessed a power far greater than that of men and of gods.

The early chapters of Exodus then detailed the encounters which took place between Moses and the Egyptian monarch. The leader of the Israelites appeared a number of times before the Egyptian king to make the demand: "Let my people go!"; yet despite the fact that various plagues were ravaging his land, the king refused to accede to this request. The text explains that this was because Pharaoh's heart was "hardened" - a statement which becomes a recurring refrain in the story. Even before Moses had returned into Egypt, God foretold that He would harden the king's heart (Exodus 4:21) and He made a similar declaration before the plagues commenced. In fact, in the twenty passages which speak of the hardening of Pharaoh's heart, approximately half ascribe this action to Pharaoh himself, but the other half to God. This raises one of the crucial issues in the Exodus narrative: that of freewill. If an irresistible divine action is taking place in Pharaoh's heart, then to what degree can the king truly be held accountable for his actions?

This complex matter can, however, be illuminated through an examination of the original Hebrew text. While in the English versions only one word is used to describe what takes place in Pharaoh's heart - "hardening" - by way of contrast two different terms appear in the Hebrew. In some cases Pharaoh's heart is indeed "hardened" (*kavod*), meaning "made heavy, unimpressionable", but at other times his heart is actually "strengthened" (*hazak*), "made firm or immovable". This variable hardening process can then be traced through the actual history of the plagues which came upon Egypt.

When Moses first came to Pharaoh together with his brother Aaron he spoke to the king in the name which God had revealed to him (Exodus 6:3): the exalted name of Yahweh, which suggested that the God of Israel was a Deity outside and beyond human categories of time and understanding. By way of contrast, the Egyptian monarch was the leader of a polytheistic nation in which many different gods were worshipped, each thought to have dominion over a separate area of the cosmos. Because these deities were thought to control the seasons and the rains, agriculture and the harvest, all life therefore depended upon their goodwill. At the same time, it was understood that the sphere of power in which any particular divinity operated was necessarily limited, so while it was possible to appease one particular god, other forces could still operate to bring disaster - resulting in the chaotic and unpredictable nature of life. When Pharaoh could not recognize the name of Israel's God within his pantheon, he dismissed the claim contemptuously, *"Who is Yahweh, that I should obey his voice to let Israel go? ... I do not know Yahweh, nor will I let Israel go"* (Exodus 5:2). He then castigated the Children of Israel as "Idle! Idle!" and ordered that their workload should be made even more "heavy" - a play on words which emphasized the main theme of the text.

Despite this disastrous result, Moses and Aaron returned and confronted the king of Egypt for a second time. When Pharaoh challenged them to show him a miracle, Aaron cast down his rod and it became a serpent, but the king then summoned his magicians who performed a similar feat; even so, the inferiority of their power was proven as Aaron's rod swallowed up their rods. Moreover, the Hebrew term for the "serpent" into which Aaron's rod was changed was not that commonly used (*nachash*) but was used for the great sea serpents which stood as a symbol of Egypt (eg Ezekiel 29:3). Accordingly Pharaoh should have understood that, when Aaron's rod swallowed up the others, it foretold the vanquishing of his empire, and the exposure of the powerlessness of all the gods of Egypt (Exodus 12:12). But he refused to consider this evidence, choosing to regard Aaron and Moses as mere wonder-workers whom his own equaled in power, and so he hardened his heart.

As a result, the king became responsible for unleashing a series of plagues upon his land and people, which gradually increased in awesome power and intensity. The calamities which fell upon Egypt featured naturally-occurring phenomena, and similar events had been experienced to a certain extent in the nation. Nevertheless, the miraculous nature of the plagues which now occurred was manifested in their immeasurably heightened degree, their coming and going at the command of Moses, and the partial manner in which they came upon the land. And yet, throughout, the focus of the text was not so much on the plagues as representing the punishment of the Egyptians for enslaving the Israelites, but rather as signs by which Yahweh would become known.

The first plague, or "stroke." Early in the morning as Pharaoh went down to the river Nile to offer worship he was confronted by Moses, who warned the king of the consequences of refusing to hear the word of the Lord. Aaron then stretched his rod over the waters and the Nile, in all its branches and canals, was turned into blood. During the flood season the swollen rivers could carry quantities of red earth and present a similar appearance, yet in this case the phenomenon was wholly supernatural, as demonstrated through its sudden appearance at the word of Moses. The fish in the river died, cutting off one of the main sources of food, nor could the people drink of the waters. But there was a further significance in this first plague. For the Children of Israel, the most traumatic aspect of their sojourn in Egypt was not the long centuries of slavery, the backbreaking labor to which they were subjected, nor even the cruelty of their taskmasters in the fields. Rather, it was the order of Pharaoh that all the baby boys of the Hebrews should be thrown into the Nile to drown. Their small bodies disappeared beneath the waters, which covered up the genocide taking place, and the Nile continued to meander on in its placid way. The fact that the waters of the Nile were now turned to blood suggested that the sin of the Egyptians was beginning to be uncovered; it was the beginning of just judgment for that greatest of all crimes. But again the king's magicians copied this feat with their enchantments - and Pharaoh's heart grew hard.

The second "stroke" was also in connection with the Nile. Aaron stretched out his rod over the waters of Egypt, and the rivers brought forth abundant quantities of frogs which covered the land, infesting even the kneading bowls and beds. The magicians once more succeeded in imitating Moses but Pharaoh was forced to ask for the intercession of Moses to remove the plague. A curious exchange then took place between the king and the prophet. When Moses asked the king at what time he should intercede to have the creatures destroyed Pharaoh did not say, as one would expect, "This very minute!" - but answered instead "Tomorrow." Moses complied with his request and as a result it was made clear to the Egyptian monarch that this unknown Deity had an uncanny ability, not only to unleash power, but also to direct it effectively and minutely. The people of Egypt then collected the dead frogs and "gathered" them up in heaps - the same term twice used for Joseph's "piling up" grain in Egypt (Genesis 41:35,49), and not used elsewhere in the Tanach. This wordplay suggested that the prosperity that Joseph brought Egypt had been repaid with evil by the subsequent Pharaohs, and that the current plague was deservedly a commensurate measure. Nevertheless, when Pharaoh saw that there was respite - he again made his heart heavy.

Stroke three - lice! - came as Aaron, directed by God through Moses, smote the dust of the earth with his rod. In vain did Pharaoh's magicians try to copy this miracle, and their forlorn efforts ended in their declaring to the king that this was "the finger of God" (8:19). But once again Pharaoh's heart was hardened and this brought to an end the first series of plagues, which had affected the waters and the soil. In the second series which now commenced the strokes came exclusively upon the Egyptians while the Israelites were exempted. This was intended to show plainly that the Lord had made a distinction between His people and the Egyptians "in order that you may know that I am Yahweh in the midst of the land" (Exodus 8:22). And with each succeeding plague it also grew evident that Israel's God wielded a might unlike anything else seen in the land of Egypt.

Stroke four commenced as swarms of flies descended, filling the houses and corrupting the land - save in the area of Goshen, where the Israelites dwelt. The swarms were the first of a number of plagues described as "heavy", an adjective which sounded an ominous echo of the process taking place in Pharaoh's heart and suggesting their intimate connection. The situation forced a concession from Pharaoh, yet after Moses entreated the Lord and the swarms were removed, he again hardened his heart. Stroke five consisted of a severe pestilence which struck the cattle and livestock throughout the land, although in the area of Goshen it was remarkable not one of the animals belonging to the Israelites perished. Yet despite ascertaining that Israel had been exempted Pharaoh's heart was again hardened. The Egyptian monarch was determined to pursue the dictates of his own desires and purposes, even while steeling himself to resist the weight of evidence concerning the awesome power of the God of the Israelites.

At this stage in the narrative another feature was introduced: up to this point, the hardening of Pharaoh's heart after each successive plague had been expressly attributed to the king himself. However, after the next stroke it was no longer Pharaoh alone who caused this process to take place. This sixth plague was to impact not only the land and possessions of the nation, but the very persons of the Egyptians. Moses and Aaron were instructed to take ashes of the furnace and sprinkle them toward heaven, which resulted in a fine dust causing boils to break out on both man and animals. Again Pharaoh resisted the evidence of this plague - but now, for the first time, it was recorded that *the Lord* "strengthened" the heart of Pharaoh (9:12). And the three strokes which followed in rapid succession, which were yet more terrible than those which had preceded, were intended to make Pharaoh know "that there is none like Me in all the earth" (Exodus 9:14).

The seventh stroke, Moses warned Pharaoh, would strike "to his very heart". It was of a different order altogether, hail mingled with fire, in Egyptian thought an impossible commingling of divine powers. It struck all that was in the field, both man and beast, destroyed every herb and broke every tree. And now Pharaoh was undone: he sent for Moses and Aaron and made his confession: *"I have sinned this time. The Lord is righteous and my people and I are wicked"* (Exodus 9:27). The Egyptian monarch had come to an apprehension of the overwhelming moral claim of the God of Israel. However, as soon as the plague was reversed he repented of his words and the familiar refrain recurred: he "hardened his heart". When Moses warned Pharaoh of the coming of the eighth plague, even the king's servants remonstrated with him for his refusal to acknowledge the destruction being wrought in their land. But the king drove Moses and Aaron from his presence.

Stroke eight: Moses stretched out his rod over the land of Egypt and locusts came up and covered the land, eating up every green thing which the hail had left. It was an inundation far more grievous than any before known, so that the land was darkened by reason of their numbers - Goshen alone being exempted. Pharaoh again confessed his sin, and for the first time asked forgiveness, entreating that "this death" might be taken away (10:16, 17). But that this was only fear of the consequences was shown by the fact that when the calamity ceased his heart was again hardened - once again through the agency of the Lord. The ninth stroke was yet more grievous than any that had gone before. A thick darkness covered the land for three days, an impenetrable, palpable blanket which was perhaps the result of a sandstorm of preternatural strength, and which made it impossible for the people to see one another or to move from their homes - although the Children of Israel had light in all their dwellings. But again the Lord strengthened Pharaoh's heart so that he would not let them go.

Is it possible at this point to come to an understanding concerning the process which has been taking place in Pharaoh's heart throughout the series of the plagues and in his encounters with Moses? The task with which the prophet had been charged was not simply to bring the children of Israel out of Egypt - but also to reveal to Pharaoh, as representative of his people, the reality of the One God who created all things and rules with justice and mercy. Only after having received an intimation of Yahweh's infinite power and goodness could Pharaoh make a moral choice to obey or disobey Him and thus be held accountable for his actions. Yet as the plagues increased in intensity, there was a real danger (ethically speaking) that Pharaoh might choose to capitulate to Moses' demands simply in order to avert any more disasters upon his land, and before he had come to a place where he could make a free moral decision in the matter. Therefore, it could be suggested that when God intervened to take action upon Pharaoh's heart, it was not to *harden* Pharaoh's heart but to *strengthen* it, thus in a sense underlining Pharaoh's own freewill in the situation - an interpretation which is underscored by the different words employed in the text.

The Egyptian king's first words to Moses were, "Who is Yahweh? .. I do not know Yahweh" - but by the end of the story he had come to know. The true tragedy of the Exodus situation for Pharaoh and the people of Egypt was that, despite having come to an apprehension of the truth, the king chose to follow the dictates of his own heart. What God did in Pharaoh was to take his power of volition, his will-energy, and use this to hasten him in the way in which he was already disposed to go. If Pharaoh had been a noble, compassionate and righteous man, with a true king's feelings for his people, he would, through the very process of strengthening his heart, have become a more beneficent ruler. Yet despite the astounding miracles performed in his sight, all the evidence he was granted of the superior power of the Israelite Deity, he became steadily more hardened in his rebellion, pride, and confidence in worldly power. He has thus became set before all ages as the irredeemable enemy of God's people, and the type of an even more formidable adversary than himself. Therefore, says Yahweh:

"For this purpose I have raised you up, that I may show My power in you, and that My name may be declared in all the earth" (Exodus 9:16, cf Romans 9:17)

Two Nights to be Much Remembered

To this day the most famous and celebrated event in Jewish history is the Exodus of the Children of Israel from Egypt under the leadership of Moses. The overriding importance of that ancient deliverance is powerfully stressed throughout the Old Testament, and retains a perennial freshness in the hearts and minds of the people of Israel. And so, why *was* that night different from all other nights?

After the ninth plague of darkness Pharaoh once again summoned Moses, and the most intense of all their encounters ensued. This time the king agreed to let the Children of Israel depart, provided they left their flocks behind as a pledge of their return, but when Moses refused the condition the king in impotent rage uttered a dire threat: "Take heed to yourself, and see my face no more! For in the day you see my face, you will die" (Exodus 10:28). But God had already revealed to Moses what would transpire, and he delivered the announcement of the tenth stroke which would come upon Egypt in minute and appalling detail. In the former plagues natural means had been utilized to visit affliction on the land; this time the Lord Himself would go out into the midst of Egypt and cause all the firstborn of man and beast to die, so that a great cry would be heard throughout the land, such as had not been heard before and would not be heard again. Thus, in this final plague death itself would be shown to be under the supreme control of Yahweh - yet during this calamity the Children of Israel would experience so profound a protection that not even a dog would bark against them.

Moses delivered his message with majestic finality but also with hot anger at the prospect of Pharaoh's subjecting his people to this final heartbreak through his stubborn willfulness. There was also a marvelous irony in the picture he painted of the courtiers of Egypt coming to bow low before him, their pride in tatters as they acknowledged the greatness of the shepherd leader from Horeb, to beseech him to depart from their land. A regal consciousness of righteous authority also flashes out in his last words to Pharaoh, the assertion that his leaving was not dependent upon the permission of the leaders of Egypt: "After that, *I will* go out" - a clear echo of the Lord's "going out" over the land.

In Goshen during the three days of thick darkness over Egypt, each household of the Children of Israel had already, on the tenth of the month, selected a lamb without blemish which was kept for four days, then solemnly slain by the head of the family. The blood was caught in a basin, then struck by means of a branch of hyssop upon the door-posts and lintels of the houses, so that when Yahweh passed through the land to smite the Egyptians, He would see the blood and pass over the door. Only when the house was secure from the destruction would the household gather round the table. Then, as the angel of death spread his wings over the whole land, within their blood-sprinkled dwellings the Israelites partook of their first Passover meal: the lamb, with unleavened bread and bitter herbs, symbol of all the bitterness of Egypt. They were to sit down to it with garments girded about them, shoes on their feet and a staff in their hands, in readiness for their departure; and as they ate their hearts were beating fast, contemplating a perilous journey to an unknown destination. For the feast they celebrated was held before the deliverance which it commemorated had been accomplished, and a whole new era was to be reckoned from it: the month of the Exodus, Abib, was thereafter to be the first month of the year.

It was at midnight that the Lord struck all the firstborn in Egypt and the sound of a great lamentation arose throughout the land, for there was not a house in which there was not someone dead, from the king's palace to the lowliest hovel, from the deepest dungeon to the cattle byre. As the horror of the tenth plague burst upon Egypt Pharaoh capitulated completely; he hastily sent for Moses and Aaron and dismissed the Children of Israel unconditionally, asking only asking that a "blessing" might be left behind. The Egyptian people themselves urged the Israelites to leave in haste, for, they said, "We be all dead men." Yet before their departure the Children of Israel had asked of their neighbors articles of silver and gold and clothing, and because the Lord had given the people favor in the sight of the Egyptians they gave them what they requested - so "they plundered the Egyptians" (Exodus 12:36). They went out also with a "heavy" amount of livestock - and the word that so often described Pharaoh's oppression and the force of the plagues then recurred to describe the substantial quantity of possessions the people took with them as they departed.

By daybreak the Children of Israel were on their march from Rameses, going out not as fugitives, but as a triumphant army. Yet because the direct road would have brought them into the land of the war-loving Philistines, they were directed to go by way of the wilderness of the Red Sea, and encamp by Pi-hahiroth between Migdol and the sea, opposite Baal-Zephon. It was here for the first time that Yahweh manifested His guiding and protecting presence to the people as He went before them by day in a pillar of cloud, and by night in a pillar of fire. The text also recorded that God had a singular purpose when He turned aside the Children of Israel from the direct route and led them in this mysterious way. At that point Pharaoh realized the people had not merely gone for a few days to offer sacrifice, but were intending to depart from his land permanently, and as he contemplated what it would mean to lose the services of that vast body of slaves, many highly skilled in different arts, was torn with regret. The inclination to pursue them at once sprang into his mind ... and God's design was to permit him to gratify that inclination, and so lure the king into the snare He had prepared for him, to complete the judgment He had determined to visit upon Egypt.

It was then that intelligence was brought to the king of the change which the Israelites had made in their route, and he at once detected it as a strategic blunder. Surrounded by mountains and with an impassable stretch of water in front they seemed closed in by the wilderness, with no way of escape from a pursuing force. This news was the very thing to persuade Pharaoh to make his preparations for chase, especially as God then hardened his heart to the greatest degree of stubbornness it yet had reached. The king quickly gathered his army, the principal strength of which lay in its six hundred chosen chariots, each drawn by two horses and carrying two warriors, as well as a vast number of foot soldiers. So it was that as the day drew to a close the Israelites in their encampment by the Red Sea saw in the distance the rapid approach of Pharaoh's army, with the rays of the setting sun gilding their weaponry and armor. It was a formidable sight, especially to a people untrained in military skills and dispirited by centuries of slavery. Eastward lay a wide body of water, to the west and south rose mountains: flight was impossible, defense out of the question, and the Children of Israel signally lost heart.

In this place of extremity of peril began the marvelous series of incidents, the greatest recorded in Old Testament history, which has ever since sustained the faith of Israel. "And Moses said ... do not be afraid" (Exodus 14:13). The danger was to the natural eye overwhelming, but the prophet knew that the pursuit of Israel by the Egyptian host was under God's sovereign control, and would lead in some way to the magnifying of His name. Moses understood perfectly that the situation was one in which the Children of Israel could do nothing, and that everything lay in the mercy and help of God. The stunning variety of the plagues he had witnessed come upon Egypt convinced him there was no limit to the resources at Yahweh's disposal. What strange form of destruction should come upon Pharaoh's army - whether the ground would open and swallow them up, or meteors fall upon them from the sky - he did not know; but he remained calmly confident that some great deliverance was on the way. Hence he continued to encourage his people with the following words:

"Stand still, and see the salvation of the Lord, which He will accomplish for you today. For the Egyptians whom you see today, you shall see again no more forever. The Lord will fight for you, and you shall hold your peace" (Exodus 14:13-14)

And the Lord rewarded the steadfast faith of Moses by revealing to him the way in which He would deliver the Israelites from their desperate plight. There was no historical precedent for such an overturning of the laws of nature, and the conception of an event of such magnitude could hardly even enter the mind or imagination. And yet, God's purposes have always embraced His desire to display His power in the situations thought to be impossible. The directions He then gave the Israelites through Moses were very simple: "Go forward." He waited till the people were shut in on every side, and then commanded them to continue in the same direction, which led onward to the sea, and beyond that the way to their Promised Land. Moreover, He promised that He would harden the hearts of *all* the Egyptians - and in this way they would come to understand that He was *Lord*. All Egypt would learn of the miraculous destruction of the army, and recognize the superior might of Yahweh, the God of Israel, over each of the Egyptian deities.

Yet the forward movement of the Israelites could take place only after the pillar of cloud moved and came between the two encampments, casting a bright light upon Israel's path while overshadowing the Egyptians with a deep and preternatural darkness. It was then that Moses descended to the water's edge and stretched forth his rod over the waves; and as he stood thus, a monument to indomitable faith, the Lord caused the sea to be driven back by a strong east wind all that night, so that the waters became divided, opening a way for the Israelites to cross.

47

One of the most dramatic and awe inspiring scenes in world history then took place. The Children of Israel, although hesitant and afraid, moved forward and began their descent into the abyss of the sea. Deeper and deeper they trod, as a strange elation began to fill their hearts, the fruit of their dawning faith. Around their ears the wind whistled and shrieked, high in the heavens the full paschal moon shone upon the heaped waters, while behind them gleamed the pillar of fire. On their right hand and their left rose the high walls of water, glassy and glistening, full of threatening power and yet mysteriously held at bay; indeed, the sea, which they had so much dreaded, formed protecting ramparts to them on either side. Hearts hammering, they continued the perilous journey, walking on dry ground in the midst of the sea, each step taking them closer to safety. And thus, supernaturally protected all the way, they completed the transit, and morning found all men, women and children securely encamped upon the far shores.

Meanwhile the Egyptians, all Pharaoh's chariots and soldiers, were bent on military glory. It was during the last watch of the night that they found the channel leading into the sea was still dry, and plunged into its depths in hot pursuit of the Israelites. Once again the Lord Himself intervened: He "looked down upon the army of the Egyptians through the pillar of fire and of the cloud, and troubled the army of the Egyptians" (Exodus 14:24). As the fire of His presence glared upon them, they were thrown into confusion. The Lord then made their chariot wheels go "heavily", so that they sank into the soft sand over which the Israelites had passed easily. The terrible conviction dawned upon the Egyptians that it was the Lord fighting for Israel, just as Moses had promised. "Let us flee" was their panicked response, and they had begun their hasty retreat when, at God's command, Moses stretched forth his hand again over the sea, and the waters on both sides began at once to return. By morning the sea had returned to its full depth even as the Egyptians raced against the advancing tide, seeking vainly to reach the shore. But the waves came on apace, and there was not a man of all those who had entered the passage into the sea that was not overwhelmed and drowned. And thus the flower of the Egyptian army perished there, as they sank beneath the waves.

The recurrence of the word *heavy* to describe the difficulties faced by the Egyptian soldiers in driving their chariots through the sea is not accidental. Rather, this provides a clue to an important truth, that the account of the plagues brought upon Egypt and the story of the Red Sea crossing are indivisible sections of one great saga, and that the event at the sea was a climax to all that had transpired in Egypt. This was not only the final act of sovereign deliverance for the Children of Israel through God's mighty power and faithful love toward them, but also revealed, by the judgments upon Egypt, that Yahweh was akin to a warrior overturning the works of oppression and tyranny in the earth. And the ransomed Israelites, safe on their far coastline, broke into a song of exultation as they recognized the greatness of the victory the Lord had accomplished. The waves of the sea were now stilled, and as the sun rose it shed its golden beams on the calm ocean beneath which their taskmasters were buried forever. A gentle breeze caressed the silver stretch of water which lay behind them, a visible sign of the final severance of the connection with Egypt.

Before they left Egypt, Moses had instructed the Israelites that they were to hold the Feast of Passover each year, as the remembrance of their redemption from slavery and birth as a nation. Over the centuries the festal meal came to form the very heart of Jewish ritual and faith, and is still observed all over the world as probably the oldest religious ceremony in existence. Even during their long dispersion amongst the nations, the Jewish people still celebrated that deliverance year by year, with indomitable hope repeating the expectation, eventually fulfilled so miraculously, *"This year, here; next year, in the land of Israel. This year, slaves; next year, freemen."* And yet, wonderful as these events were, their true import lies in the adumbration of an even greater deliverance which would take place many centuries later. The Exodus was seen in

49

the New Testament as a prototype of the greatest redemption of all, the redemption of the souls of men and women from bondage to sin, accomplished by Jesus Christ through His cross and resurrection. Just as the children of Israel went down into the sea and came up again, so Jesus descended into the grave and rose again, bringing freedom from death for those who joined their lives to Him in faith and love.

Nevertheless, it could be argued that, as Moses stood on the shores of the Red Sea and spoke those immortal words to the Children of Israel, "Stand still and see the salvation of the Lord," he was actually looking down through the centuries to see the fulfillment of the deliverance of which the Red Sea crossing spoke in type and shadow. He looked ahead to see the parting of the sea, and foresaw in that wondrous event the salvation accomplished by Jesus - *Yeshua* - through His death, burial and resurrection. It was the signal wonder of that vision which caused him to command the Israelites to stand still and *behold*: a recommendation that in the events which would transpire for them they might see delineated, through the fixed gaze and singular focus of faith, an even greater salvation yet to come. It is this interpretation alone which can explain the strange contrast that exists between Moses' first command to *stand still* and his subsequent order to *move forward*. It is remarkable also that this is only the second time in scripture that the word *salvation* had been used. The first time was Jacob's exclamation in Genesis as he also gazed into the dim mists of the future: "I have waited for Your salvation, O Lord" (Genesis 49:18) - the expression of his longing desire for the coming of God's redemption, which alone could save his descendants from the afflictions he knew awaited them.

It was at the Last Supper that Jesus revealed the true and transcendent meaning of that first Exodus: that He Himself was the true "Passover Lamb," whose sprinkled blood protects the world from judgment, and whose death brings deliverance for His followers from a more terrible bondage than that of Egypt. Like the Passover, the Lord's Supper was established before the deliverance it celebrated was accomplished. On that last night with His disciples, before He endured the cross and shame, Jesus called upon them to always remember His body broken and blood shed for them. In calm consciousness of the unique significance and power of His atoning sacrifice, He put aside the ancient deliverance by the shores of the Red Sea and instituted a new rite, calling upon His followers to henceforth partake of the Lord's Supper as commemorating His own death.

The Lord's Supper is predominantly a memorial feast, but in it there is also a prophetic element. All three Synoptic Gospels record that during the meal Jesus gave a mysterious promise to His disciples: that the time would come when He would drink the fruit of the vine new with them in the Father's kingdom. In that calm and heavenly realm, they would gather together around the festive table with unalloyed joy, and gaze upon the King in His beauty, their faces reflecting the radiant light of His glory. Surrounded by those whom He has redeemed and won for Himself through the greatness of His love, He will fill the brimming wine cup, and as it passes from lip to lip perfect rapture shall fill each heart, nor shall they go any more out, for death and sorrow and pain, all the former things, will have passed away.

THE FORTY DAYS AFTER EASTER/PESACH

The Psalm of the Shoah

After Passover days of recollection come thick and fast in Israel: *"On Holocaust Remembrance Day we mourn the price of powerlessness; on Remembrance Day for the Fallen of Israel's Wars we mourn the price of power, and on Independence Day we celebrate our improbable resurrection."*

The first of these times of intense remembrance is *Yom HaShoah*, or Holocaust Remembrance Day. On this occasion the nation as a whole seeks to address this inescapable issue: the genocide of the Jewish people which took place during World War II under the Nazi regime. This was an event of such magnitude that it is legitimate to ask whether it may have been foretold in the scriptures. A number of passages have been suggested as describing the unprecedented scale of the suffering, amongst them the remarkable Psalm 102.

The superscription of the psalm reads as follows: *"A prayer of the afflicted, when he is overwhelmed and pours out his heart before God"*. The Church fathers believed the one speaking in the passage to be Jesus, so the whole psalm may be looked at as a prediction of His sufferings and subsequent exaltation. Although Christ was chosen for the Messianic role of establishing God's kingdom, He first endured a great number of ordeals - in the same way as did the writer of the psalm, who after enumerating his sorrows confessed to God that *"You have lifted me up and cast me away"*. The reason given for this is God's indignation and wrath – although it is noticeable there is nowhere any personal admission of wrongdoing. Therefore he cried out: *"O my God (El), take me not away in the midst of my days"*. And the answer finally came, in the form of a statement of God's eternal power and majesty:

> *"Of old You laid the foundation of the earth,*
> *And the heavens are the works of Your hands:*
> *They will perish, but You will endure ...*
> *You are the same, and Your years will have no end"* (Psalm 102:25-27)

The contrast between the description of extreme affliction and ascription of utmost glory eventually emerges as the most striking aspect of the psalm. Moreover, as the images of suffering are examined more closely they appear to be of a very singular nature. This individual is enduring unimaginable difficulties: his days are consumed like smoke; his bones are burned like a hearth; his heart is broken; he has lost his appetite; his bones cleave to his skin; he has become like the lonely sparrow on the housetop; his enemies cast reproaches upon him and curse him; they are sworn to his destruction; he eats ashes like bread, and mingles his drink with weeping. In short, these are descriptions which remind the reader in vivid detail of the experiences undergone in the Nazi death camps.

The anguish of these individuals is brought graphically into the present at Yad Vashem, the Holocaust Memorial located at Mt Herzl in Jerusalem. This was first established in 1953 with the goal of documenting the history of the Jewish people during the Shoah and perpetuating the memory of victims for future generations. A new state-of-the-art museum was opened in 2005, designed by Canadian-Israeli architect Moshe Safdie in the shape of a prism and consisting of ten different galleries illuminated by a long skylight. Here the personal experiences and feelings of the Holocaust victims are emphasized through photographs, documents, works of art, and items found in the camps and ghettos. Other memorials and monuments on the hillside setting include the Hall of Names, containing over three million names of those who perished in the Shoah, Yad Layeled, commemorating one and a half million Jewish children, and the Avenue of the Righteous Among the Nations with over

2,000 trees planted in honor of non-Jews who risked their lives to save Jews from the Nazis. The Hall of Remembrance is an imposing vault-like structure with walls made of grey basalt boulders brought from the Galilee region, and the names of 22 Nazi extermination sites engraved on its mosaic floor. Here an eternal flame burns from the likeness of a broken bronze goblet, continuously lighting the Hall with a soft glow, while before it stands a stone crypt containing the ashes of Holocaust victims brought to Israel from the camps. No sound, but a vast stillness permeates the immense stone room.

Visiting the Yad Vashem Museum is a challenging and emotional experience for the one million individuals, world leaders and dignitaries who pass annually through its doors. One Christian visitor who came to the shrine noted the photographs which showed the hangings, lynchings and burnings of Jews, and the pictures of emaciated men, women and children imprisoned behind bars. As the eyes of those waiting to be slaughtered gazed out at him, he was arrested with a wondering thought: *"Our Lord was a Jew,"* he later wrote, *"and I see Christ crucified in Yad Vashem."*

There are a number of scriptures which indicate a similar understanding: that the suffering of the Jews during the Holocaust may be identified in some way with that of Christ upon the cross. This might be regarded as a consequence of the fact that the people of Israel have always retained their status as servant of the Lord (Luke 1:54), and as such are linked with God's ultimate Servant, Jesus, in a profound and inescapable way.

In the book of Romans, Paul expressed his doctrine, the heart of his gospel, in the words of the prophet Habakkuk: *"The one who is righteous by faith will live"* (Romans 1:17 LEB). He claims this assertion was designated by God to mean the righteousness, not of the law, but of faith in Christ. This argument then leads to the dense statement of Romans 3:21-26, where Paul declares that God "justifies the ungodly" by setting forth Christ as the propitiation for their sins. Subsequently he enlarges upon this theme by identifying God as the One "who gives life to the dead and calls into existence things that are not" (Romans 4:17), who possesses a life-giving power which can bring a son to Abraham when he is past the age. It is this same omnipotence which has raised Christ from the dead, and God now calls those who are spiritually dead to the promise of new life through faith in the One who is Himself the Resurrection and the Life. It therefore emerges that hope in the promise of God who raises the dead is the true hallmark of faith.

Romans chapter 9 through 11, where Paul turns to the question of the Jewish people, is not a digression from this theme but rather the crowning section of his argument and an impassioned plea on behalf of his brethren. He acknowledges that in the present situation of the Jews there is something largely beyond human responsibility; in fact, we are in the presence of a mystery. There is a direct relationship between the fault or rejection of the Jews and the salvation of the Gentiles; however, the rejection or casting aside of the Jews is not the end of the story, for this will ultimately issue in their reacceptance - an eschatological renewal which will take place through that same resurrection power of which he has been speaking. And, since their rejection meant the reconciliation of the world, their reacceptance will mean nothing less than "life from the dead", an ultimate raising up which refers not only to the final destiny of Israel but also to the whole of humanity. It is possible, therefore, to see strong suggestions of a connection between the death and resurrection of Christ and the rejection and acceptance of Israel.

The church herself is a "mystery" which can be understood only in her relationship to Israel, who precedes her in election and to whom still pertain "the adoption, the glory and the covenants " (Romans 9:4). The Gentile believers have been grafted into the covenant as wild branches into an olive tree, to use Paul's vivid terminology, whereas the people of Israel form the natural branches. The Apostle therefore emphasizes the need for members of the church to forswear arrogance and cultivate an attitude of humility toward the chosen people. It was through His cross that Jesus broke down the dividing wall of separation between these two entities, making them into one (Ephesians 2:14). The unity of Jews and Gentiles thus brought about constitutes one of the fundamental purposes of salvation – and the great reconciliation accomplished there should be realized in mutual love. As a result, Paul urges his readers to a way of life that would be filled with power to reveal the truth of the gospel and provoke the Jews to jealousy. Yet has the church fulfilled this mandate, or has she not rather, over the past two thousand years, emphasized the division she was supposed to overcome?

When the terrible history of anti-Semitism throughout the centuries is reflected upon, it becomes devastatingly clear that the Jews have suffered greatly within the Christian world itself, and most particularly in our own day and time in the very heart of Europe. The Nazi genocide of the Jewish people can be considered for many reasons the most calamitous event in history - but has not as yet made a corresponding impact upon our theology. The church indeed bears a heavy responsibility for the conditions that made the Holocaust possible and this is a recognition which cannot go without repentance: "the tempest that fell on the Jewish people is at the same time a judgment that has fallen on the Christian world". And yet, above all, this is the disaster in which Israel experienced not only the silence of the Gentiles but also the silence of God - perhaps the same abandonment which Jesus experienced on the cross, expressed in His cry: "*My God, My God ...*".

Hannah Senesh was a young Jewish woman who was sent on an assignment by the British Army during World War II to help rescue Hungarian Jews about to be deported to Auschwitz. Parachuted into Yugoslavia, Senesh was arrested at the Hungarian border, then imprisoned and tortured, but refused to reveal details of her mission; she was eventually tried and executed by firing squad. She wrote a poem in her secret diary in 1942, just before she died. It is the best known of her songs, *Halikha LeKesariya* ("A Walk to Caesarea"), commonly known as *Eli, Eli* ("My God, My God"); it affirms the eternal power of prayer and is often sung in ceremonies marking Holocaust Remembrance Day in Israel.

The Psalm of the Lord's Appearing

....

Days of sad commemoration finally give way in Jerusalem to a time of rejoicing: the glad ceremonies of *Yom HaAtzmaut*. On this, their Independence Day, the people of Israel celebrate the miraculous rebirth of their nation - out of the ashes of the Holocaust and after the devastating experience of World War II. Considering the fact that the Hebrew Scriptures were written by and for the people of Israel, it is surely appropriate to ask whether this astonishing event may also have been foretold in the Bible. Once again, Psalm 102 provides a key to unlocking the answer.

The psalm was most probably written as the Jewish people were mourning the loss of their homeland during the first exile in Babylon - nevertheless, it seems that the ancient and very specific prophecies it contains are only now being fulfilled in the modern era. The psalm clearly strikes an eschatological note, stating that the things set down in it *"shall be written for the generation to come"*. In Hebrew, the words "generation to come", or *l'dor acharon*, actually mean "the last generation", suggesting the psalm could not be comprehended fully before the arrival of the time of the end.

The first verses of the psalm describe the sufferings of an afflicted individual which in their precise details bear remarkable parallels to the experience of the Jews during the Holocaust. But then, suddenly, there is a marked change in tone. Even as he is becoming overwhelmed by his adversities the psalmist turns to God and begins to proclaim His greatness and everlasting power. As he does so a new awareness arises in him, which issues in an inspired prophecy:

"You will arise and have mercy on Zion; for the time to favor her, yes, the set time, has come" (v 13).

He is predicting that a special moment in history which has been definitely appointed and set aside will finally arrive, when God will remember and honor the gracious promises He made to His people, most especially those concerning their regathering to Zion. And indeed, in 1948, as the nations were still stunned by the revelation of the attempt to exterminate the Jewish people in their very midst, the sovereign state of Israel came into being. The return of the Jewish people to their ancient homeland after almost 2,000 years of exile is an event unprecedented in history. It may best be understood not as the result of heroic leadership, nor of Zionism, although both have played their part, but as an act of God's powerful intervention in world affairs.

According to the psalmist, this mercy which God shows occurs in response to the love of His people for Jerusalem: *"For,"* he writes, *"your servants take pleasure in her stones, and show favor to her dust"* (verse 14). God's servants love first of all that quintessential feature of Jerusalem - her stones. It was over her rocky pathways that King David led his people in procession, that the prophets delivered their fiery messages, and Jesus Himself walked with His disciples. From the stone walls surrounding the city and from the massive Western Wall (Kotel) countless prayers have ascended over the centuries. Day by day the sun falls upon these ramparts, gilding them with gold at dawn, then with various shades throughout the day until a rosy flush suffuses them at dusk, inspiring the refrain: *Yerushalayim of gold, of bronze, of light.*

This love for Jerusalem is one which persists through seasons of disfavor also: according to verse 14 God's servants also care for the very *dust* of Zion. When the city of Jerusalem was destroyed by the Babylonians, there were those who returned and with passionate determination sought her rebuilding. During the second great dispersal of the Jewish people, after the Romans razed the city and Temple in 70 AD, this longing for Zion continued unabated – poignantly expressed by Jewish poet Judah HaLevi, writing in exile in Spain during the twelfth century, who yearned to water the dust of Jerusalem with his tears and press his lips to her stones.

With the departure of the Jewish people from *Eretz Israel* the land experienced many centuries of decay and by the nineteenth century travelers were noting the extreme barrenness of the region. Yet as the story moved toward the birth of the Zionist movement Jewish hopes of a return to their homeland became strongly supported by countless Christians who had read and believed the biblical promises. Many of these Christian Restorationists carried out extensive work in Palestine in the fields of surveying, mapping and geography: as true lovers of her dust they thus pioneered the work of archaeology in the Holy Land. They also helped pave the way for return by laboring to improve Jerusalem with the introduction of modern infrastructure, schools and hospitals. But it is since the re-establishment of the State of Israel in 1948 that Jerusalem has truly been transformed so that this city, which in the 1880's Mark Twain called a "neglected, forlorn, religious relic that no one cares about", is now a vibrant, beautiful and growing metropolis, home to a million citizens, site of numerous cultural, religious and political institutions – and a continual focus of world attention.

The writer of Psalm 102, who had foreseen this restoration, unfolded further the prophetic implications of this time of favor: *"When the Lord shall build up Zion ..."* (it is the *Lord* who drew these dedicated individuals to the land in a divinely mandated process) ... *"He shall appear in His glory"* (verse 16). When Christians see the land of Israel and the city of Jerusalem given again into the hands of the Jewish people they can then look for that "blessed hope" which has sustained them for two millennia: the return of Jesus in a Second Coming which will differ markedly from His first. That was one of lowliness and obscurity in which He suffered much rejection as He accomplished His task of redeeming the world; this next advent, however, will be filled with "power and great glory" as He appears before the nations accompanied by the holy angels. It is then that very eye shall see His majesty and transcendent power, for it shall be as *"the lightning that flashes out of one part under heaven shines to the other"* (Luke 17:24).

The time of this return, the consummation of world history, is pinpointed even more precisely in this astonishingly visionary psalm when it is remembered that it is written for "the last generation". In other words, it may be that the rebuilding of Zion and the Second Coming will each transpire within the span of a single generation *"...and the people which shall be created shall praise the Lord"* (verse 18). The word "created" here, Hebrew *bara*, means "a new creation", the same word used in Genesis 1:1 when God "created" the heavens and the earth. And as God shows this favor by restoring Zion, so, according to verse 15, *"the nations shall fear the name of the LORD, and all the kings of the earth His glory"*.

Going Ahead to Galilee

···

ccording to Luke's Gospel, during a period of 40 days following
Easter Sunday the Risen Christ appeared to His followers and
spoke to them of "things pertaining to the kingdom of God"
(Acts 1:3). Some of these encounters took place in Jerusalem - but the
Gospels highlight another meeting place as well. Before His death,
Jesus promised His disciples, "After I am raised, I will go ahead of you
into Galilee" (Matthew 26:32). The angel who met the women at the
tomb early on the resurrection morning urged them to "Go quickly and
tell his disciples that He is risen from the dead and is going before you
into Galilee" (Matthew 28:7), and this instruction was later reiterated
by Jesus Himself. Why such special insistence upon this location? To
answer this question, it is necessary to gain first of all an historical and
geographical understanding of the region.

Galilee today is one of the most famous place-names in the world, but
this was not always so. It was first mentioned in the Old Testament in
connection with Joshua's conquest of the area, although the Israelite
tribes who settled there continued to co-exist with their Canaanite
neighbors. Later, King David united the northern and southern tribes
into one kingdom with the capital at Jerusalem, but after the death of
Solomon the ten tribes in the north broke away. Their kingdom, Israel,
then became subject to rulers from a number of different dynasties,
while the descendants of David continued to reign over Judah in the
south. Under a succession of ungodly kings in both realms many of
the people turned to false worship and prophets began to warn of a

coming judgment. In somber words, the prophet Isaiah forecast a time of impending distress and disaster for the people:

"They will look to the earth and see trouble and darkness, gloom or anguish; and they will be driven into darkness" (Isaiah 8:22)

These words vividly describe the terrible fate which actually befell the citizens of the northern kingdom in the 8th century BC, when the region was invaded and conquered by Assyrian armies, the people deported, and the land forcibly resettled with foreigners. The area that had been the homeland of the ten northern tribes, including Zebulun and Naphtali, then became "Galilee of the nations" (from Hebrew *Galil* signifying a "circle" or "circuit") and stripped of its identity as part of the promised land. It must have seemed a forcible declaration that God had turned away from His people and "lightly esteemed" them. But suffering and distress were not Isaiah's last words. Precisely in those lands which had experienced the death-dealing Assyrian invasion a great light would shine, and the darkness that covered the region would be dispelled by the blazing forth of this brightness. Its revivifying light, full of divine glory and radiance, would bring hope and consolation to the peoples:

"... by the way of the sea, beyond the Jordan, in Galilee of the Gentiles: the people who walked in darkness have seen a great light: they that dwell in the land of the shadow of death, upon them a light has shined" (Isaiah 9:1-2)

In the first part of this passage, Isaiah was denoting the territories that Israel had lost to Tiglath Pileser III in the earliest Assyrian campaign; the expression "by the way of the sea" probably referred to the road from Dan to the sea at Tyre which marked the northern border of Israel at the time of the conquest. The first result of this great light shining over the peoples would involve the defeat of their Assyrian oppressors, just as Midian had been defeated in days of old. This would enable the exiles to return to their homelands, traversing through the same territories

65

on the way. The mighty Assyrian Empire was indeed conquered by the Babylonians - but there was no subsequent edict issued to the ten northern tribes allowing restoration. Babylon in turn was conquered by the Persians and in 333 BC Alexander the Great swept through the region. Thus the land continued under foreign domination until a period of independence arrived under the Maccabees. During the first century BC the Hasmonean rulers from this family attempted to reunite the Galilean area with the south, transporting Jewish families to the region and giving them large tracts of the beautiful fertile land.

Could this development be considered the fulfillment of Isaiah's prediction of a glorious future time, when the tribes of Israel would be safe from their enemies and their land prosperous? If so, it did not last very long, for shortly thereafter the area was once again groaning under the yoke of oppression, this time that of the Romans. When and how, therefore, was Isaiah's prophecy to be accomplished? The key is to be found in the verses which follow. The oracle of the great light shining upon a people in darkness does not end there, but rather forms a preliminary introduction, an ascending note to a yet more illustrious passage which promises the birth of a descendant of David: "Unto us a Child is born, a Son is given ..." (Isaiah 9:6). This larger Messianic context suggests that the prophecy could refer to an even greater deliverance - one that only the Messiah could bring.

Early in his Gospel, Matthew cites this verse in relation to the ministry of Jesus. After informing his readers that Jesus arrived in Galilee, and chose not to settle in his hometown of Nazareth but in Capernaum by the sea, he writes:

"This was to fulfill what was spoken through Isaiah the prophet: 'The land of Zebulun and the land of Naphtali, by the way of the sea, beyond the Jordan, Galilee of the Gentiles— The people who sat in darkness have seen a great light, and upon those who sat in the region and shadow of death light has dawned'" (Matthew 4:14-16).

Although John's Gospel places Jesus in Jerusalem at the beginning of His mission, Matthew and the other Synoptics present Jesus' ministry as commencing in Galilee. Throughout his Gospel, Matthew continues to stress Jesus' Galilean connections: there He grew up, there the greater portion of His active ministry occurred, and His disciples also came from that region. Jesus, he says, went "throughout *all* Galilee," teaching, preaching, and healing, and gathered a following from a wide geographical area including Syria, the Decapolis, and beyond the Jordan. Through his citation of the Isaiah scripture Matthew wanted his audience to know that Jesus' arrival in Galilee was a deliberate choice on His part, which involved the fulfillment of prophecy and formed another demonstration that Jesus was the promised Messiah. What did the Evangelist recognize about the spiritual significance of this association with Galilee which caused him to lay so much emphasis upon it? Two ideas suggest themselves.

In 53:2, Isaiah had given a further prophecy about the coming Messiah: that he would grow up as "a root out of dry ground". Perhaps, for Matthew, the identification of Jesus with Galilee was an integral part of the Messiah's first coming in humility and lowliness. For the Jews of Judah and Jerusalem, Galilee was not considered a likely soil for the appearing of the Messiah, nor did early rabbinic references suggest this possibility. Capernaum, moreover, was hardly the kind of great city which could be expected to operate as headquarters for the long-awaited Deliverer. Galilee was not just geographically far from Jerusalem, its people were considered spiritually less pure than those in the south, and there was the seemingly insurmountable problem of the mixed racial composition of the region. In short, it was a scandal that the Messiah should come from Galilee. Yet it was this very debasement which made the people feel more strongly their need of a Savior (Matthew 9:13), so it was this same region which acquired everlasting fame through His presence, ministry, and miracles among them.

It was appropriate, too, that the One destined as a "Light to the Gentiles" should minister chiefly on the borderland of Israel. Matthew shows Jesus' activity centered around the Sea of Galilee, a busy thriving region where towns with large populations crowded the shores and fleets of sailing boats covered the waters. The account of Jesus' words and deeds is set against a rural background involving sowing and reaping, mending nets and fishing. Here beside the lake He made His irresistible call to His disciples: "Follow Me, and I will make you fishers of men".

Yet just beyond those waters were the surrounding Gentile areas, with imposing cities that boasted stately forums, amphitheatres and temples. The Greco-Roman influences in the region pressed hard upon the simple life of Jewish tradition pictured in the Gospels. Glimpses of that other world are to be caught everywhere: in the figures of centurions and publicans, in the story of the demoniac crying that his name was Legion, in the parables of opulence and wealth, servants and masters, and in the customs houses on the tollways - from one of which Matthew was called. It is to this mixed world, situated on the threshold of an even wider realm, that the disciples return to meet the Risen Christ, and from there He sent them to carry the light of His truth to all the nations.

The Branch of Jesse

··

M atthew, the First Evangelist, also detects a singular importance which is to be attached to the fact that Jesus came from Nazareth. At the beginning of his Gospel, as a kind of frontispiece, Matthew details Jesus' genealogy as son of Abraham and son of David, and then devotes significant space to describing the tumultuous events in the early life of "the one who is called Christ". He tells the story of the birth of Jesus in Bethlehem of Judea and the flight of Joseph and Mary with their young Child into Egypt. This was to escape the murderous wrath of Herod, who instigated the slaying of the firstborn children in Bethlehem to prevent the emergence of another "King of the Jews". After Herod died an angel appeared to Joseph assuring him it was safe to return to the land of Israel, "for those who sought the young Child's life are dead" (Matthew 2:20). Matthew relates that Joseph then took Mary and the Child and came back to Israel; however, when he heard that Archelaus was reigning over Judea in place of Herod, he was afraid to go there. There was good reason for his apprehension.

The Jewish historian Josephus provides a significant amount of information about this son and principal heir of Herod the Great. After his father's death in 4 BC, 18-year-old Archelaus found himself poised to take over the kingdom. Even before he had been confirmed in this position by the Emperor, however, Archelaus had managed to alienate his Jewish subjects. A popular uprising had begun in Jerusalem when a number of rabbis, who had torn down a golden eagle placed by Herod on one of the Temple gates, were burned to death. Archelaus ordered out his whole garrison to deal with the insurrection and in the massacre that ensued three thousand were left dead within the Temple precincts. Although Archelaus was subsequently appointed Ethnarch of Judea by Augustus, he failed in his brief reign to redeem the house of Herod. Rather, his mixed Idumean and Samaritan lineage as well as his tendencies toward cruelty and tyranny continued to provoke the populace, nor did he possess any of the leadership gifts of his father. Eventually a united deputation of Jews and Samaritans prevailed upon Rome to have Archelaus removed and he was sent into exile in 6 AD - the end of independent rule in Judea.

Therefore, Matthew informs his readers, Joseph determined to leave the environs of Jerusalem and Judea and travelled north to Galilee:

"And he came and dwelt in a city called Nazareth: that it might be fulfilled which was spoken by the prophets, He shall be called a Nazarene" (Matthew 2:23)

Throughout his Gospel Matthew demonstrates a fondness for alluding to Old Testament scriptures he believed to have been fulfilled in the life of Jesus. However, there is actually no prophecy in the Old Testament which states the Messiah will be "called a Nazarene". What, then, can Matthew possibly be suggesting? A solution to the puzzle may be found in the fact that, contrary to his usual practice, Matthew here refers to "prophets" in the plural - that is, he is pointing to a prophetic *theme* rather than an individual prediction. And in fact the Greek word he uses, *nazoraios,* has definite echoes of some very significant terms found in the Hebrew Scriptures.

The best explanation of the origin of this name appears to be that which traces it to the word *netzer* in Isaiah 11:1, which reads: "There shall come forth a rod out of the stem of Jesse, and a branch (*netzer*) shall grow out of his roots". Matthew believed that this promise had been fulfilled in Jesus, who was descended from Jesse's family, and who by dwelling at Nazareth would be called "a Nazarene", or "*Netzer, the Branch*". The little town of Nazareth in lower Galilee, mentioned neither in the Old Testament nor in Josephus, was probably so called from its insignificance: a small twig in contrast to a stately tree, and accordingly somewhat despised: "Can any good thing come out of Nazareth?" (John 1:46). Here the royal scion of the house and lineage of David could grow to manhood, far from the machinations of the Herodian family in Jerusalem and other centers of power. Moreover, the idea of Christ as the divinely placed "Branch", insignificant in its shooting forth, but destined as the Fulfiller of the Messianic task was true to the whole subsequent history of Christ.

As well as *netzer* there is another Hebrew word translated "Branch", which further elucidates the significance of the title. This word, "*tsemach*", is one of the most prominent of the names by which the Messiah was to be called, as suggested by its inclusion in the interwoven tapestry of blessings and petitions that Jews pray three times a day. The 15th of the Eighteen Benedictions is a prayer for the rise of the Messianic king, called "The Branch of David". There are also four major scriptures in which the Messiah is introduced under this title in the Old Testament (Isaiah 4:2; Jeremiah 23:5; Zechariah 3:8; Zechariah 6:12-13). According to these verses the "Branch" to come shall be of the house of David; he will be a righteous judge, a king and a priest; he will save Israel and Judah and build the Temple of God; and in him the Gentiles will trust. In him are attributes both divine and human, and he is associated with ideas of beauty and glory as well as those of lowliness and servanthood. It is this collation of terms and images which functions to describe the multifaceted nature of the expected Messiah.

The Evangelists provide very few details about Jesus' years in Nazareth, where He grew up in the hiddenness and obscurity suggested by the Matthean text. It is nevertheless possible to make some suggestions about his experiences there, how these impacted Him and helped prepare Him for His ministry. Galilee was a cosmopolitan setting, located close to great commercial centers and open to impressions and influences coming from a wider realm. The richness and beauty of the Galilean landscape also contrasted sharply with the hard, rocky terrain of Jerusalem in the south. In ancient times, as now, Galilee was Israel's most fertile region, known for its sunny, temperate climate, its vineyards and orchards watered by abundant streams, and the wildflowers which covered the slopes each spring. The town of Nazareth itself lay in a valley where its small houses, sheltered by green hills on each side, appeared as "a handful of pearls in a goblet of emerald". Yet as a boy Jesus could have climbed to the "brow of the hill on which the city was built" (Luke 4:29) and looked out on a vast panorama, akin to a picture book in which he could see illustrated all the vivid drama of His people's history.

To the south, the great plain of Esdraelon, scene of immemorial battles, was traversed by caravans carrying goods for trade between Egypt and Syria. Just a little way east lay Mount Gilboa where Saul and Jonathan were slain, their shields "vilely cast away", and further still was the great rift valley down which coursed the River Jordan with its many associations for the people of Israel. Westward could be glimpsed the long wooded ridge of Mount Carmel where Elijah had confronted the prophets of Baal, beyond which glinted the azure waters of the Mediterranean. Looking north were the highlands of Galilee, with the Sea of Gennesaret set as a blue jewel in their midst, and rising above these the snow-tipped mountains of Lebanon. But in Nazareth the young boy must also have become aware of, and deeply touched by, the glories of the natural world which surrounded Him, which thereafter lent vividness and color to his teaching. For Jesus, this was His Father's world, and He saw the gentle flowers adorning the field as providing a splendor which surpassed that of Solomon; in the deepest parts of His being He received the impression of God's love and care for all His creation, assuring Him that there was a special providence even in the fall of a sparrow.

Thus Jesus grew up in Nazareth instructed by both the Book of the Law and the Book of Nature. Over them both He bent His kindling look, searching heart and limitless power of thought, so that all His learning coalesced into words and teaching suffused with a matchless grace, and a power that would cause type and shadow to emerge in living color, open radiant glimpses of the Kingdom of Heaven to His hearers, and penetrate heart and soul as no teacher before or since. Henceforth Jesus would be known to all the world by the distinctive designation, *Jesus of Nazareth.*

The Intertwined Miracles

··

T he roads of Galilee are one of her most singular features. The region is crossed by many of the world's famous highways, paths which long ago were trodden by the patriarchs, trade routes along which exotic wares were conveyed from one end of empire to another, and broad thoroughfares over which the chariots of Assyria and Rome thundered. But these byways have become metamorphosed in our collective historical imagination. Their present-day significance is perhaps best explained by Scottish theologian George Adam Smith, who traveled extensively throughout the region on horseback during the late 19th century. In his classic work *The Historical Geography of the Holy Land* he noted that:

"It was up and down these roads that the immortal figures of the Parables passed. By them came the merchant seeking goodly pearls, the king departing to receive his kingdom, the friend on a journey, the householder arriving suddenly upon his servants, the prodigal son coming back from a far-off country."

Along the roads leading from Jerusalem to Galilee, around the year 33 AD, an unremarkable group of Galileans might have been glimpsed as they made their way north. Their conversation as they walked revealed they were still somewhat bewildered by the events which had taken place recently in Jerusalem and uncertain of their future, but at the same time a radiant new hope was burning in their hearts.

Their journey would eventually bring them to the plateau rising above the Sea of Galilee, from where they could behold the length and breadth of the lake, seemingly shaped like a harp. It is because of this fortuitous resemblance that the Sea is called in Hebrew *Kinneret* (from *kinnor*, a harp), a musical name which evokes the beauty of her sparkling waves. Surrounding and girdling the expanse of blue waters are verdant hills which at dusk become cloaked in shades of violet, while at night the stars seem to light the sky with a special brilliancy and luster. This favored region was famed for its abundant fruitfulness; according to Josephus the area had soil so rich that all sorts of trees would grow upon it and he lists palms, figs, olives, walnuts and grapes. Proof of that luxuriance could be seen as the small group descended the slopes surrounding the Sea, which were adorned with a wealth of flowering plants, gardens and orchards.

A Kinneret Road

Memories would have crowded in upon them as they walked. Their Master, Jesus, holding the crowds entranced by the seashore, speaking words which though "heaven and earth pass away" would never pass away, and moments of intimate fellowship as He unfolded to them the inner mysteries of the Kingdom of God. And of course there were the miracles, the "deeds of power", they witnessed. One particularly memorable event took place on the very road on which they walked as they made their way to Capernaum. The account of it would later appear in all three Synoptic Gospels.

Jesus' fame had spread far and wide and He was at the height of His popularity, so that even Gentiles who had heard of His miraculous healing power were coming to Him from the surrounding countries. As He trod along the dusty roads beside the lake that day, great crowds thronged him. Then came to Him one of the rulers of the synagogue, named Jairus, who fell at Jesus' feet and implored Him to come and heal his 12-year-old daughter who was just then at the point of death; moreover, she was his only child. Jesus accompanied the ruler but, as they were on the way, a woman who had been afflicted with an issue of blood for 12 years came up behind Jesus in the crowd. Pressing through the multitude, she managed to reach out and touch His prayer shawl, for, she said to herself, "If I shall just touch the hem of His garment I shall be made well".

As she did so, instantly "the fountain of her blood" dried up and she knew she had been healed. But Jesus was aware that power had flowed out of Him. He turned to see her who had done this thing and the woman came forth trembling to confess before all the crowd what had happened. Jesus then commended her for her faith: "Daughter, your faith has saved you," He said to her, "Go in peace." Jairus must have been half mad with apprehension and fear for his daughter by this stage and, indeed, a messenger arrived at that point to inform him not to "trouble the Master" any further, for his daughter had died. Jesus instantly reassured the stricken father and they proceeded to the house. Here was "a tumult" and much weeping and wailing, but He remonstrated with them, "Why make this commotion and weep? The child is not dead but sleeping." Having put out the mourners, and taking only the girl's parents and three disciples, He entered the room where she was lying, and taking her by the hand spoke the words, *Talitha Cumi!* - "Little girl, I say to you, arise!" - and the girl rose up and walked.

As a double healing miracle the narrative was striking enough in itself. In all three Synoptic versions, the account of the woman with the flow of blood is intertwined with the story of the healing of Jairus' daughter through the literary device of intercalation. This strategy, in which an author opens with one story, interrupts it to tell another, and finally returns to complete the first story, allows each narrative to be interpreted in the light of the other. Why do the Gospels present the two stories in this way? Very early on, some of the Church Fathers noted that the central theme in both narratives was that of restoration and new life, and that many of the details in the accounts dovetailed, especially the number 12 which has a special significance in the scriptures. The woman had her issue of blood 12 years and the little girl was 12 years of age when she died, reminiscent of the fact that there were 12 tribes of Israel and 12 apostles of the church. The Fathers therefore gave the whole narrative a spiritual or allegorical interpretation related to both Israel and the church, with the woman representing the Gentiles and Jairus' daughter the Jewish people.

For many centuries, even before their exile from the land, God's chosen people had been waiting for a Messiah who would bring deliverance, healing (Isaiah 53:5) and blessing to the nation. But the illness of the daughter of the synagogue during her 12th year suggested the polity of Israel was at that point spiritually moribund and ready to die at the very time when she should have borne spiritual progeny. Jairus represented the faithful remnant of his people who recognized the Messiah and implored His aid and healing power for the nation. Jesus, who had come for His own, hastened to his house - but on the way was interrupted as the woman with the issue of blood claimed His complete attention.

The woman had an illness which rendered her ritually unclean according to Leviticus 15:19, and in this situation she symbolized the Gentile nations as a whole. Moreover, she had suffered from her condition for 12 years - that is, from the time Jairus' daughter had been born - suggesting that the Gentiles had been deemed unclean from the moment Israel had been constituted as a nation. This was because the same giving of the Law at Mount Sinai that had created Israel had also exposed the spiritual exigency of the Gentiles: "the Scripture has concluded all under sin" (Galatians 3:22). As a result, the woman had actually no right to approach Jesus - or any Jew - but in her desperate need she nevertheless pressed in to touch the border of His garment. Instantly she was purified through the outflow of His power and love and as a crowning blessing Jesus addressed her as "daughter" - an honor given to no other woman in the Gospels. It signaled she had been brought into the covenant and accepted as belonging to the people of God.

But in this delay, alas, the daughter of Jairus dies. The synagogue leader held on in trembling faith until Jesus finally reached his home and, taking the little girl by the hand, raised her to new life. To Him the little girl was just sleeping, to be awakened at the time which had been foreordained, through His word and the touch of His hand. As a result of the experience Jairus became *illuminated* by the revelation of the resurrection power of Jesus, as his name had prophetically foretold, and understood that the same love and mercy which had healed his daughter had also been extended to the Gentile woman. As a whole, the narrative is therefore a dramatic illustration of the course of salvation history which Paul explains clearly in Romans chapters 9 through 11: that Israel would first believe, then the fullness of the Gentiles would come in, and finally all Israel would be saved.

The purpose of God, who loves the whole world He has created, was always to draw all the nations into His kingdom, but this intention was at first hidden in His election of one nation: Israel. To her He had committed the "the glory, the law, the covenants, and the service" (Romans 9:4) to prepare her as a vessel through whom His light and truth would shine to the ends of the earth. He also promised His people that He would send them a Messiah, one who would redeem them from oppression and bring all Gentiles to join Israel in worship and obedience to God. For this great Deliverer all faithful Israelites waited, but did not foresee the tragic development that would ensue: that they themselves as a nation would reject the Messiah. It was hidden to their view that a long interval would intervene between his first coming in humility and the second in glory, just as two mountain ranges from afar seem to merge into one and the long distance between them is concealed. As a result they entered a long period of national eclipse and suffering.

Israel's rejection of her Messiah appears to human reasoning a puzzling enigma, a fatal overthrow of God's program to extend His Kingdom reign of mercy and love throughout the earth. However, the non-acceptance of the gospel by the Jews instead became the occasion of a marvelous new demonstration of divine grace and wisdom, for it was their fall which made possible the salvation of the Gentiles (Romans 11:11). The church which sprang into being simultaneously with the casting off of the chosen people was a new creation of God's love and power, called from all peoples and nations to carry out His beneficent purposes during the period of Israel's disfavor. Just as the woman who touched Jesus' garment was healed and could no longer hide herself, so the church is presently in the world as a light and a witness, testifying of the grace of God which has brought salvation and anticipating the Second Coming of the Messiah.

Paul also reveals in Romans that, within this eschatological framework, it is the salvation of the Gentiles which will eventually play a key role in bringing the Jews to recognition of their Messiah. God's tender heart toward the people He foreknew will not allow Him to cast them off, and the gifts and callings He bestowed upon them so lavishly are without repentance. When the fullness of the Gentiles has come in God shall arise and have mercy on His beloved people, their lands and fortunes shall be restored, and from Zion as a fountainhead streams of blessing shall flow into all nations. "For," says the Apostle, "if their being cast away is the reconciling of the world, what will their reacceptance be but life from the dead?" (Romans 11:15).

The restoration of God's people through whom the nations are to be blessed is presently taking place - for those who have eyes to see. It is an assurance that all the ancient predictions of the prophets shall come to pass and that every land and kingdom will be filled with the knowledge of God. Jew and Gentile are thus comprehended together in God's matchless plan for the ages:

"For God has concluded them all in unbelief, that he might have mercy upon all. O the depth of the riches both of the wisdom and knowledge of God! how unsearchable are his judgments, and his ways past finding out!" (Romans 11:32-33)

Universal Dominion and
a Universal Task

....

Where, amongst the scenes of His former ministry, were the disciples to meet with Jesus in Galilee? According to Matthew Jesus had "appointed" a certain mountain for this encounter. In the final chapter of his Gospel the Evangelist then relates what transpired at this epochal event – most probably the occasion Paul also mentions (1 Corinthians 15) when the Risen Jesus appeared to more than 500 of His followers at one time. It was then He spoke to His disciples the words which set the stage for subsequent world mission and the evangelizing of all nations in the Name of the Father, Son and Spirit. Is it possible, twenty centuries later, to locate the site of that encounter?

The most prominent physical landmark which can be discerned today around the Sea of Galilee is Mount Arbel, towering over the western shore of the Sea of Galilee in the vicinity of ancient Magdala, home of Mary Magdalene. Below the sheer face of the mountain lies Wadi Hamam, named for the doves with pink-grey feathers whose wings may still be seen today fluttering in the valley. This was a natural access route into the lake area and a road probably used by Jesus Himself as He travelled back and forth to Cana and Nazareth from Capernaum, the centre of His ministry in Galilee.

Arbel has only one mention in scripture which suggests a rather dark and turbulent history, associated with the struggle for political dominion which afflicted the region so continuously. Hosea 10:14 reads:

"Therefore tumult shall arise among your people, and all your fortresses shall be plundered as Shalman plundered Beth Arbel in the day of battle; a mother dashed in pieces upon her children". This describes the manner in which Assyrian invaders mercilessly killed many Israelites by throwing them from the steep sides of the mountain. Arbel was also a primary site of the Jewish resistance against Herod the Great in 39 BC during the period when the Idumean king was rising to power, and once again became a scene of great slaughter. As the Jewish fighters were sheltering in caves on the sheer north face of the mountain, Herod let his men down in baskets and fished them from their hideouts, forcing them off the cliff to their destruction; he then went on to conquer the city of Jerusalem.

Today the precipice of Arbel provides a challenge for hikers and mountain climbers, yet if they attain its summit they are afforded a breathtaking view which also showcases most of the areas in which Jesus ministered. Far below lie the towns of Capernaum, Bethsaida, and Korazin; while to the north, beyond the Mount of Beatitudes, the panorama extends to encompass the landscapes of Tsefat, the Golan Heights and even on a clear day the snowy peaks of Hermon. Southward is the distinctive outline of Mount Tabor; while away to the east is the mountainous region of the Decapolis – the beginning of the Gentile regions.

If this was indeed the place where Jesus met with His disciples, it was a sublime setting for the world-wide mission He entrusted to them. From these heights He commanded them to go forth bearing His gospel to all the nations of the earth, so that all peoples, ranging from the most unenlightened to the most cultured, throughout the unfolding ages of history, would be enabled to enter into covenant relationship with the Triune God. It was a task so vast as to be almost beyond comprehension. But the authority of Jesus to deliver such an assignment to His followers was disclosed in the preface to this charge, the declaration of His own majesty and co-equality with God the Father: *"All power is given unto Me in heaven and in earth"* (Matthew 28:18 KJV).

Because these words have become so familiar, it is possible to forget how truly astonishing they were. Only a few weeks before Jesus gave this commission it seemed His work had failed irrevocably and that He had "spent His strength for nought" (Isaiah 49:4). Despite a ministry attended with much initial success and acclaim His nation had turned against Him; the religious leaders had denounced Him and adjudged Him worthy of death; all the weight and authority of the Roman Empire had ratified this sentence so that He was made to suffer the most cruel and ignominious of penalties, crucified between two malefactors; while His own disciples forsook Him and fled. The whole world had united in rejecting Him and believed that His crucifixion and burial signaled the final destruction of His mission.

Yet now with royal emphasis the Risen Jesus asserts His omnipotence in heaven and on earth. Unseen but tangible a crown of victory adorns His brow, His words are majestic and gracious, and His commands carry supreme authority. Those who had failed Him in His hour of need He now appoints and sends forth as His messengers, not merely to His own nation of Israel, but to all the peoples of the earth, to bring them the knowledge of salvation. The weapon with which they are to conquer the hearts and minds of men and women is the message of Christ crucified; and they are to be sustained in this mission not through worldly power, wealth or eloquence, but above all through the Lord's own Presence with them, "even to the end of the age".

Matthew's account conveys the sense of awe which gripped the disciples as they listened to these commands. And yet a jarring note is struck: "they worshipped, *but some doubted*". From whence did such unbelief spring, even as the words of the Risen Christ fell upon their ears?

Their uncertainty can be explained through a consideration of Jesus' final discourse in the Upper Room on the night He was betrayed, when He told the disciples that "He who loves Me will be loved by My Father, and I will love him and manifest Myself to him" (John 14:21).

Following this, Judas (not Iscariot) asked, "Lord, how is it that You will manifest Yourself to us, and not to the world?" In these, his only words recorded in the Gospels, Judas was clearly thinking of outward physical disclosure. The common Jewish expectation of the time was for a Messiah who should establish an earthly kingdom: how then could the Lord sit on the throne of David and rule the world without disclosing His identity to all His subjects, as well as the religious authorities and the powerful Romans?

Judas' question almost certainly expressed one of the deepest perplexities troubling the hearts of the Twelve. However, the query gave Jesus the opportunity to explain further what He wanted them to understand. *"If anyone loves Me,"* He tells them, *"he will keep My word; and My Father will love him, and We will come to him and make Our home with him"* (John 14:23). He was revealing that there is a kind of inward unveiling of God's presence which could only be recognized and received by those who love and obey Him as Lord and Savior.

To these Jesus manifests Himself, shining the light of His glory upon them, and giving to them an ever-clearer revelation of His glory in God's eternal kingdom and the splendor and power of His approaching rule over the nations. They, therefore, shall with ever-increasing eagerness be looking for and hastening the coming of their Lord; and it may even be that He will soon return as that Traveler from a far country, to take up His throne in Jerusalem and exercise His dominion of *shalom* over all the earth.

Girded with Divine Strength

On the western shores of the Sea of Galilee is a place called Tabgha, where there is a church built out of grey basalt stones located beside a small rocky beach. Here, in the early morning, the sight of the sun rising over the waters is spectacular. After the first faint lifting of the darkness on the far side of the Sea a pale radiance gradually suffuses the eastern sky and then grows in intensity. A pearly sheen begins to steal over the waters - until finally, with a fanfare of gold and rose, the sun flings itself over the hills and lays a path of fire across the lake.

This place is traditionally held to be the scene of another resurrection narrative, recounted in the 21st chapter of John. This story of the fishing trip undertaken by the disciples on the Sea of Tiberias and their encounter there with the Risen Jesus was clearly considered of great importance by the Apostle, and he describes it with a wealth of detail. He begins the passage by telling his readers that Jesus "manifested" Himself to His disciples; that is, His appearance was a divinely-granted revelation of His presence and power, just as He had promised them. Moreover, Jesus appeared to His disciples on the shore as dawn was breaking, and the shining of the morning light after a long night of darkness reinforces the dominant ideas of the passage.

A Kinneret Morning

The central figures in the narrative which unfolds are the Beloved Disciple (John) and Simon Peter, who leads the fishing expedition but is still haunted by the remembrance of his threefold denial of the Lord on the night when He was betrayed. Peter's fall was tragic indeed: despite having proclaimed his unshakeable love for Jesus and his willingness to endure imprisonment and death for His sake, he had forsaken Him in His most critical hour. And yet it was a fall which had been surveyed prophetically by Jesus: His disciple did not appear to Him as "the rock" but rather as a frail human surrounded by a host of mortal dangers of which he had no awareness - a life that Satan intended to sift like wheat. In the tremendous battle over Peter's soul, Jesus only was the Rock, who prayed for Peter that his faith would not fail, so that his repentance and bitter tears had their source in Jesus' unexpected, miraculous act of grace.

And now, this one whom Christ had called as a fisher of men had returned with a number of the other disciples to his old trade – yet all that night they cast their nets fruitlessly. But then - morning came, and there on the shore stood a Figure - not clearly discerned in the hazy light of dawn - and the disciples did not know that it was Jesus. He called out to the tired men and gave them a directive, *"Cast on the right side of the boat"* - and then they brought in a tremendous multitude of fish, so they were no longer able to draw it into the boat. It was the Beloved Disciple who alone was able to discern the identity of the Stranger on the shore. "It is the Lord," he said to Peter. Peter's impetuosity, his eagerness to come to Jesus, is pictured vividly as he "girded" himself (*diazonummi*) with his garment, for he was "naked", and cast himself into the sea.

The fact that Peter had to wrap an outer garment around himself before plunging into the water seems an unusual detail for the Evangelist to include. It is perhaps intended to awaken an echo of an earlier story in the Gospel - the footwashing scene in chapter 13, where John recounts how Jesus "girded" Himself (*diazonnumi)* with a towel, symbolizing that

He was taking upon Himself the form of a servant. The implications of this are drawn out in the scene which now follows.

Peter, having reached shore, was followed by the other disciples in the boat; he then single-handedly drew the net to the land, full of great fishes; Jesus invited them to dine and became Host to the small band. After they had breakfasted there commenced the memorable interview in which Jesus restored Peter in indescribable grace, His three queries as to whether Peter loved Him corresponding to Peter's three earlier denials. Jesus' intricate questions were designed to penetrate Peter's psyche to the very depths. "Do you love (*agapao*) Me?" He asked the disciple twice; that is, "Do you have that deep and unchanging veneration for Me that you professed in the Upper Room?" Peter answered twice, "Yes, Lord, I love (*phileo*) You" – that is, "I love You with affection and devotion" - and made no claim to the highest form of love.

However, the third time Jesus asked whether he loved Him, He used the disciple's own word, *phileo*, and Peter was stricken. The Discerner of Hearts had turned the unbearable searchlight of His gaze upon his innermost being, and he was learning that he did not even begin to know his own self, that the Lord alone could judge his heart. "Lord, you know all things; you know that I love you," he responded. He would no longer speak or boast of his own ability to love but rather depend utterly upon Jesus' all-encompassing, all-forgiving love for himself. But this was more than a restoring, it was a preparation for a whole new level of service. "*Truly, truly, I say to you,*" Jesus continued to Peter – words which conferred much solemnity on what was to follow - "*when you were younger, you girded (zonnumi) yourself and walked where you wished*" - it was the third use of this word. What does it signify?

Jesus was telling Peter that in his earlier days, that is, before he became a disciple of his Lord, he had accomplished his enterprises through his own desires, energy and determination. In this way, he had been the natural leader of Andrew, James and John and the others in the fishing fleet at Capernaum, in this way he had instigated the fishing expedition by night, and so also he had just now elected to gird himself for the task of swimming to Jesus' feet. The revelation is of Peter's self will, which is so conspicuous in his character, the source of much of his individuality, but also of much of his weakness. But a great change was coming over Peter as a result of the fiery experience through which he had passed: he was sensing that he was no longer the master of his destiny, that his natural initiative and courage were being transformed through a new power which was taking hold of his life - a divine principle of love which would alter the focus of his whole being and eventually remake him completely.

Peter was still to be a fisher of men, but he was also to have a new role – that of feeding the flock which belongs to the Good Shepherd. Peter the impetuous, the brave, the strong, was called to an enlarged sphere as Peter the tender-hearted, the compassionate, the loving. So came the fourth and final use of *diazonummi* as Jesus completed His prophetic word to His disciple: *"When you are old,"* He told him, *"you will stretch out your hands, and another will gird you, and carry you where you do not wish to go"* (John 21:18). As Peter entered a long career of tending God's flock, he would be "stretching out his hands" in imitation of Jesus' ministry of extending blessing or healing to those in need. And this willing laying down of his life, the surrender of his strength and gifts in the service of others, would be preparing him in spirit for a final entire submission. When his days drew to their close he would again stretch out his hands, allow another to bind him and lead him to the violent martyr-death reserved for the prince of the apostles. But even as he yielded up his life in utter human weakness, he would at the same time be wrapped about, girded mightily, with divine, supernatural strength.

Peter's First Letter, written in view of his approaching death, is shot through with allusions to the marvelous grace that had come to him and remade him: *true grace, manifold grace, all grace, prophesied grace, multiplied grace, life-giving grace*: all that is needed when passing through trials is found in the grace of God. Yes, says Peter, *"All of you gird yourself with humility to serve one another, for God resists the proud but gives grace to the humble"* (1 Peter 5:5).

He had come to understand that the surpassing crown of beauty in one's character was this humility that girds itself for service, just as Jesus did when He washed the disciples' feet and transformed the towel, the sign of slavery, into the sign of nobility in the kingdom. And through the Gospels and Epistles this understanding comes to us, also bringing light and truth, just as the early morning rays had illuminated the Figure on the shore.

SHAVUOT AND PENTECOST

Fire in the Heart

In the first book of the Bible, Genesis, the reader is intimately engaged in following the journeys and vicissitudes of a single family, that of the patriarchs, Abraham, Isaac and Jacob. But when the Book of Exodus is opened, it seems one is thrust into an entirely different universe, for this sweeping narrative comprehends vast national events and eventually takes on aspects of a cosmic drama. Within its pages is located the archetypal liberation story, touchstone and inspiration for a thousand threatened minorities since that time. The echoes of those thundering words, "Let My people go", spoken by one of the greatest leaders the world has known, have sounded through all succeeding centuries. Through the power of its images, Exodus has retained an overarching impression in the consciousness, not just of Israel, but of all the nations which have been nurtured in its teachings. Filled with revelatory light and power, these ultimately provide a testament of God's sovereign hand at work in the world, governing events and guiding history. But they also enrich the individual soul, for they delineate a Deity filled with tender care for His people, who bends a compassionate eye upon the suffering and afflicted, and whose heart is open to their cry.

After being drawn onto this larger stage, the reader is alternately dazzled and appalled by the scale of the events which transpire in a few short chapters. The story begins with the Children of Israel in bondage in Egypt, then moves to the account of their attempted annihilation through the drowning of the male children and the rescue of the future deliverer Moses from the water. The man of God is then discovered in the desert, where the fiery theophany prepares him for return to Egypt and his task of liberation. A titanic clash takes place between two leaders who represent fundamentally opposed worldviews; one is ruler of the most powerful nation on earth, the other a shepherd from the desert, guiding a powerless, dispirited flock. Plagues of a world-threatening intensity straddle the land, until the angel of death "spreads his wings on the blast", while the blood of the lamb on the doorposts shelters the Israelites. Bound for the Promised Land, they undertake their flight into the desert with Pharaoh's chariots in hot pursuit, before the Red Sea splits to let them pass. All the way through, a common feature linking the episodes is the elemental image of fire, which appears in the coruscating blaze of the burning bush, in the guiding pillar of God's presence with His people, and at Mount Sinai when the Law was given.

These are events of singular magnitude, but the revelation given in Exodus also attests to the interwoven nature of personal and national affairs, as it traces the developments which take place in the soul of the hero, Moses. It did not seem a promising start for one who would prove the great deliverer of his people: the baby son of an enslaved nation, floating on the River Nile in his ark of bulrushes. But the infant in the small boat was rescued by Pharaoh's daughter and brought up as her child in the royal palace of Egypt, so he became "*learned in all the wisdom of the Egyptians, and mighty in words and deeds*" (Acts 7:22). He then appeared to throw away the privileges conferred upon him, as he chose to identify himself with the Children of Israel. As he went out to visit his brethren one day, upon seeing an Egyptian overseer strike one of the Hebrew slaves, he killed the man and hid the body; when he discovered the deed was known he fled to the wilderness. He was there for another forty years, tending his flock under the vault of heaven, beholding daily the grandeur of the rugged mountains, and baring his soul to the influence of the Creator's majesty. Here in the desert he surely acquired a measure of the dauntless spirit he would need for his life's mission. For there was a greater turning point ahead.

One day, in a solitary scrub bush in the wilderness, there gleamed to him a wondrous sight: the Angel of the Lord appeared to him in the midst of a bush which burned with fire, and yet was not consumed. There is a mystery here: a striking contrast between the humility of the bush and the divine glory which irradiated it, the fire that blazed without destroying its object. Moses was caught and held by this vision, and made his fateful decision – he *turned aside*. It was a moment of destiny which altered his life, the course of a whole nation, and indeed the world. Though trembling and afraid, he fixed his gaze upon those flames, filled with an unearthly brightness, as their flickering light streamed into the limitless desert sky. Had there come to him a transcendent awareness that the fire would not burn *but would change him*?

The medieval Jewish commentator Rashi noted the similarity between the Hebrew words for flame, "*lehava*", and heart, "*lev*", and for him this evoked questions about the relation between fire and the human heart, which is the inner place of transformation. The volatile element of fire both fascinates and allures and so the burning bush compelled Moses to come closer; at the same time, there is an instinctive fear of its immense destructive power and thus he was also told, "Do not come near". What was the danger he was being warned against? If the flame which burns so vehemently does not extinguish its object, it must nevertheless have a radical effect upon the matter it is engulfing. It seems therefore possible that the text is hinting at a radical idea, that of *transmutation*, and that it was this thought, of which Moses became subliminally aware, that drew him near to the heart of the flame.

It was also this overwhelming experience which prepared Moses for the first great task before him – to return to Egypt and deliver God's people from their oppression and bondage. He was fearful and reluctant, with a sense of utmost inadequacy: "Who am I that I should go to Pharaoh?" he asked, and God assured him, "I will certainly be with you". Moses offered a further objection, saying that the Children of Israel would surely ask him to identify the God who had sent him. "What shall I say to them?" he asked, and God's answer came: "I AM WHO I AM. Thus you shall say to the Children of Israel: I AM has sent me to you." The Hebrew version of the name God disclosed here is more properly understood as being in a future tense: "*I will be what I will be*". According to Rashi, God is therefore saying in these words: "I shall be with them in this anguish as I shall be with them in future crises." God, who alone knows the future, saw that nations and individuals throughout the course of history would face many devastating situations, but His power would be present to respond to the need and answer the cry for help.

Moses returned to Egypt and, despite his sense of shortcoming, despite the recalcitrance of his own people, mounted a siege against all the might of Egypt. In the encounters which took place between the two leaders, Pharaoh's heart became yet more hard and obdurate, yet all Moses' self-consciousness vanished. His steadfast endurance in the face of opposition, his unswerving fidelity to God's command, are incomparably striking and, as this history is traced more fully, it is impossible not to marvel at the breadth of his courage.

In response to Moses' request that the Children of Israel should be permitted to depart from Egypt for three days in order to worship, Pharaoh at first issued a refusal; but then, under a strong degree of compulsion as the plagues ravaged the nation, made a concession, "You may worship in your own way - but you must do it in the land". Moses' answer stressed their determination to go three days journey into the wilderness, in accordance with the divine command. Pharaoh then continued to negotiate, urging that, if they must go outside his land, they should not go far away. Once again the response came, which insisted upon the journey to the desert. Further seeking a compromise, Pharaoh proposed that, if they must go themselves, they should leave their children behind. This subterfuge Moses refused to consider for a moment, and reiterated his firm declaration: "We and our children". Finally Pharaoh's last desperate appeal was made, that they should leave their cattle - and to that the sublime answer was given: *"There shall not a hoof be left behind."*

Thus the Children of Israel finally departed from Egypt under Moses' indomitable leadership. The prophet recognized that God had brought them out of the "iron furnace" (Deuteronomy 4:20), a place of cruel smelting, but he faced an even more radical challenge ahead: Sinai. Fifty days after coming out from Egypt the Children of Israel arrived at this mountain, where one of the most dramatic events in their long history would unfold. The account of the giving of the Law in Exodus Chapters 19 and 20 impresses the reader with its description of the powerful evidences of God's presence among His people:

"So it came about on the third day, in the morning, that there were thunderings and lightnings and a thick cloud upon the mountain, and the sound of the trumpet was very loud, so that all the people who were in the camp trembled. Now Mt. Sinai was completely in smoke because the Lord descended upon it in fire ..." (Exodus 19:16,18)

At the Festival of Shavuot the people of Israel celebrate the giving of the Torah, and affirm the traditional Jewish belief that the Ten Commandments were spoken by God and heard in the presence of their forefathers at Sinai. The revelation of the Law, and the many supernatural phenomena which accompanied it, was an historic occurrence publicly witnessed by those who stood at the foot of the mountain; and the experience of this unique event was then transmitted from parent to child and from them to succeeding generations as an unbroken chain. The Torah way of life, revealed in a vast, empty desert to a people who had only recently been liberated from slavery, introduced hundreds of new laws and practices and brought about a complete revolution in the lives of individuals, families and the entire nation. It has also preserved the Jewish people and served as their guide through aeons of tumultuous human history.

It was the experience at the burning bush that prepared Moses to face the fire on Sinai, to ascend the mountain and spend forty days and nights in the presence of God, receiving from Him the two tablets of stone engraved with the Ten Commandments. During his journey he had been transformed from timorousness to courage through faith in the One who had sent him, who had promised him "I will be with you" - just as Jesus had assured His disciples of His presence with them to the end of the age. Yet Moses' pilgrimage was not over, and the divine principle of fire would continue the work of transformation in his heart.

Fear and Love at Sinai: The Fundamental Revelation

Some time after he led the Children of Israel out of Egypt, Moses became engaged in another very singular conflict - perhaps unique in the history of the world. And his adversary in this battle? None other than God Himself! The archetypal struggle which occurred between them centered upon the revelation of a fundamental biblical truth - the character of God. Chapters 32-34 of Exodus follow the trajectory of Moses' intercession on behalf of the Children of Israel, and the final outcome reveals with shining clarity the true nature of the Deity with whom they had to do.

When Moses first came to the Children of Israel on his mission as deliverer, he brought them amazing promises from God: *I shall release, I shall save, I shall redeem, I shall take you to Me as a people*" (Exodus 6:6-7) - but the Israelites were unable to take in these words, so broken and demoralized had they become through their hard labor in Pharaoh's service. Subsequently they witnessed the overthrow of Egypt's armies in the sea and tasted manna from heaven in the wilderness; then, as they reached the base of Sinai, heard God's message to them though Moses: *"'You have seen what I did to the Egyptians, and how I bore you on eagles' wings and brought you to Myself"*(Exodus 19:4).

Yet the Children of Israel were seemingly unable to gaze through the shifting shape of events to perceive a heart yearning over them with tender kindness and goodness. And now they were faced with an unprecedented new challenge, to obey the commands which God imparted - yet the very proclamation of the Law had thrown into sharp relief their inability to keep it. There was only one mighty force which would have made them able to bear the demands of Sinai - *love*. But their trust in God's providential care had vanished swiftly as a mirage in the desert.

At this point in the tale Moses left the people, ascended the mountain, and was there forty days and nights as God gave the laws of the new polity of Israel - rules which, if they should keep them, would bring them blessing and life (Deuteronomy 4:40); He also placed in Moses' hands the two tablets of stone with the Ten Commandments. Sinai, wreathed in darkness and flame, was a scene of "cloud and majesty and awe". For the Children of Israel standing at the base of the mountain it was too much to bear. They fashioned a gold calf and threw themselves with abandon into its worship - anything to blot out the memory of those terrifying new strictures. On the mountain, God informed Moses of the idolatry of the Israelites and declared His intention to destroy them, while promising that He would make Moses himself great.

God's words were abrupt, and His willingness to abandon the people He had brought out of Egypt bewildering and shocking. In fact, His statements do raise a major issue for the defenders of the biblical record. It is sometimes asserted that the God of the Old Testament, in contrast to the gracious Father of the New Testament, is a Deity of vengeance and wrath. The person who assents to the teachings of the New Covenant is convinced in his or her heart that God is a Being of infinite love and compassion. Therefore, if the Hebrew Scriptures set forth a Deity filled with anger and bent upon judgment they have clearly failed in their purpose. But there *is* a way out of this impasse: is it not possible that God, in dealing with the Children of Israel, placed Himself in this difficult light, in a blaze of anger and wrath, that He might cause men and women to see the seriousness of the sin which hindered their lives and ultimately brought destruction? But this was only for one clear goal:

that He might at the same time reveal His unfathomable mercy and grace to a people with no former conception of it.

In the unfolding of this revelation, everything depended on the character of the man whom God had raised up as intercessor for his people - Moses. For, in order to accomplish the purpose of unveiling His heart, God first appeared to set Himself up as Adversary to the prophet. In the encounters which took place between them, it was imperative for Moses to hold on to his belief in the steadfastness of God's love, for only in this way could he bear the weight of intercession and endure under such tremendous testing. This was a new challenge for the prophet - perhaps even greater than that of confronting the might of Egypt. Through their interchanges, charged with tension, Moses pressed on in faith and as he did so his love for the people and trust in God's goodness coalesced in burning integrity; there also developed in him that very understanding of the divine nature which God wished him to convey to the Israelites. The reader who follows the course of his intercession is taken on a staggering journey, for these prayers lead as far beyond the conventional notion of pleading for others as the clouds float high above the earth.

FIRST INTERCESSION

Moses' compassion for his people was evident from the first description of his adult consciousness, when he went out to his brothers and felt immediate empathy for their suffering. Yet after the transgression at Sinai he became far more deeply apprised of the tendencies of their hearts. On the mountain, after God reproached him concerning *"your* people whom *you* brought out of the land of Egypt", Moses then faced God with the same courage and boldness of speech with which he faced Pharaoh. He refuted the charge they were his people, threw back responsibility for them upon God, then poured out his soul in entreaty for them: "Why, O God, should Your anger blaze against Your people?" he asked, appealing to God's program of salvation, His reputation among the nations and the promises He made to the patriarchs. Nor did he at any stage deign to give the thought of his own advancement a moment's notice. And the Lord relented from His purposes.

SECOND INTERCESSION

Moses then descended the mountain with the two tablets of testimony in his hands, but when he saw the calf and the dancing he smashed the gifts in anger. The following day he announced to the people that he would go again to the Lord, "for", he said, "perhaps I can make atonement for your sin". A realization was dawning in his heart that something more was needed for restoration of right relationship beyond even the sacrificial offerings - some kind of ransom which could lift away guilt. This new apprehension called forth an extraordinary response: the offer of his own life to gain forgiveness for his people. In ringing words, as though throwing down a gauntlet to the Deity, he demanded: "Blot me from Your book that You have written". And although this offer, filled with the spirit of noble self-sacrifice, was one which God refused, yet He answered the unspoken appeal: the Children of Israel were permitted to go up to their land as originally promised.

THIRD INTERCESSION

But in the Israelite camp the suspense and mourning lingered - for God had stated that He Himself would not go with them but instead send an angel. Moses could not let the matter rest and went to the Lord again. And now the very heart of his intercessory appeal was reached:

Then Moses said to the Lord, "See, You say to me, 'Bring up this people.'
But You have not let me know whom You will send with me. Yet You have
said, 'I know you by name, and you have also found grace in My sight.'
Now therefore, I pray, if I have found grace in Your sight, show me now

Your way, that I may know You and that I may find grace in Your sight. And consider that this nation is Your people (Exodus 33:12-13).

Moses cast himself utterly upon the mercy and grace of God which he had experienced personally as the grounds for hoping that the Lord might look upon Israel with favor - and the answer which came to him was overflowing with comfort: "My presence shall go with you, and I will give you rest." Yet these words came as an assurance for Moses alone, and the prophet refused to be content with such an answer. He continued to entreat earnestly for the extension of the promise to the entire nation, closely identifying himself with them, and reiterating "I and Your people" as if he would have no blessing which was not shared by them. Then finally, in a statement sublime in its defiance, he declared: "If Your presence does go not with us, carry us not up hence." Moses was laying everything that was at stake on this one play, this tremendous gamble. For him, Israel's essential distinction from other nations was that she had God in her midst, and if this was not so naught else mattered. And the result of this audacity, this chutzpah? God acceded unconditionally to his request, at the same time making abundantly clear it was for Moses' sake that the divine presence was once again granted to the people as a whole.

Fourth Intercession

The astounding consciousness of God's favor, the benevolence of this answered prayer, awakened in Moses a desire which soared beyond the present circumstances: "*Show me, I pray Thee, Thy glory,*" he beseeched. Was it not to this point that God had been leading him all along? After receiving a favorable answer, the prophet ascended the mountain again and was hidden in a cleft of the rock:

And the LORD passed before him and proclaimed, "The LORD, the LORD God, merciful and gracious, longsuffering, and abounding in goodness and truth, keeping mercy for thousands, forgiving iniquity and transgression and sin ... (Exodus 34:6-7)

These are the immortal words Moses was given which describe the "thirteen attributes" of God. This shining array of virtues, this radiant galaxy describing the fundamental aspects of God's character, is the very centerpiece of His revelation to humankind. He is a God of truth and justice, but the divine mercy and grace which are prominent in this enumeration are the reflection of His overflowing heart of love and the true mantle of His glory. Here was given to the Children of Israel an altogether new view of Deity on earth: a God who offered free forgiveness for trespass and lawbreaking. The Law had unveiled the mystery of sin and death, the terrible propensity of the human being to transgress together with the stern penalty which would accrue. Yet at the same time it revealed the all-surpassing power of God's mercy and forgiveness: so that for Israel, and all who would enter a covenant of faith with Him, the institution of sacrificial worship would make the way for restoration of relationship and blessing.

Israel's sin had thus called forth God's redeeming mercy. Despite the visible, terrifying splendor of the theophany on Mount Sinai, the true disclosure of God's character lay in this proclamation given at the same time the Law was instituted - words which, filled with musical notes of grace and compassion, were a foreshadowing of the New Testament declaration that "God is love".

FIFTH INTERCESSION

Thus, at Sinai, was granted to one man a realization of God's presence and glory so far as flesh and blood were able to bear. This revelation led to a new response on Moses' part:

So Moses made haste and bowed his head toward the earth, and worshiped. Then he said, "If now I have found grace in Your sight, O Lord, let my Lord, I pray, go among us, even though we are a stiff-necked people; and pardon our iniquity and our sin, and take us as Your inheritance" (Exodus 34:9)

For the first time when interceding for his people, Moses switched to the first person plural in a prayer which indicated he had come to a place of full identification with the Children of Israel in their sinful, estranged state. It also conferred upon the prophet a measure of the same divine glory he had just witnessed, so that when Moses finally descended again from the mountain with the second set of tablets in his hands this radiance shone from his face, an astonishing witness to the people below.

This light bathing Moses' countenance was given to him as he came to share in the sacrificial love of God. Although the Lord had appeared initially appeared as his Adversary, the prophet had seen the apparent hardness of His heart melt into the rivers of overflowing grace He desired to display to the people. Through the rest of his long life's journey, Moses came to understand ever more clearly that God was a *consuming fire* (Deuteronomy 4:24) – but that this fire was one of *love* – the flame in the heart, *lehava lev*, that burns but does not consume. The Book of Deuteronomy recorded Moses' final discourses to his people, in which he taught that, behind all the laws, edicts, and stern demands for holiness, was a heart filled with grace and mercy. God's laws, Moses insisted, were the outcome of His love, and it was also love alone which enabled a person to keep those commandments - love for God with all the heart, soul, and strength (Deuteronomy 6:5).

In his intercessions, Moses had demonstrated that his own glory, his very life, was worth nothing to him while his brethren were shut out from the blessings of the covenant. In the great Lawgiver we see, as in a glass dimly refracted, the image of the prophet greater than Moses in condescension, in graciousness, in love that yearns over His people. The lofty principle of intercession reaches its supreme height in Jesus Christ, who also binds Himself closely with His people, who accepts nothing from the Father's hand for Himself alone, who also appears continually before God saying "I and Thy people", and whose prayer for them prevails.

The Crowning Revelation

....

J ust outside the southern walls of the Old City of Jerusalem lies the broad promontory known as Mount Zion, a name around which cluster so many associations and longings, both earthbound and heavenly. According to biblical history, David captured *Metsudat Tsion*, the fortress of Zion, and made Jerusalem the capital of the united tribes of Israel; here also he transferred the Ark of the Covenant and Solomon later built the great Temple on Mount Moriah. Through the succeeding centuries the word *Zion* came to encapsulate additional meanings as a name for the city of Jerusalem and the nation of Israel as a whole, but was especially attached to the hill on the southwest of the city. It also came to possess spiritual connotations: viewed as the dwelling place of the Lord's presence, source of Messianic blessings, and the throne of the future Anointed King who would one day rule over all the nations of the earth.

Passing through the high gate leading to Zion's hill on a late spring day, one is greeted by a warm south wind, laden with scents of pine and jasmine. From this eminence it is possible to gaze past the southern contours of Jerusalem, still at this time of year cloaked in emerald, over the immense abyss of the Jordan Valley into a seemingly boundless distance, delimited by tawny mountains tinted with ochre and violet. Here memories tug and fret at the corners of the mind, visions of prophets and kings, armies and wandering peoples, which swirl up out of the past to crowd the landscape and make their present felt insistently. The student of history and the biblical narratives is caught and arrested at this point, charmed, as the mind wanders through its hall of remembrances. Here time coalesces - past and present dovetailing. From Sinai to Zion, a great distance - geographically, historically and spiritually - has been traversed. But the events which took place on Mount Zion were the culmination in many ways of the otherworldly trajectory set in motion at Sinai.

A complex series of buildings crowns the hill, structures rooted very firmly in history, amongst which are sites venerated by both Jews and Christians, most especially those found in the ancient building located at the center of this arrangement. On its lower level is a shrine associated with the burial place of King David and sacred to the Jewish people, while on the floor above is a large room known as the Cenacle, where, according to Christian tradition, Jesus met with His disciples for the Last Supper. The Gospels relate that this meeting took place in a large furnished "Upper Room", often identified as belonging to the house of Mark and his mother Mary; it seems that in this location the disciples also gathered after the crucifixion, here the Risen Lord twice appeared to them, and here they gathered for prayer in the days between Ascension and Pentecost.

Although the Evangelists do not detail the location in Jerusalem of the house containing the Upper Room, other historical sources suggest that it may have been situated on Mount Zion. The first strong evidence to this effect comes from a fourth-century bishop named Epiphanius, who stated that when the Roman emperor Hadrian visited Jerusalem around 130 AD a small "church of God" and seven synagogues existed on Mount Zion. This "church" could only have been a Judeo-Christian synagogue, for the building of churches was prohibited during the first three centuries of the Christian era. Working with this information, and adding other historical and archaeological data, it is possible to construct a possible scenario for the building of this sanctuary, and to trace its fluctuating fortunes through the eras that followed.

The earliest followers of Jesus in Jerusalem were all Jews, who clung to their Judaic heritage, considered themselves part of the wider polity of Israel, and continued to worship in the Temple. However, this mixed community of Hebrew and Hellenistic Jews may well have assembled together in the large home, presumably aristocratic and wealthy, which features so prominently in the Gospels and Acts, and here the earliest church councils may have been held, led by James, "the brother of the Lord". But this pattern of life was violently disrupted when the First Jewish Revolt against the Romans broke out in 66 AD. The members of the Judeo-Christian community in Jerusalem fled at this time to Pella in Transjordan, as Jesus had instructed them, before the Roman general Titus burned the Temple and destroyed Jerusalem in the year 70. When, after this time, the Jews were permitted to return to their devastated city and rebuild, it is likely that the Judeo-Christians also made their way back and gathered again at the meeting place around which clustered so many of their sacred memories.

This historical reconstruction is given added weight by the testimony of tenth-century Alexandrian Patriarch Euthychius, who wrote that the Judeo-Christians "returned to Jerusalem in the fourth year of the emperor Vespasian". This was 73 AD, the year Masada, last outpost of Jewish resistance, had fallen. The Patriarch then added that they "built there their church". That is, they constructed a Judeo-Christian synagogue, very possibly on the site where the building containing the Cenacle is located. Archaeological evidence shows that this building is constructed over the ruins of a first-century synagogue, and the theory is given additional weight when building stones of the original period, which can still be seen on the outside face of the synagogue, are examined. These large ashlars from the Herodian period were not originally carved for this structure. Perhaps, as the Judeo-Christians constructed their sanctuary over the ashes of the villa with the Upper Room, they used some of the magnificent stones from the ruined

Temple. Their synagogue became known eventually as the "Church of the Apostles" and "Mother of all Churches".

According to church historian Eusebius, the Judeo-Christian community in Jerusalem flourished for some decades after this time, presided over by a series of bishops "from the circumcision". However, after the year 135 AD this line of Hebrew bishops came to an abrupt end, the same year the Second Jewish Revolt was suppressed by the Emperor Hadrian. All Jews were banished from Jerusalem on pain of death, and the city was rebuilt as a Roman colony named Aelia Capitolina. Yet it seems that the intrepid Judeo-Christian community continued to maintain its presence on Mount Zion, perhaps because they had opposed the messianic claims of Bar Kochba, leader of the Revolt.

In the early fourth century, after embracing the Christian faith, Roman Emperor Constantine embarked on an ambitious program of church building, commissioning a number of sanctuaries in the Holy Land of great size and splendor. These new religious structures laid the foundations for Jerusalem's impact on European consciousness for centuries to come, and the city became an intense focus of Christian pilgrimage. But as the Christian faith spread throughout the Roman and Byzantine worlds, Christians began to move further away from their Hebraic roots, while the state church of the Empire took control of sites in the Holy Land and appointed subsequent bishops of Jerusalem. Historical records suggest a separation between Judeo-Christians and Gentile Christians in the Holy City itself - but indicate at the same time that efforts were made to heal the rift.

Toward the end of the fourth century, Byzantine emperor Theodosius 1 (379-395) commissioned a large sanctuary on Mount Zion, which was constructed beside the Church of the Apostles. At the consecration of this church, around 394, Bishop John II of Jerusalem was said to have delivered a sermon filled with Judeo-Christian symbolism, focusing on the celebration of Yom Kippur, and also blessing the altar of the Church of the Apostles - an act said to bring reconciliation between the Judeo-Christians and the rest of the Jerusalem church. John II also enlarged the Theodosian sanctuary, creating a magnificent octagonal structure which became known as Hagia Sion. However, over the following centuries the whole complex on Mount Zion was destroyed and subsequently rebuilt a number of times. It seems likely that the room known as the Cenacle which survives to the present day was constructed by Crusaders, who also incorporated the walls of the ancient synagogue in their church. After the 16th century, when the Turks captured Jerusalem, the room was transformed into a mosque, and a *mihrab* (prayer niche) as well as stained glass windows with Arabic inscriptions added.

Since 1948, Mount Zion has been part of Israel. The area was a particular focus of religious interest from 1948 through 1967 while the Old City was in Jordanian hands, thus rendering inaccessible the Western Wall of the Temple. During the War of Independence in 1948, considerable fighting occurred on and around Mount Zion, during the course of which a shell exploded in the building housing the traditional tomb of King David. Israeli archaeologist Jacob Pinkerfeld was given the task of repairing the damage, and as he did so also gave the site an archaeological examination, making some amazing discoveries. As well as finding the niche of a first-century synagogue, he uncovered three earlier floor levels: Crusader, late Roman or early Byzantine, and the original stone pavement; in the lowest layer he also found pieces of plaster with graffiti marked on them. Tragically, Pinkerfeld was killed in a Jordanian attack on the 1956 Archaeological Convention at Ramat Rachel, south of Jerusalem. A team of Franciscan experts later published an interpretation of the Greek letters NCBI on the graffiti-marked plaster: they may be translated as "Conquer, Savior, Mercy".

This discovery seems to reinforce Mount Zion's claim to be the seat of the Apostles and the earliest *ecclesia* in Jerusalem. Moreover, since at least the fourth century the site of the Upper Room has been drawing pilgrims, and few places in the city can point to such an enduring tradition.

The Cenacle today may well mark the place where Jesus held the Last Supper with His disciples, an event of paramount importance within the Christian tradition, around which the central rite of the faith is built. On this occasion was revealed the means whereby the covenant which God had made with His people at Sinai was to be ratified. It was here also that Jesus uttered the High Priestly prayer recorded in John's Gospel, the richest glimpse the New Testament affords of the love of Christ towards His people. It was perhaps for these reasons that the writer of the Letter to the Hebrews chose to contrast Mount Sinai with Mount Zion, suggesting the ways in which the latter transcends the former.

He emphasizes, first of all, that the Hebrew Christians to whom he is writing had not come to the mountain that burned with fire and was wreathed in blackness, causing those who heard God speaking the "Ten Words" out of the tempest to draw back in fear. Rather, in these last days, God had spoken through His Son, the perfect image of His goodness and love, to reveal the glory of the realm to which He invited those who believed in Him and at which, in fact, they had already arrived. In musical phrases filled with light and beauty the inspired author delineates ten aspects of the contrast between Sinai and Zion (Hebrews 12:22-24). *You have come*, he writes, *to*

Mount Zion - and the city of the living God - the heavenly Jerusalem: They have gathered to another center entirely, the dwelling place of the Divine presence, illuminated with the unfading brightness of the Shekinah glory, the place of ultimate rest and *shalom* as glimpsed from afar by the patriarchs and seers. On this sacred height, adorned with towers and palaces as David's city of old, dwells everything lovely and good and true; it breathes an air of inviolable serenity, and is indwelt by countless numbers: Mount Sinai stood in the great and terrible wilderness, but Mount Zion is the centre of a cosmopolitan city. Therein is found ...

An innumerable company of angels: The Christians are invited to partake of the festive gathering held in heaven where the angel choirs are assembled in ranks around the throne of grace; here also they may join with *the general assembly,* or *panegyris.* This word, found nowhere else in the New Testament, refers to the great convocation of the Greek city states around Mt Olympus every four years, with all that suggests of concord, excellence and mutual purpose. They share together also with *the church of the first-born who are enrolled in heaven:* Those who were firstborn among the Hebrews enjoyed pre-eminence of rank, and their members were individually consecrated to God; so also the Christians have attained this lofty position; their names "are written in heaven" and their citizenship in this realm is assured, though they have not as yet passed through the shining gates.

They have also come to - *God the Judge of all ...* The same God of Israel who descended on Sinai, limitless in justice and holiness, is now approached with joy and confidence by numberless worshippers in the heavenly courts; these are - *the spirits of just men made perfect.* Those who have come through a stern conflict are experiencing now a wondrous peace, arrayed in bright linen and crowned with victory. In this beatific rest above, all longing is fulfilled, sorrow vanquished, love perfected, so that they shine forth like the stars of heaven, dwelling together in consummate fellowship. And how is this? *For,* says the writer, *You have come to ..... Jesus the Mediator of the new covenant.*

The crowning excellence of the new dispensation is the revelation of the Son of God; the trumpet blast of Sinai has faded, and in its place there is One who invites His people in golden tones: "*Come unto Me ...*". Jesus, who shared the experience of His people, who triumphed on their behalf and has brought many sons to glory, is now is at the center of the universe, worshiped by the assembled multitudes. They have been brought near through: *the blood of sprinkling,* washed from their sins and made whiter than snow through the One who loved them and gave Himself for them, so that Christ and His shed blood are the ground of all their blessings, and the sum of all.

113

The Upper Room and The Ultimate Petition

Visiting the Cenacle today one finds a graceful room, high-ceilinged, with slender columns - but otherwise quite empty. Nevertheless, with a little imaginative reflection it is possible to envision the figures of Jesus and the Twelve reclining around the festive table on that Passover evening so long ago. This is especially true because the scene is familiar through countless works of art, most notably Leonardo's classic picture. However, when the events that took place at that famous Last Supper are examined through the lens of the four Gospels, they present some very different aspects. And it is only when they are looked at in the light of the scriptures as a whole that their fullest significance may be drawn out.

Jesus and His disciples had passed through the streets of Jerusalem, crowded with pilgrims come for the feast, as they made their way to the house where a guest-chamber had been prepared. Passover, the annual celebration of God's deliverance of the Children of Israel from slavery in Egypt, was a time when not only the past was remembered, but future deliverance also anticipated, so both national and religious feelings were running high. But Jesus was surrounded only by His small band of followers as they gathered together in the intimacy of the Upper Room. As they celebrated the Passover meal together, He surprised them with an unforeseen action, something completely different from the usual ritual of the feast. He took bread and broke it, then said, "This is My body, given for you", then in the same way, after supper, He took a cup of wine and said, "This is My blood of the new covenant, poured out for you." Mysterious words and actions! - the significance of which can be discovered only through turning again to the history of Israel recorded in the Hebrew Scriptures.

On the Way to the Upper Room

The Old Testament had been marked by a series of covenants, in which God declared His sovereign, electing purposes towards His people, and the people, on their side, promised to do all that God commanded. The inaugural covenant with the nation of Israel as a whole had been made at Mount Sinai; yet before this covenant was set in place, even before God brought the Children of Israel out of Egypt, He had made a series of promises to them through Moses:

*I WILL **bring you out** from under the burdens of the Egyptians*
*I WILL **rescue you** from their bondage*
*I WILL **redeem** you with an outstretched arm and great judgments*
*I WILL **take you** as My people* (Exodus 6:6-7)

The arrangement of these promises in a series of first-person verbs, emphasizing God's determination to carry out such mighty deeds of deliverance, is very striking. The Jewish rabbis later denoted these promises as the "four redemptions", and they gave rise to the custom of drinking four glasses of wine at the Passover Seder, one for each of the succeeding declarations. These rise in a gracious crescendo, moving from a focus on rescue from an external enemy to the intimate relationship to be created between God and His people as a result of His saving acts. The fourth promise "to take" is the Hebrew verb *laqah*, used many times in the scriptures, but in this particular construction denoting a marriage relationship, suggesting the profound depth of relationship God desired would exist between Himself and His people. He is declaring Himself as the Divine Bridegroom, announcing His intention to "take" His bride from her Egyptian captors. "Then," He says, "you shall *know* that I am the Lord" (verse 7), using the Hebrew verb "to know" which suggests not intellectual knowledge, but rather the consummation of a relationship in mutual love.

The whole Exodus drama describes the means by which God fulfilled His promises to the Children of Israel. Having brought the people out, and gathered them to Himself at Sinai, God gave them the words of

His commandments through Moses, and as one the people promised solemnly, "All that the Lord has said we will do", a pledge then sealed with sacrificial blood (Exodus 24:8). But - generation after generation, even after the Israelites entered their promised land, the people failed to keep their vows, in essence rejecting the relationship with God established at Sinai - and as a concomitant came the overthrow and exile of the nation. Both northern and southern kingdoms were taken into captivity, and Jerusalem with its beautiful Temple was destroyed by the Babylonians in 586 BC. It appeared that Israel's role as God's chosen people had come to a tragic end.

It was at this moment of seemingly irrevocable national disaster that the prophet Jeremiah delivered a message to the people in a series of oracles known as "The Book of Consolation". Jeremiah did not simply hold out the hope for restoration of those privileges that had been lost, but foresaw a future more illustrious than anything Israel had yet experienced. An unprecedented hope had stirred in his heart, the vision of a new day dawning, when out of the ashes of the old religion a new and living faith would arise. Despite the divine suffering over the infidelity of His chosen people, God would restore the nation and reestablish the relationship that was broken. His announcement was of a new covenant, introduced with a note suggesting wonder: *"Behold,"* He said,

The days are coming when I will make a new covenant with the house of Israel, not according to the covenant that I made with their fathers in the day that I took them by the hand to bring them out of the land of Egypt; My covenant which they broke, although I was a husband unto them, says the Lord:

I WILL put my law in their minds
I WILL write it on their hearts
I WILL be their God
I WILL that they shall be My people

I WILL that they shall all know Me, from the least to the greatest
I WILL forgive their iniquities
I WILL remember their sins no more (Jeremiah 31:31-34)

This is one of the great passages of the Hebrew Scriptures, the only place where the term "new covenant" appears, unfolding a spiritual future which would impact all peoples and nations. This new covenant would be permanent and final, dependent on God's faithfulness alone and not upon the erring and fragile recipients of His promises. Inaugurated by a great act of forgiveness in which the overflowing grace in the heart of God would appear, it would have power to melt the most resistant heart, and call forth an answering love to the God who does not deal with His creatures on terms of strict, legal precision, but who pardons at His own cost.

When Jesus took the cup at the Passover Supper and spoke the words over it which instituted the new covenant, He was directing the thoughts of His disciples to the words of Jeremiah as the prophecy which, above all others, He had come to fulfill. It was an apocalyptic moment in the quiet hush of the Upper Room, the point in time for which all Israel had watched and waited for so long. As the immortal words fell from His lips, it became disclosed that all the promises of the covenant were to be sealed through the breaking of His body and the shedding of His blood. After this, and as the time of Jesus' passion drew very near, it seemed that a veil was drawn aside, granting a glimpse as at no other time of His innermost heart, and the intense desire for His own which had prompted His entire mission. In this penultimate moment, the flame of love in His heart seemed to burn with a new ardor, finding expression in the "High Priestly" prayer for His disciples which He uttered at the close of the meal.

As recorded in the 17th Chapter of John's Gospel, Jesus prayed thus for His own: that they might be kept safe from the world, that they might be sanctified, and that they might be drawn into a mystic union which reflected His own unity with the Father. But then came a marked change in His address to God. Having exhausted all that could be asked for His disciples here on earth, He then, as it were, extended His gaze into eternity, and uttered His final petition, intended to crown and go beyond all He had previously asked. No longer did He say, "I pray", but, in a striking change of tone, said, "Father, I *will* ..." an expression which, as used by Him here, is unique. There were two things which He expressed as His will in this royal fashion. First, He asked *"that they also whom Thou hast given Me be with Me where I am."* Because they were the Father's gift to Him, His followers were indescribably precious in His sight, and His great longing was that they might be with Him always - so that, He says, *"they may behold My glory"*.

The glory which Jesus had possessed from eternal ages past as the Word of God, co-equal with the Father in heaven, had not been seen by His disciples as He embraced His mission of salvation upon earth. That *doxa* had flashed out only momentarily as He went about "incognito", as He took upon Himself the form of a servant and humbled Himself to the most shameful of deaths, the death upon a cross. The glory He now desired that His followers should behold was His perfect glory, not only as Son of God but also as Son of man, the weight of honor adorning the brow of the risen, ascended and conquering Savior after the completion of His work. Their joy in beholding His transfigured humanity in perfect union with His eternal divine nature, as He poured upon them the radiance and light of His love without hindrance or bar, would constitute for them the ultimate beatitude of heaven. If the Queen of Sheba, overcome by the glory of Solomon, exclaimed, "Happy are thy men, happy are these thy servants who stand before thee, and that hear thy wisdom" (1 Kings 10:8) so much more inexpressible must be the gladness of the redeemed in the vision of that love. Further still, to behold this glory is to partake of it: for then shall be fulfilled the words: "we shall be like Him, for we shall see Him as He is" (1 John 3:2).

This sublime statement of the will of Jesus comprehended the highest goodness He could desire for His followers, the sum total and glorious goal of all He had come to accomplish for them through His atoning death. This was a destiny planned from all eternity, for which humanity was created, and which alone is able to satisfy the hearts of men and women. Well did Jesus know all that was so soon coming upon him, yet He thought nothing of His own suffering as He brought His disciples the ineffable truths which would fill their hearts and minds long after He was physically departed from them. In the record of those hours in the Upper Room was set forth a length, breadth, height and depth in the love of Christ for His people which transcends human understanding. Higher than this, thought cannot aspire. Moreover, in the expression "I will" is all the creative power to bring to pass the thing desired - not just for those who heard Him that night, but for all who would believe on Him in the ages yet to unfold.

The Way of the Messiah

"*Lord, this shall never be to You*" – that was Peter's declaration when Jesus first revealed to the disciples the necessity of His suffering and death. Although Peter's knowledge that Jesus was Messiah came not by "flesh and blood" but was revealed from above, the destiny of the Messiah as one of ignominy and shame was beyond his comprehension. And when Jesus spoke of the cross that stood in His pathway, toward which He was resolutely treading, the disciples drew back in horror; everything in their souls rebelled against this disclosure. If the cross had any glory it was veiled from their sight; they could perceive in it only failure and shame - and according to worldly standards they were perfectly correct. When it finally occurred, the crucifixion of the One they believed to be the Messiah on that Passover Friday was to them the epitome of disaster; all their hopes and dreams lay shattered - it seemed irrevocably.

It was only after the resurrection, during the forty days during which the Risen Jesus appeared to them and taught them of all things pertaining to the Kingdom of God, that their understanding began to be opened in previously undreamed-of ways. And the manner in which He unveiled these truths? He led back His disciples back to the Hebrew Scriptures, as the sole way in which He could enlighten them concerning God's master plan for humanity. As He unfolded the words of Moses, the Psalms and the prophets, they began to perceive what no earthly wisdom could discover: that the pages of scripture, from beginning to end, were suffused with one great light and dwelt upon one matchless theme. Before their gaze, out of the myriad of types and shadows which foretold his coming, emerged one luminous Figure, the sum and culmination of all the Old Testament pictures. It was to him the feasts of Israel were pointing, he was prefigured by kings and prophets such as David and Moses, and shown forth in narratives which predicted the circumstances of his life in minute detail. Here was unfolded the significance of his mission, as well as the necessity of his advent: a full and rich portrait of the One who should accomplish God's promised salvation for the world.

Yet an apparent contradiction runs all the way through the prophecies which speak of the coming Messiah, for while on one hand he is represented as a majestic leader, the Son of David in whom all nations would be blessed, they also represent him as experiencing terrible agony and seeming defeat, rejected by his own people, and suffering a violent death. This lowly Messiah was set forth during all the period of Israel's history, and the themes of atonement and sacrifice weave their scarlet thread through all the narratives, twin aspects of suffering and glory as intricately laced together as a double-stranded necklace of pearls. And so the scriptures taught *two* comings of the *one* Messiah: the first in humility and affliction, the second in power and glory, after which He would take up His throne and reign from Mount Zion over all the earth.

As the pages of scripture yielded up their inmost meaning, and the events, types and persons of the Old Testament became transfigured in this light, the disciples came to understand this mystery of the way of the Messiah, and so equipped for the task set before them. They were to testify that Jesus was God's Anointed One, but this could be accomplished only by explaining the *meaning* of this title: the depiction of the Messiah found in the Old Testament concerning His works, suffering, death and exaltation. As such, they were sent to preach Christ *according to the scriptures*. Yet these chosen witnesses of Christ needed something further. Before He ascended Jesus commanded them to wait in Jerusalem until they were "endued with power from on high". They kept their ten-day vigil before the Feast of Shavuot, the memorial of the giving of the Law on Mount Sinai - but there was no precedent for what came to pass on that day.

Acts Chapter 2 records that, when the day of Shavuot had "fully come", the disciples were gathered together, when there came a sound "like" a rushing wind – yet not a wind – and flames "like" fire – yet not fire – which appeared on the heads of each of the disciples. The insignia of Sinai were there, but the terror was alleviated – rather, the disciples were bathed in the divine presence which had descended upon them, crowning them with fire and light. This opened a fountain within the depth of their beings, which issued forth in ecstatic words, so that they extolled the "wonderful works of God" with heightened powers of language – not just to the Jewish citizens of Jerusalem, but to every people group "under heaven" gathered for the Feast. And when some mocked – "these men are filled with new wine" - Peter stood up with the Twelve and delivered the first gospel message of the new era - the declaration of the fulfillment of prophetic scripture in the life and death of Jesus of Nazareth. And in this preaching, all the types and figures of the Old Testament were illuminated in the dawning light of the New Covenant day.

Peter began his Pentecost sermon by speaking to *the men of Judah, and all who live in Jerusalem*, and quoting to them the prophecy which appears in the Book of Joel (3:1-5), that in the last days God would pour out His Spirit upon all flesh. What had just taken place, declared Peter, was the fulfillment of this promise. Then he turned his gaze to:

"Jesus of Nazareth, a Man attested by God to you by miracles, wonders, and signs which God did through Him in your midst, as you yourselves also know" (v 22)

Jesus had an earthly ministry authenticated by God the Father by means of His miraculous deeds – He healed the sick, forgave the sinful, subdued the adverse powers of nature, defeated Satan, raised the dead: His life on earth was throughout a manifestation of love, as He went about doing good to all who were suffering in mind, body or spirit. In His sinless and perfect humanity the eternal life which is in God had appeared to humankind – and yet the world rejected Him. And so Peter continued:

"Him, being delivered by the determined purpose and foreknowledge of God, you have taken by lawless hands, have crucified, and put to death" (v 23)

It was not those steeped in ignorance and folly who had thus slain God's Messiah, but those possessing human culture in its highest aspects: Romans nurtured in Greek wisdom and philosophy, as well as the Jewish leaders possessing the scriptures which delineated the fullest portrait of the One to come. All men, Jews and Gentiles, rejected the Bearer of infinite love - and yet, while it had been human hands that crucified God's Son, the death of Jesus had also taken place through the sovereign determination of God. The sinful will of man had met in the cross with the omnipotent love and wisdom of the Father, who was working out His eternal plan of salvation through the death of the Anointed One:

"…whom God raised up, having loosed the pains of death, because it was not possible that He should be held by it" (v 24)

According to Peter, the Resurrection of the Messiah sprang out of the same divine necessity as his death and had also been foretold in the scriptures; in Psalm 16, David had stated his faith that God would not abandon him in the grave, nor "allow His Holy One to see corruption". This indeed expressed the king's hope and assurance of eternal life, yet went far beyond anything David could claim for himself: he had rather to be speaking of Another, greater than he.

"Therefore being exalted to the right hand of God, and having received from the Father the promise of the Holy Spirit, He poured out this which you now see and hear" (v 33)

The Ascension also, declared Peter, was part of the prophetic course of the Messiah, and he cited Psalm 110 to demonstrate that here, once again, David's words could never apply to himself: it could only be the Anointed One who was exalted to this supreme place. The bodily Ascension of the Risen Lord introduced a whole new range of heavenly benefits, because from the right hand of the God He now sent forth gifts to His people, so that the Messianic age anticipated by the prophets had already begun.

The clear declarations of the Hebrew Scriptures concerning the history, character and mission of the Messiah thus corresponded in every detail to Jesus of Nazareth, proving not only that He was the One who had been promised, but also that the predictions of the prophets given hundreds of years earlier had been exactly fulfilled. Jesus, then, was the Christ - but He was also *Lord*, a sharer in Deity. Accordingly, Peter summoned *"all the house of Israel"* - priests, rulers, and people – to *"know assuredly that God has made this Jesus, whom you crucified, both Lord and Christ"* (v 36). Such was the authority and boldness with which the apostle spoke to the assembled Jerusalemites ... and this fearless champion of Jesus, "this undaunted arraigner of the nation's crimes", was the man who, only a few weeks earlier, had capitulated to the questioning of a servant girl!

As Peter addressed the house of Israel with words like blazing spears, his listeners were cut to the depth of their being (the Greek word *katanyssoma* which appears only here in the New Testament means "to be smitten in the heart with sorrow", or "pained vehemently in the mind"). The scene they had witnessed, together with the fiery words of explanation, produced a deep conviction of conscience, which in turn gave rise to the anxious question, *"What shall we do?"* Peter's answer laid down two conditions: repentance and baptism, but he went on to assure his hearers they might all possess the gift of the Spirit - "*for the promise is to you and your children, and to all who are afar off, as many as the Lord our God will call*" (v 39) - a promise for all future generations, and all peoples. In the roll call of the nations represented in Jerusalem for the Feast of Shavuot, Luke had listed proselytes, Cretans and Arabs – Gentiles as well as Jews - and three thousand new disciples were added to the church that day, a number that remarkably paralleled the three thousand who had perished at Sinai in the incident of the Golden Calf. A new work of God had begun: the creation of the church as a body composed of both Jew and Gentile (Ephesians 3:1-7) - a mystery, something that not only did not exist previously, but had never before been revealed.

Peter and the other disciples had come to understand the deep meaning of the death and resurrection of Christ: not as a scandal, but as the wonderful revelation of the wisdom and mercy of God, through a plan pre-established from all eternity, and announced by the prophets. Above all, Jesus had laid down his life out of love, even for those who had rejected and denied Him, and now this infinitely wonderful Person was sitting at the right hand of the Majesty on high, mediating blessings to men and women from the centre of the Godhead. Peter himself had been overwhelmed with an answering love for his Lord, and this love was the driving force of his courage on the day of Pentecost. The cross of Christ was the heart of his proclamation, and the power of his message inseparable from its paradoxical character. And to this day the witnesses of Jesus have been given the sword of the Spirit to proclaim the living Word of the Cross, until He shall return in power and glory to take up the throne of His father David.

The Teacher Come From God

The Book of Acts records that there were 120 disciples of Jesus present in the Upper Room on that dramatic day when the Holy Spirit descended in flames of fire. Besides the apostles and Mary the mother of Jesus, who else may have been there? The Gospels provide some tantalizing clues suggesting that one of the most distinguished citizens of the city may also have been present on that singular occasion. They also provide a paper trail which, some 2000 years later, helps to trace the sequence of events which may have led this person to so openly throw in his lot with the followers of the Nazarene.

The second chapter of John's Gospel describes some of the events taking place at the beginning of Jesus' ministry: He was in Jerusalem for the feast of Passover, and had caused a sensation in the city, showing signs among the people, and casting the moneychangers out of the Temple. These developments led up to the narrative of Chapter Three: the story of one who "came by night" to Jesus. As the full Passover moon was shining over the darkened streets of Jerusalem, a silent figure made his way through the narrow alleys to a certain dwelling place. He ascended the outer staircase to the guest chamber on the roof, threw back the cloak which covered his face, and announced himself to the charismatic Galilean whose words and deeds were causing such a storm in the city. This was one Naqdimon Ben Gurion, a Pharisee and a member of the Sanhedrin, possessor of great influence and wealth and also a person of historical note, mentioned in the Talmud. His Greek name Nicodemus translates as "ruler of the people".

It is no wonder that Nicodemus wished to mantle his visit to Jesus under cover of night and darkness. It was a very compromising action for a Sanhedrin member to take, for with Jesus' first dramatic cleansing of the Temple a rift had been created between Himself and the Jewish leadership, setting in motion a drama that would lead inexorably to its climax. But the terrible finale was, at that point, still far in the future. And there in the lamplight on that quiet Jerusalem evening one of the most extraordinary conversations ever recorded took place.

"Rabbi," began the visitor, "We know You are a teacher *come from God* ...". In those words, Nicodemus gave away the fact that he was not alone among the Pharisees in being powerfully impressed by Jesus' actions. Steeped as they were in Old Testament prophecy, there had perhaps sprung into their minds unbidden the remembrance of One clothed with zeal like a garment who would come suddenly to his Temple; and who, in his blazing consciousness of the holiness of the Lord's house, offered unprecedented evidence of entire consecration to God. Nicodemus' words echoed also the announcement of the Messiah's mission of atonement found in the Hebrew Scriptures: "*Lo I come*, in the volume of the book it is written of Me" (Psalm 40:7; cf Psalm 118:26). Yet Jesus heard not merely the words of Nicodemus, He knew what was in his heart and to this issue He went directly: "Truly, truly, I say to you ..." He said, indicating He was about to convey a truth of great solemnity, "... except a person be born from above, he cannot see the kingdom of God."

In that one sentence Jesus swept away all that Nicodemus stood for, and demanded a fundamental reorientation of his life and thought. To many Jews, to be born within the commonwealth of Israel *was* to be born into the kingdom of God, yet Jesus' declaration implied that Nicodemus' status as a scion of Israel, together with all his attainments in knowledge and virtue, was not sufficient to gain him entrance to heaven. The Kingdom of God is a realm so entirely apart, so transcending all earthly comprehension, that to partake of its goodness is beyond human effort and power. Therefore, it can be entered upon, not through moral or intellectual endeavors directed toward spiritual enrichment, but only through the entire renovation of the person's being as the result of a sovereign divine action.

That the Pharisee was stunned by what he heard may be inferred by the entire inadequacy of his subsequent question: "How may a man be born again – can he enter his mother's womb a second time?" In answer, Jesus repeated His first solemn declaration, but this time substituted the words "of water and spirit" for "from above". At that point, the spring breeze rustling through the narrow Jerusalem streets may have caused the flame of the lamp to tremble and Jesus, the Master of language, adapted the metaphor for His teaching. Did Nicodemus hear the sound of that wind sweeping through the city? Although he heard its voice, he knew neither whence it came, nor where it was going: so indeed, averred Jesus, was every person born of the Spirit quickened and directed by a Power beyond human comprehension.

Yet for Nicodemus this seemed to involve an even greater mystery, and he questioned further, "How can this be?" Jesus' answer came as a gentle rebuke: "Can you really be *the* teacher in Israel and not understand these things?" Should he not, as the most prominent teacher of the Jewish faith, have been aware of the Old Testament promises which predicted this very regeneration of which Jesus was speaking, awaiting the fulfillment of prophecies such as Isaiah 44:3: "I will pour water on him who is thirsty, and floods on the dry ground; I will pour My Spirit on your descendants ..."

At this point in the conversation, Jesus assured Nicodemus that: "We speak about what we know and testify about what we have seen ... but you people [Israel] do not accept our testimony." Jesus' use of the words "we" and "our" was in emphatic contrast to the opening words of the Pharisee, "Rabbi, *we* know", indicating His own absolute divine knowledge of God as One who had come "from the bosom of the

Father". He continued to further express His surprise at the Pharisee's lack of comprehension, "I have spoken to you of earthly things and you do not believe; how then will you believe if I speak of heavenly things?" The doctrine of regeneration from above through the Spirit of God was clearly, according to Him, to be considered an "earthly" matter; He alone, as the Son of Man who came from heaven, could disclose the mysteries of that realm. What were the heavenly truths He had come to bring?

The first of these concerned the revelation of the Messiah and his God-given task, which Jesus chose to now set forth (as He did so often) under a figure from the Hebrew Scriptures. Numbers 21 tells of how the Israelites had been complaining against God in the wilderness, so that fiery serpents were sent among them and many were bitten and died. God then instructed Moses to make a bronze serpent and set it on a pole, so that anyone bitten by one of the deadly creatures could merely look up at the serpent and be healed. The story was clearly emblematic of the nature and power of sin, first producing pain and finally causing the people to perish. Yet the fact that the Israelites were to gaze at the serpent for their healing, the very thing which had brought destruction, seemed incomprehensible. But Jesus unfolded the inner meaning of the story to Nicodemus: just as the brazen serpent was lifted up, so the Son of Man also would be lifted up, so that all who lifted their gaze to Him in faith would be saved - for the remedy which God provided was the Son of God appearing in "the likeness of sinful flesh" and "becoming sin" for His people.

Nicodemus had received already at this point received an "embarrassment of riches" in the way of divine truth. But Jesus was gently leading the Pharisee to yet a further understanding, a revelation which rose above all He had thus far taught as does the final towering peak in a great mountain range. This way of redemption that God had provided, He told Nicodemus, was a demonstration of the love He bears toward *all* whom He has created, and His desire that *all* should attain to the happiness and glory of eternal life in His kingdom. This assurance of divine graciousness was delivered through a statement transparent in its simplicity yet breathtaking in its majesty, which has shone with an incomparable luster over the past two millennia: *"For God so loved the world ..."*

But this declaration fell on the ears of the first hearer with an even greater shock value – for the assertion that God's love extended, not just to the people of Israel, but to *the world* was literally beyond the comprehension of many Jews – and not only this, but as a concomitant there was also the *possibility of perishing.* Yet if Nicodemus uttered any further protests, they went unrecorded; his whole world was shaken, and one wonders what thoughts jostled in his mind and heart as he made his way back to his home. To him had been granted the privilege of listening to immortal truths in a unique one-on-one interview with the One sent from the Father; as they lay in his mind like divinely planted seed, did they germinate, blossom and bear fruit in his life? The paper trail following Nicodemus' connection to Jesus and His followers continues in the 7th Chapter of John's Gospel.

It was midway through Jesus' ministry and He was again in Jerusalem, this time for the Feast of Tabernacles, when He stood up and made His great appeal to the people: "He that believes on Me, as the Scripture has said, out of his heart will flow rivers of living water" (John 7:38). The Evangelist clarified that Jesus was speaking of the Spirit, "which they that believe on Him should receive" - combining the same thoughts of new life through water and spirit which were the subject of the night discussion in John 3. It is highly likely that Nicodemus, as one of the leading members of the Sanhedrin, was present at the festival as Jesus made this offer. Immediately following this occasion the council of chief priests and Pharisees convened, desiring to arrest Jesus; and at this point, although Nicodemus did not express outright faith, he nevertheless stood up boldly to plead for just treatment for the Galilean (John 7:51).

Yet it was in his third and final appearance in John's Gospel, the day of the crucifixion, that the true character of Nicodemus shone forth most brightly. Now his faith was no longer hidden as he came together with Joseph of Arimathea, bringing a great weight of myrrh and spices to give the body of Jesus a royal burial. And as the Pharisee took down His lifeless form from the cross, it perhaps then rushed upon him with blinding clarity the meaning of Jesus' words of "lifting up".

When all this evidence is considered together, it seems highly probable that this faithful nobleman who featured at all the critical junctures of Jesus' life was also present on the Day of Pentecost, to hear the sound of the rushing wind from heaven, and with the other disciples to experience the upspringing of a divine fountain within the heart. If this be so, then the story of Nicodemus is surely one of the most fascinating accounts of conversion to be found in the scriptures. Moreover, his distinguished name lives on in present-day Jewish history, for the first Prime Minister of the modern State of Israel, David Ben Gurion, took his Hebrew name from the illustrious family to which Nicodemus belonged.

Yet, over and above the details concerning Nicodemus' personal journey of salvation, there is a richness in the account of his meeting with Jesus by night which has caused it to become imperishable. Apart from the fact it sets forth some of the greatest doctrines of salvation, it is pervaded with images of things divine and heavenly, conveying the sense that it has in some way descended "from above". And throughout, Jesus has opened a vista of "the length and breadth and depth and height" of the love of God – revealed above all in the lifting up of the Son of Man and the fountain of the Spirit thus opened for humanity. Here is seen the fullness of this gift – God's beloved Son, who came from highest heaven to save His people; the breadth of the gift – to the whole world, so that the promise of salvation has been borne over azure seas to the four corners of the earth; and the length of the gift – the words that promise everlasting life to those who believe on the Son of Man have been carried down through the ages, and will continue until the glory of the promise merges into the light of endless day.

And thus to all time, shining in the world's darkness as did the lamp in the shadowed streets of Jerusalem, are the words of eternal love, spoken by the Teacher come from God as the essential Gospel message to all peoples.

BEIN HAMETZARIM-BETWEEN THE STRAITS

Comfort in Dire Straits

hakespeare spoke truly of the Jewish people in his words, "*Sufferance is the badge of all your tribe*". Therefore, the Christian who desires to respond to God's call, "*Comfort My people*" (Isaiah 40:1), wishes also to know how best to offer consolation to those who have endured so much in their long history. Surprisingly, an answer can be found through reading the very texts in which Israel recalls the darkest moments of her existence.

During the days of high summer in Israel, the benison of radiant sunlight pours unremittingly from a cloudless sky. In Jerusalem an intoxicating blend of scents - rosemary, lavender and jasmine - spills from the gardens onto the streets and tourists fill the narrow lanes and bazaars of the Old City. Meanwhile on the coast in Tel Aviv a warm salt-laden breeze wafts over the endless blue Mediterranean and holidaymakers crowd the cafes and restaurants that line the streets near the sea. Yet at this same time comes a period of trepidation and sadness for observant Jews, and a withdrawal from all outward appearance of festive celebration. This is a consequence of the fact that, historically, the three weeks after the summer solstice have proved a season in which extraordinary calamities have befallen the people of Israel. This 21 day period, between 17 Tammuz and 9th Av, is the time known as "Between the Straits" – *Bein HaMetzarim* – a phrase taken from the Book of Lamentations (and from which is derived the English term "dire straits"):

"Judah is gone into captivity, under affliction and hard servitude; she dwells among the nations, she finds no rest: all her persecutors overtake her between the straits" (Lamentations 1:3)

According to Jewish tradition, Moses shattered the tablets on the 17th of Tammuz after he came down from Sinai and found the people worshiping the Golden Calf - yet an event considered even worse than this occurred on Tisha B'Av (Ninth of Av). On this date it was decreed that the original generation rescued from Egypt would be denied entrance into the Promised Land because of the Sin of the Spies, considered the "unpardonable sin" of the Torah because it involved *unbelief*, and as such became prophetic of other misfortunes of Jewish history. Twice upon this same day the Temple was destroyed, first by the Babylonians in 586 BC, and later by the Romans in 70 AD. Following this latter event the Jews were sent into exile, and then, during their long Diaspora over the past 2000 years, there were many other tragic occurrences on this date. Accordingly, the period "Between the Straits" culminates with a national day of mourning on Tisha B'Av, when the Book of Lamentations, *Megillat Eichah*, is recited plaintively during the evening service - Jeremiah's eyewitness account of the first destruction of Jerusalem by the armies of Nebuchadnezzar.

Jeremiah had exercised his ministry in Judah throughout a forty-year period after the northern kingdom of Israel had already passed away. Throughout this time the prophet saw Judah falling ever deeper into idolatry and rushing headlong to a similar calamity, even as he warned the people out of a heart filled with anguish. Yet when the Babylonians finally destroyed the city, when the Temple was burnt, the king driven into exile, his children slain and his people scattered, the citizens were completely unprepared. They believed their city had been chosen by God as His dwelling place, and were as astonished as though the sun had fallen from the sky.

Although Jeremiah had foreseen these things, when the disaster occurred his heartbreak could not have been greater. The ruined city lay silent with grief before him, and he was compelled to take up his pen and describe her sufferings. His task was to determine the real significance of this dramatic reversal in the fortunes of Judah, and yet the profound questions raised in Lamentations delineate the fundamental issues which engage all peoples and nations. Like the brilliancy of a diamond shining out from rocky surrounds, its great themes emerge in solemn splendor through the sad cadences - divine sovereignty and human responsibility, justice and judgment, the yearning for mercy and the hope of renewal. Above all, the unbearable pathos of the recognition that these calamities had descended because of human culpability pervade the lines:

> *"The crown has fallen from our head,*
> *Woe to us, for we have sinned!"* (5:16)

How was it possible for Jeremiah from his grotto, at this time of unprecedented suffering, to hold out hope to the Jewish people – and to future generations?

Lamentations is a tiny book in the Hebrew Bible, consisting of five poems, each of which looks at the destruction of Jerusalem from a different perspective. It opens with the Hebrew word *eicha*, meaning "how," which is typical for the beginning of a lament: David used it in his dirge over the death of Jonathan: *"How the mighty have fallen in battle!"* The first chapter, comparing the present deserted state of Zion with her glorious past, is one of the darkest pictures in all scripture: the city is portrayed variously as widow, mother, princess, vassal, mourner, shamed and despised woman; the one-time princess is now under hard servitude, the roads to Zion once filled with traffic are now empty, her former friends and lovers have become enemies. The repeated refrain, *"There is no one to comfort"*, evokes her complete desolation of spirit. And thus:

> *"She weeps bitterly in the night;*
> *Her tears are on her cheeks .."* (1:2)

Chapter 2 is a vivid eyewitness portrayal of the fall of Jerusalem: palace and stronghold, altar and sanctuary, ramparts and walls are broken down under the might of a relentless hand. The splendor of Israel is cut off, and the kingdom, its rulers and people are dishonored. None are spared, prophet and priest are silenced, elders and maidens are bowed to the ground and the description of pitiful suffering culminates in the picture of children who are swooning for hunger in the streets. Well might passersby shake their heads in wonderment at the daughter of Jerusalem, saying:

"Is this the city that was called
'The perfection of beauty,
The joy of the whole earth'?" (2:15)

With Chapter 3, however, there is a sudden change in perspective; it does not focus upon the destruction of Jerusalem, nor does it start with *eicha* as do chapters 1, 2 and 4, but rather with the words, *"I am the man who has seen affliction"*; thus, it becomes distinctive as a personal lament. Additionally, it contains the only voice of explicit hope in the book:

"This I recall to my mind,
Therefore I have hope.
Through the Lord's mercies we are not consumed,
Because His compassions fail not" (3:21-22)

Yet Chapter 4 plunges back into billows of despair. The most striking feature of this section is the contrast between the former glory of the Holy City and its present abasement: the city itself is like tarnished gold; her nobles, who were "brighter than snow and whiter than milk", are now blacker than soot; the sons of Zion, once esteemed of great worth, are now like earthen sherds; while mothers, deranged by the torments of famine, have boiled their own children for food. The destruction of Jerusalem is so complete it astonishes the kings and peoples of the earth; while the last chapter reveals Mount Zion, the place of revelation, as a desert where jackals roam. It closes on a poignant note, asking the desperate question that echoes throughout the whole book: *"Why do you forget us forever, and forsake us for so long a time?"* (5:20).

Lamentations looks at the ruin of the city and probes into it exhaustively from various angles - yet nowhere in the five poems is there a clear movement from grief to renewed expectation as is found in the psalms of lament. In fact, in all 154 verses of the book, there is only one explicit mention of hope - and there is an even greater theological tension residing at the heart of the poem, created by the recurrent use of the phrase *"He has ..."*. Chapter 2, in particular, depicts in vivid language what the Lord has done to His own people: He has *"humiliated, thrown down, destroyed without mercy, cut down, killed, poured out his fury, abolished festivals and Sabbath, spurned king and priests, scorned his altar, disowned his sanctuary and laid Zion in ruins"*. He had kindled a fire in Zion which not only consumed the city, but devoured its very foundations. The devastation of Jerusalem and the punishment of the Judahites could not be viewed as primarily the result of the Babylonian invader, but rather as divine judgment, and it was this which gave an additional depth to the tragedy.

At this point, the author's anguished question in 2:13 seems to express his ultimate yearning:

"How shall I console you? To what shall I liken you, O daughter of Jerusalem? What shall I compare with you, that I may comfort you, O virgin daughter of Zion?"

Yet the answer to this question is actually to be found imbedded within the text itself, which contains the interpretive keys to unlock its hidden message and so reveal the comfort and hope it holds out. The artistic composition of Lamentations features a remarkable literary device, utilizing the Hebrew alphabet of 22 letters. The first four chapters are composed in acrostic fashion, with each new verse beginning with a

141

succeeding letter of the alphabet – save for one puzzling aberration. In Chapters 2, 3 and 4, two of the letters have been transposed – usually the letter *ayin* comes before the letter *pe*, but here the order is reversed, and *pe* precedes *ayin*. Could it be that the reversal of the two letters is a deliberate literary choice by the author in order to make a theological point?

In understanding the significance of this transposition it is crucial to understand that the letter *pe* also stands for the word "mouth", while *ayin* means "eye" - making it possible that Jeremiah is highlighting the unpardonable sin of the Old Testament, the Sin of the Spies, who gave a bad report of the land to the children of Israel, saying that:

*"All the people whom we **saw** in it are men of great stature; there we **saw** the giants ; and we were like grasshoppers **in our own sight**, and so we were **in their sight…**"* (Numbers 13:32-33)

They had respect to the sight of their eyes rather than belief in the power of God to overcome their enemies, a fault reminiscent also of the first sin in the Garden of Eden, when the woman *"**saw** that the tree was good for food"*. Perhaps, then, through this literary device, the writer is indicating symbolically *that the "mouth" should precede the "eye"*, and anticipating the need for faith which is so dominant a feature of the New Testament.

The confession of faith which comes from the heart must necessarily precede the sight of the eyes; so that faith becomes *"the substance of things hoped for, the evidence of things not seen"* (Hebrews 11:1). It is faith alone which can gaze steadily at ruin and destruction, even such a ruin as that described in Lamentations, and trust in the power of God *"who raises the dead and calls those things which do not exist as though they did"* (Romans 5:17). It is that world-altering possibility which Jesus was always looking for in His disciples, and rejoicing to find. "When the Son of Man comes", He asked, "will he find faith on the earth?" But there is much more comfort yet to be discovered in the pages of Lamentations …

The Weeping Prophet

···

T he Book of Lamentations is the saddest book of the Hebrew Bible, but, when it is read carefully, lines of great solace and beauty begin to resonate through their dark packaging. In particular, a very intriguing literary feature may be discovered in Lamentations 5, the climax of the book.

There is no alphabetic acrostic in this section, as in the other chapters, but some verses near to the conclusion seem to express the tension which has been echoing throughout the whole text. Verse 19 is a great confession of the Lord's sovereignty, affirming His reign of righteousness and justice will endure to all ages; but following closely upon this the anguished question of verse 20 recapitulates the theme of the extreme suffering His people are enduring, and seems to revert to despair:

> *19 You, O Lord, remain forever; Your throne from generation to generation.*
> *20 Why do You forget us forever? And forsake us for so long a time?*

A closer perusal reveals that these lines have been carefully composed to form a hidden message, a "mini-acrostic" which is crucial to the interpretation of the work. Verse 19 embraces the first half of the Hebrew alphabet, *Aleph* to *Kaph*, by using an *aleph* word ("You") to start the first half of the verse, and a *kaph* word ("throne") to start the second half; in the same way verse 20 encompasses the second half of the alphabet, *Lamedh* to *Tau*, using the *lamedh* ("why") to begin the first part line and *tau* ("You forsake us") to commence the second half. Through this device the writer may be subtly suggesting that the suffering of Israel

143

is under God's sovereign control, and this exclusive dominion will not permit abandonment of the nation He has chosen.

This idea finds confirmation through consideration of the two Hebrew verbs in the second line, *shakach*, "to forget," and *azab*, "to forsake", in a rare combination which is found elsewhere only once in the Hebrew Bible, in Isaiah 49:14: "But Zion said, 'The Lord has *forsaken* me, And my Lord has *forgotten* me.'" The answer to this sorrowful allegation is found in the Lord's immediate exclamation: "Can a woman *forget* her nursing child, and not have compassion on the child of her womb? Surely they may *forget*, yet I will not *forget* you!" - an implicit response to Jeremiah's complaint. It is also David's cry in one of his psalms: "My God, my God, why have you *forsaken* me?", the same words which Jesus uttered on the cross: *"Eloi, Eloi, lama sabachthani?"* It is this cry which finally answers Jeremiah's question, for it puts the cross at the center of the whole book of Lamentations.

This emphasis is reinforced by an examination of the central section of the book, Chapter 3, which has an intensified acrostic pattern, with not just one but three verses starting with each succeeding letter of the alphabet. Here, instead of describing the calamities of the nation, the writer seems to point to himself: *"I am the man that has seen affliction"*, he begins his elegy, identifying himself completely with the sufferings of his people, as though they belonged to himself alone. Although he had been consistently rejected by his people, and despite the fact they have brought their sufferings upon themselves, he nevertheless is overwhelmed with grief for them when the calamity he predicted finally occurs, exclaiming: *"My eyes overflow with rivers of water for the destruction of the daughter of my people"* (3:48). It is a prophetic anticipation of a similar outpouring of compassion which will be seen hundreds of years later.

All four Gospels describe the triumphal entry of Jesus to Jerusalem on Palm Sunday. His disciples had brought a colt and placed Him on it, and as He rode into the city the multitude paid Him homage with waving branches and hosannas, even as His disciples exulted in shouts of joy emulating the angel songs of the night of His birth: *"Blessed be the King that comes in the name of the Lord: peace in Heaven and glory in the highest"* (Luke 19:38). Yet in the midst of the acclamation Jesus paused on the brow of the Mount of Olives to look over the Holy City which lay spread out before Him in the bright sunlight, with the great Temple gleaming with white marble and gold in its midst. It was one of the wonders of the ancient world, so that the rabbis declared that "he who had not seen Herod's Temple had never in his life seen beauty". Yet as Jesus surveyed the scene, one overpowering emotion mastered any feeling of admiration for its glory. His prophetic soul knew that, despite all those rich and precious adornments of God's House, there would not be left one stone upon another that would not be thrown down (Matthew 24:2).

And so, at the sight of Jerusalem and its great and beautiful Temple He wept with a deep inward anguish, all His divine compassion called forth towards the beloved city which was about to reject Him: *"Oh that you had known, even you, at least in this your day, the things which belong to your peace!"* (Luke 19:42). The name of Jerusalem signified peace, yet that peace, that shalom, was bound up with the recognition of her Messiah and His way of mercy and love. Before another week had passed, the Sovereign who had come to His city would be enthroned upon His cross, wearing the scarlet robes of His Kingship. And so the tears ran down Jesus' face even as He rode in triumph in the midst of His followers, sorrowing for the fate which would befall this people who knew not "the time of their visitation".

The ruin which Jesus foresaw with great historical accuracy and detail was summed up in a sentence of indescribable sadness: *"Your house is left unto you desolate"* (Matthew 23:38 KJV). The story of the destruction of Jerusalem in the year 70 as told by Josephus remains one of the most potent narratives ever set down. In the last battle of a six-year campaign, the Romans legions under Titus, a force of nearly 100,000 men, slaughtered perhaps half a million people in the city, so that the narrow streets literally ran with blood, until the carnage culminated in the final, climactic burning of the Temple Sanctuary:

"Grief might well be bitter for the destruction of the most wonderful edifices ever seen or heard of, both for its size and construction and for the lavish perfection of detail and the glory of its holy places. Through the roar of the flames as they swept relentlessly on could be heard the groans of the falling, held in the iron embrace of war: such were the height of the hill and the vastness of the blazing edifice that the entire city seemed to be on fire, while as for the noise, nothing could be imagined more shattering or more horrifying."

But the central elegy in Lamentations which is a prophetic forecast of Jesus' weeping over Jerusalem also affirms a great truth which emerges in limpid clarity from its pages: the understanding that "in all their affliction He was afflicted" (Isaiah 63:9). Jeremiah's lament is above all a foreshadowing of the Passion of Jesus Christ, and the essential clue to this truth is offered in its first line: "I am the **man** who has seen affliction by the rod of His wrath".

Although there are a number of different words for "man" in Hebrew, the particular word used here by Jeremiah is *gever*; this is a term signifying strength and nobility as possessed, for example, by David's "mighty men". The last time this word is used in the Hebrew Scriptures it appears in this way: *"Awake, O sword, against My shepherd, against the man (gever) who is My equal,' says the Lord of hosts"* (Zechariah 13:7) - it is the Messiah who is the ultimate *Gever*. The use of this term also anticipates a scene from the Gospels: when Jesus was standing before Pilate, the Roman Governor presented Him to the people in the words, "Behold the Man!" The similarity of the phrases suggests the central truth of the whole scriptural record: that Jesus is the One who had come to stand in the place of His people and bear the punishment they themselves deserved.

The final interpretation of Jeremiah's suffering is therefore to be found in the suffering of Jesus, the One who could say more truly than the weeping prophet, *"Behold and see if there is any sorrow like my sorrow which has been brought on me"* (Lamentations 1:12). The sin which deserved God's just wrath has spent itself on Christ, so that a message of compassion might be given to the daughter of Zion - the glad tidings of mercy renewed each morning, of love which is everlasting. The daughter of Zion had done naught to deserve pardon, but God had chosen her, and entered into covenant concerning her, that He would never leave nor forsake her. In His sovereign grace, He had preserved deliverance for the beloved city, would bring back His people, and in time to come would rekindle their faith and hope. In this way Jesus was able to affirm to the people, even as He wept, that a wonderful confession of faith upon their lips would precede the sight of their eyes – their Messiah would return to them in the fullness of His glory, even as they made their great proclamation: *"Blessed is He who comes in the name of the Lord!"* (Matthew 23:39).

These are treasures of consolation, promises to be clung to in moments of great darkness, when a tide of sorrow threatens to sweep away all that is held dear and precious – and they are not just for the Jewish people. In a world racked by war and violence, Lamentations reveals itself as a book for the whole human condition. And those who trust in the suffering Messiah it sets forth hold on in hope to the great message of comfort discerned in the lines of the book, believing that the *Gever* who is God's own equal, who has borne the afflictions of His people and also triumphed over them through His cross, has the power to bring both personal and national redemption. And, at the promised time, He shall return again in undisguised majesty to take up His throne in Jerusalem, end the days of mourning, and renew all things.

Elul and the Theme of Love

....

The great theme of consolation continues to be traced out as the Jewish liturgical year continues. The Sabbath immediately following *Tisha B'Av* is called *Shabbat Nachamu*, the Sabbath of Comfort, based on the reading from the prophets that begins *Nachamu, nachamu ami*, "Comfort, comfort My people" (Isaiah 40:1). According to the rabbis, the word is repeated in order to assuage the sorrow for both Temples that were destroyed. Then comes the beginning of Elul, the last month before the High Holy Days, and throughout this period the overarching idea is *love*. In Hebrew, the first letters of the phrase found in Song of Songs 6:3, *"Ani l'Dodi ve Dodi li"* – "I am my Beloved's and my Beloved is mine" - spell the word Elul. It is believed to be a time when the depth of love in the heart of the Divine Bridegroom toward His bride, Israel, is revealed in new ways.

In the Tanach God presented Himself in many ways to His people - as King, Lord, Redeemer, Provider - but one great designation transcended all others. The prophet Isaiah disclosed the way in which God chose to reveal Himself supremely as he wrote: *"For your Maker is your husband — the Lord Almighty is his name"* (Isaiah 54:5). It was God's desire to enfold the people to Himself in a marriage covenant, and it was this which above all set forth the intensity and depth of His love for them, as well as the staggering condescension of the divine purpose in entering such an exclusive relationship. The scriptures delineate the unfolding history of the people of Israel with their God in terms of a marriage betrothal, following times of mutual love as well as periods of separation as a result of unfaithfulness on the part of the affianced bride. It is a chronicle marked by betrayal, suffering and contrition, yet shot through with gleams of glory: the revelation of the steadfastness of God's love toward His covenanted spouse that will not allow Him to finally abandon her.

The New Testament writers built on these conceptions as they transferred the nuptial imagery of Bridegroom unhesitatingly to Jesus, whom they identified as One had come to woo and win His bride, while the Apostle Paul especially emphasized the "great mystery" which is the transcendent unity to be accomplished between Christ and His church. But it is only when the final pages of the Bible are reached that the great purpose toward which the unfolding revelation of God's love has been proceeding is blazoned forth. Revelation 19:9 describes how the author, John, was exhorted by an angel of God to write a new beatitude to be recorded for future ages: *"Blessed are those who are called to the marriage supper of the Lamb"*. It was the announcement of the consummation of the ages, when the perfected union of Christ and His people should be celebrated and the true Bridegroom, the King in His beauty, revealed to all.

But herein lies a puzzle: why is this supreme occasion described not as the marriage supper of the *King* or the *Messiah*, but of the *Lamb?* And why is it that of all the divine titles accorded to the Jesus in both Old and New Testaments it is this name which is bestowed upon Him at His wedding? And finally, why do the scriptures also indicate that the bride, the one destined to share His throne, is to be identified as "the Lamb's wife"? The answer to these queries may be discovered by travelling back through the pages of the scriptures and discovering the contexts in which the image of the lamb appears.

At the very commencement of the Hebrew Scriptures, in the first pages of Genesis, a shepherd named Abel appears on the scene, pictured as bringing the firstlings of his flock - a lamb - to God. It was this costly sacrifice involving the shedding of blood which caused Abel to find acceptance with God. Only a few chapters later in Genesis 22 comes the story of the Binding of Isaac, the soul-shaking account of the way in which Abraham's dedication to God was tested by the command to offer his son Isaac as a "holocaust" on a mountain God would show him. There on the slopes of Moriah, as the two "went on together", Isaac asked of his father the question, "Where is the lamb for a burnt offering?" And it was then that God drew back the veil and permitted the patriarch to see down through the centuries and give the great answer of faith: that God Himself would provide the lamb.

During Israel's struggle for freedom from slavery in Egypt the lamb featured again: on that dark night when the angel of death spread his wings over the land the chosen people remained safe within their houses as the blood of the lamb, splashed on doorposts and lintels, protected them. And then, when the Children of Israel were finally in their Promised Land, the *tamid* or lamb of the daily offering was sacrificed both morning and evening in the Temple (Exodus 29:38-46), a creature without blemish burnt in its entirety on the altar as God's provision for the continual protection and cleansing of His people.

The 53rd Chapter of Isaiah plunges the reader deep into the heart of the mystery of God's plan of salvation for humanity, manifested in the character and identity of His Servant. This saving figure comes not with dazzling armor and battle sword, nor with ten thousand legions of angels - rather, he assumes the character of a *lamb*. The prophet must often have seen the gentle animal led in silence to the altar to be slain and that was the incomparable image which came to him. This Servant, although unique and beloved of God, was nevertheless *"led like a lamb to the slaughter"*, enduring great agony of soul and the bitterness of death to make expiation for the sins of His people. Yet throughout the whole course of his unparalleled sufferings this meek, unresisting lamb "opened not his mouth", neither complaining against God for yielding him up, nor reviling his accusers for punishing him without cause.

Rather, he accepted the punishment for human iniquity and laid down his life willingly, with the unexpected and contradictory result that this weak and suffering Servant brought health, shalom and cleansing to Israel and the nations.

When the New Testament is turned to the same image recurs in the context of the first presentation of Jesus to the people. The beginning of John's Gospel records that when John the Baptist was at Bethabara beyond Jordan he saw Jesus coming to him and made the great declaration: *"Behold the Lamb of God, which takes away the sin of the world"* (John 1:29). The familiar concept of "lamb" was here extended in an entirely new way: to suggest that this lamb possessed a unique relationship with God and functioned as His personal agent of redemption. Yet the Baptist's statement seems to be at odds with some of his other pronouncements and one might well ask exactly what he intended to convey.

The Baptist's preaching as recorded in the synoptic Gospels placed a strong emphasis on judgment and he clearly expected that God's Coming One - the Lamb - would function to bring swift retribution to his enemies, would "thoroughly purge His threshing floor and ... burn up the chaff with unquenchable fire" (Matthew 3:12). After he was imprisoned for rebuking Herod Antipas concerning his adulterous marriage with Herodias, it appears John also entertained serious doubts concerning Jesus' Messiahship - again suggesting he was expecting a Deliverer who would sweep away unrighteous and oppressive rulers in the land. It seems likely, therefore, that John's idea of the lamb was related to images found in apocalyptic literature appearing in the intertestamental period. In these well known works, some of the great heroes of Israel such as David and Judah Maccabee were depicted as horned lambs, an image symbolic of power and victory. The Baptist very probably conceived of Jesus as just such a conquering lamb, one who would purify the world of sin not through a sacrificial work of atonement, but through a great act of eschatological judgment at the end of history.

Nevertheless, John is given great prominence in the Fourth Gospel as a true witness to Christ, and it may well be that in this utterance he was speaking beyond his own knowledge as an inspired prophet of the tradition of Israel. When combined with the Evangelist's emphasis in later chapters upon Jesus as the true Passover lamb, the statement becomes a powerful theological affirmation in which the metaphor of the lamb reaches its crowning point, denoting one who should sum up in himself all previous sacrifices and offerings. The word "Behold" in John's statement strikes a note of amazement and wonder. He looks beyond the bounds of Israel, and presents the Lamb for the *whole world*, indicating that Christ's redemptive purpose embraces both Jew and Gentile. Jesus was the innocent sacrificial lamb sent from God whose death would provide a full and sufficient expiation for the sins of all people.

When the Book of Revelation is reached, it is discovered that the term "Lamb", in this case the unusual word Greek *arnion* meaning "little lamb", is by far the most widely used designation for Jesus, to whom it refers 29 times. As the spectacular visions unfold John is lifted to heaven and sees "in the midst of the throne" a Lamb still bearing the marks of sacrifice. Yet the Lamb of Revelation is not a figure of weakness. Rather, it was through His lamb-like character that Jesus had become the All-Conquering One who now has "seven horns", symbolic of absolute power, and "seven eyes" indicating perfect omniscience. The elders, the living creatures, the redeemed saints, every order of beings bow down and worship the Lamb as One who is infinitely worthy to receive wisdom, glory, riches and honor. The key to history is the slain Lamb of Revelation who alone is able to open the sealed book and bring God's redemptive purposes for humanity to their conclusion.

Yet according to Revelation 13:8, Jesus as the slain Lamb also existed *"from the foundation of the world"*. Before the vaporous clouds condensed into suns and stars and shone their light into the dim recesses of space, before the bright earth itself with its rich sea-girdled lands was hung "upon nothing", before all the great unfolding events began to stride the aeons of time, even then, in the solemn councils of eternity past, the decree was ordained and the course of the Lamb was fixed as Representative, Substitute and Sacrifice for the children of men. And the incomparable wisdom of the divine plan shall be demonstrated when it is brought to ultimate fulfillment on the day to which all things are hastening, when the Lamb shall take to Himself in everlasting union those whom His Father gave Him from the beginning, accompanied by a great multitude singing:

"Alleluia! for the Lord God omnipotent reigns! Let us be glad and rejoice, and give Him glory, for the marriage of the Lamb has come, and His wife has made herself ready" (Revelation 19:6-7)

Therefore, it is as a Lamb that Jesus will celebrate the marriage supper with His bride, the church, because it is as the Lamb He has most fully displayed His love to her. The true extent of this divine ardor was not revealed as He went about doing good, as the pearls of wisdom fell from His lips and men and women were redeemed from disease and darkness by His deeds of power, though these indeed played their part and foreshadowed His ultimate service. The incontrovertible proof of His love was that He was led as a lamb to the slaughter and poured out His blood for her, when He endured the nails and the spear, the crown and the thorns, the cross and the grave, in order to save His people from destruction. The love of Jesus was set forth supremely not in the Transfiguration, not in the Triumphal entry, but at Gethsemane, Gabbatha and Golgotha.

Moreover, it is as the Lamb that Jesus is best loved of His people. As Christ reigns from the throne of the universe He radiates all the effulgence of the divine glory and possesses untold power and majesty. Yet it was in His character as the gentle Lamb who laid down His life for her that He first compelled the love of His church: it is the One lifted up on the cross who alone has power to draw all men to Himself, and it is His suffering and death which is the irresistible magnet that compels their worship. Moreover, it is as the Lamb that Jesus is most closely joined to His people. Jesus drew very near to His own when He took their nature upon Himself, became bone of their bone and flesh of their flesh. But when He took their sins upon Himself and bore them away it brought a union with His church closer than any other which can be conceived, the unbreakable union of Christ with souls redeemed by His blood.

At the marriage supper of the Lamb the heavenly Bridegroom will demonstrate to the whole cosmos that He loves His bride to the furthermost bound love can go. And as a final triumph of Jesus' act of redemption, the bride at His side will be conformed to His likeness, reflecting His peerless beauty and raised to a superlative dignity. At this supreme feast of love, well might she then exclaim with overflowing joy: *"My beloved is mine and I am his"*.

Glory on the Mountain Top

liyah! This Hebrew word meaning "ascent" or "going up" evokes all the yearning, passion and hope which has filled the hearts of so many Jewish people over the centuries - the longing to return to Zion. After the establishment of the State of Israel in 1948, great numbers of those who had been scattered among the nations began arriving in their new homeland from the four corners of the earth. The Soviet Union, however, placed severe hindrances in the way of Russian Jews who wished to make this aliyah, causing the "Prisoners of Zion" and refuseniks to embark upon an underground struggle full of suffering and heroism. With the collapse of communism the Iron Curtain finally swung open, and since that time approximately one million Russian émigrés have arrived in Eretz Israel.

The impact of this unprecedented influx from the north has been felt in every sphere of cultural and political life. Highly skilled and educated, the Soviet Jews have made a significant contribution to the technological boom which has transformed Israel's economy; at the same time they have created a vibrant Russian subculture, maintaining their own range of newspapers and social media, and adding another layer of complexity to an already multifaceted society. Overhearing the Russian language in streets and cafes, observing the pervasive signs in Cyrillic, or browsing supermarket shelves stocked with vodka, herrings and Baltika beer, it is possible for fleeting moments to imagine oneself in St Petersburg or Moscow rather than the Jewish homeland. And there are other reminders also, in Jerusalem, of the lingering influence of Imperial Russia.

In the latter part of the 19th century, as the power of the Ottoman Empire declined, various European powers sought to gain a foothold in the Holy Land. The Russians, too, purchased an area to the north of the Old City walls which had been used by the Ottoman army as a parade ground. On this expansive plot, later known as the Russian Compound, they built an extensive array of facilities for the many thousands of Russian pilgrims arriving in the land: hospices, a church, a hospital, almost a miniature city. But the most impressive Russian construction was located on the Mount of Olives: the Church of St. Mary Magdalene, with seven golden, onion-shaped domes projecting brilliantly against the backdrop of green foliage which covers the lower slopes. One may climb a little way up the winding path which leads to the summit, enter through tall gates and discover one of the most distinctive places of worship in Jerusalem. Set in beautifully tended gardens, the magnificent structure has solid, graceful lines and a classic exterior with Roman-style arches; it also offers a breathtaking panorama of the Old City.

One of Russia's most remarkable saints lies buried in state within the church, Russian Grand Duchess Elizaveta Fyodorovna, who has a unique and enthralling story. Born in 1864, the granddaughter of Queen Victoria, she became famed throughout Europe for her beauty and eventually wed Grand Duke Sergei of the House of Romanov in an arranged political marriage, adopting the Russian Orthodox faith. Her brother-in-law, Czar Alexander III, initiated the building of the Mary Magdalene Church in memory of his mother, and Elizaveta arrived in 1888 to attend its consecration. During the lavish ceremony, she went up on the Mount of Olives, and on seeing the view from there over the city experienced a spiritual revelation; from then on she became the moving spirit behind all the Russian building in Jerusalem, and brought in some of Russia's leading artists to decorate the church.

In 1905 Elizaveta's husband Sergei was assassinated in the Kremlin by a Socialist revolutionary. This seemed to her the terrible fulfillment of a prophecy she had made after the Grand Duke had expelled 20,000

Jews from Moscow: "God will punish us severely". The event marked a turning point in Elizaveta's life: *"I am leaving a glittering world where I had a glittering position, but with all of you I am descending into a greater world - the world of the poor and the suffering."* Now she gave away her jewelry and sold her possessions, and with the proceeds opened the Martha and Mary home in Moscow to foster the charitable deeds of a group of nuns called the Sisters of Love and Mercy. Yet political events in Russia were spiraling out of control. In 1918 Bolshevik revolutionaries executed all the Czar's family by firing squad, and Elizaveta they thrust blindfolded into a disused mineshaft, then tossed in grenades. Here she perished, but her body was brought by those who revered her on a long and difficult journey to Jerusalem, where she was buried as she had requested in the Mary Magdalene Church.

The interior of the church is exquisitely simple; shades of brown and cream predominate, and it is also decorated with a profusion of icons. The use of icons (Greek *eikones*), sacred images representing Christ, the Virgin and the saints gained in popularity in the early church, especially in the eastern provinces of the Roman Empire, and are to the present day regarded in the Orthodox Church as a medium of divine grace which can deepen the experience of communion with God. One of the most popular subjects for icons is the Transfiguration of Christ, a major feast in the Orthodox Church, celebrated each year in August. The Eastern theologians insist that the story of the Transfiguration lifts the reader into a realm full of divine mystery and wonder. What can be learned from them concerning this astonishing narrative?

The New Testament presents accounts of the Transfiguration in each of the Synoptic Gospels (Matthew 17:1-9; Mark 9:2-9; and Luke 9:28-36). The context is the same in each case: Peter, as spokesman for the disciples, had just made his great confession of the Messiahship of Jesus at Caesarea Philippi; and Jesus, while affirming Peter's declaration, had immediately begun to unfold to the disciples the destiny which awaited Him. The revelation that, far from ushering in a glorious Messianic kingdom, He was to experience public rejection and die a shameful death was beyond their power to grasp, and their hearts became suffused with foreboding. Some days later Jesus took Peter, James and John and went up onto "a high mountain apart" - most likely one of the towering peaks of snow-capped Mount Hermon which was so close to Caesarea. They made the steep ascent, reaching the solitary heights as evening drew on and the brilliant stars began to cluster overhead, while a pale moon perhaps cast an unearthly radiance over the scene. The disciples sank into a heavy slumber, and awoke to perceive a sight for which nothing in their experience or in the history of Israel had prepared them.

For there, before them, Jesus became transfigured, so that His face shone like the sun and His clothes became whiter than snow and glistening, filling the night with glory. The Evangelists struggle to find terms to convey the exceeding brightness of the light in which He was enveloped, an effulgence which nature suggests, but to which it does not attain. Luke, who so often referred to Jesus praying, imparts the information that the twofold change in Jesus' countenance and garments took place "as He prayed". It was during this time of heavenly communion that the veil of His flesh became transparent and illuminated as if unable to conceal the radiant indwelling divinity, like white light glowing within the translucent shell of an alabaster vase. And with this "metamorphosed" Jesus appeared two of the greatest figures from the Old Testament, Moses and Elijah, talking with Him.

In the Hebrew Scriptures, there are numerous manifestations of the *Kavod Adonai*, the *Shekinah* glory of the Lord, images of flame, light and cloud signifying all the awesome, mystical power of God's presence and holiness. Already in Exodus this glory appeared to Moses in a visible fashion in the burning bush, then as a cloud by day and a pillar of fire by night as Israel was led out of Egypt. When Moses came down from Mt. Sinai after conversing with God, his face glowed with such brilliance that the people could not bear to look at him - yet the light which shone on Moses' face is to be understood not as something which he himself projected, but rather as a divine splendor bestowed upon him. But when Christ shone with radiance brighter than the sun, He was showing forth in His countenance the *Shekinah* glory of God – the transcendent light He possessed through His oneness with the Father, a glory He chose to conceal while upon earth, but which never ceased to be a part of His essential nature.

The image of the Deity as luminous, possessing "Uncreated Light", is central to Eastern spirituality. In icons of the Transfiguration the huge aura surrounding Christ is called a "glory", and He is always the central Figure in the scene, as the One who alone could dwell in the heart of that divine radiance. Moses and Elijah are often seen standing on its outer edge: each in their lifetimes had experienced a revelation of God's glory on another mountain, Sinai, and thus were enabled to draw near the fiery brightness without being consumed. As for the disciples, the different postures in which they are portrayed reflect the degree to which they were able to bear the revelation of Christ's glory. The Orthodox theologians assert that, as they contemplated the transformation of Jesus' countenance and body, they did so not with corporeal eyes but only through the enlightening power of the Holy Spirit - for it is impossible that the supernatural glory and kingdom of the Father could be projected forth in any sort of mundane light.

Suddenly a cloud passed over the mountain and enwrapped the group like a luminous veil. A nameless awe and terror gripped the disciples, together with an inchoate desire to prolong the vision. As happened so often, Peter then became the spokesman for the others, in his confusion not knowing what he was saying: "Rabbi, it is good for us to be here; and let us make three tabernacles: one for You, one for Moses, and one for Elijah" (Mark 9:5). Peter was perhaps thinking of the Feast of Tabernacles, during which time the Jewish people would construct and dwell in small shelters or "booths" in remembrance of their years of wilderness wandering. Probably he also associated the tabernacle with a manifestation of the divine Presence as experienced by Moses.

On Mount Sinai Moses had received instructions to construct the Tabernacle which would accompany the Israelites as they journeyed through the desert, the same Tent of Meeting that would be filled with the cloud of the divine glory (Exodus 40:34-38). The most common Hebrew word used to refer to the Tabernacle of Moses, *mishkan*, is derived from *shakan*, which means to "pitch a tent" and it is from this root that the word *Shekinah* is drawn. In the New Testament, the word σκηνή (*skéné*) is a Greek term whose oldest and primary meaning is "tent", but other meanings include "dwelling-place", and "temple"; it was also the word used in the Septuagint to denote the Tabernacle. *Mishkan, Shekinah,* and *skéné* are thus related etymologically by means of the common consonants "s k n", and also linguistically because each serve to reveal the Divine Presence: the *mishkan/skéné* provided the place where the *Shekinah* might dwell amongst humanity upon earth.

That there is indeed such a close interconnection between the *skéné martyríou*—the Tent of Meeting or Witness—and the *Shekinah* who dwelt there, and Christ as the *skéné* within whom the *Shekinah* dwelt, as revealed in the Transfiguration, is made clear in the Prologue of the Fourth Gospel. It seems certain that the Apostle John, the only Evangelist present at the miracle on the holy mountain, was remembering this occasion as he wrote: "*....and the Word became flesh and tabernacled (eskénósen) among us (or 'pitched His tent among us')*". He then continues: "*We beheld His glory, the glory as of the only begotten of the Father, full of grace and truth*" (John 1:14). In other words, Christ's body was a *skéné* that dwelt on earth, through whom the radiance and beauty of the *Shekinah* glory of the Father was finally revealed. As the writer of the Letter to the Hebrews expressed it: God "*has in these last days spoken to us by His Son, the brightness of His glory and the express image of His person*" (Hebrews 1:1-3).

The account of the Transfiguration ended as a Voice came from the cloud, saying, "*This is my beloved Son, in whom I am well-pleased. Hear Him!*" (Matthew 17:5). According to Luke, the cloud was "bright" and yet it "overshadowed" the disciples, a reminder of the cloud which filled the Temple, in the glory of which the priests could not stand to minister. As they heard the Voice speaking, the disciples fell on their faces. It was a message to them from heaven of the most solemn import, affirming the testimony Jesus had given them concerning the way of His Messiahship and the necessity of His death. Their trembling hearts needed such encouragement as they walked with Him the road that led to the cross; it was of vital importance that they should be able to remember, as they saw His face marred and crowned with thorns, that it had once shone like the sun, and that He had been clothed with light as with a garment.

And so the Voice was urging them: "Listen to Him!", as He reveals His way of suffering and death; "Listen to Him!", as He tells of rising from the dead and overcoming the grave; "Listen to Him!", as He tells of His return in glory, to take up His throne and rule over Israel and all the nations of the earth.

The Church of St Mary Magdalene

The Theme of Exodus

....

J esus did not stand alone in the glowing radiance that bathed Him on the Mount of Transfiguration. As the purple shadows gathered on Hermon, the disciples had fallen into a deep slumber, and when they awoke they saw Him conversing with two figures who made a powerful impression upon them. In some mysterious way, they were able to recognize in their forms and faces the august lineaments of two major representative persons from the Old Testament. One had ascended flame-encircled Mount Sinai to commune with God forty days and nights, and brought back to Israel her law: Moses; the other was the prophet who called down fire from heaven and led straying Israel back to the one true God: Elijah.

What had called forth these mighty dead, and of what did they talk with Jesus on that sequestered height? It was certainly not to apprise Jesus of the cross which cast its shadow over His pathway; Jesus Himself had forecast His suffering and rejection in minute detail to the disciples some eight days earlier. What then was the matter so dear to their hearts, which carried such great import, that they had come from an unseen world to stand on the snowy slopes of Hermon?

Most fortunately, despite the fact that the disciples were still heavy with sleep, certain unexpected words fell upon their ears, which only much later, in hindsight, were understood. Luke the Evangelist recorded those words for posterity and so divulged this priceless information: the subject of the mysterious communication which took place on the mountain top. This was nothing less than the central event of time and eternity, the great purpose for which Jesus had descended from Heaven: *"And behold, two men talked with Him, who were Moses and Elijah, who appeared in glory and spoke of His decease which He was about to accomplish at Jerusalem"* (Luke 9:30-31).

The term used by the heavenly visitors to denote Jesus' death was the Greek word *exodus* which literally means a departure or "going out". Its appearance in this unusual context suggests a fact overflowing with significance: that Jesus would pass from earth to heaven and make His return to the place from whence He had come, not overcome by any adverse force or power, but of His own free and sovereign will. Further than that, He should "accomplish" this as a task to be fulfilled, a glad surrender to the exigencies of a divine purpose set in motion from ages past: that One would come from the Father on a mission of redemptive love, to save a world sinking under a weight of sin and unable by any means to lift itself. Who could accomplish such a task? None other than God's own equal: this has always been the orthodox testimony of the church.

During the great fourth century debate on the nature of Jesus Christ, Church Father Gregory Nazianzus made the following statement: *"That which was not assumed is not healed; but that which is united to God is saved"* - that is, he was saying, Christ had to have been fully human in order to accomplish the task of redeeming humanity. According to Gregory's doctrine of the Incarnation, when God had clothed Himself in human flesh it was necessary for Him to take upon Himself all the attributes of the human being, for whatever He did not take upon Himself would not be saved. Therefore, Jesus had assumed every aspect of a mortal being so that through His redemptive work He might bring "healing" to men and women in the totality of their bodies, souls and spirits. Although Gregory thus asserted Christ was fully human, he also emphasized that Jesus did not cease to be God when He became a man, nor did He lose any attributes of His divine nature.

Thus, as the Lawgiver and the chief of the Prophets stood either side of the transfigured Christ with His radiant face and glistening robes, they formed an eloquent tableau, as if affirming that this was the One whom they had seen from afar, and that though He came after them He was before them; that in Him all types and shadows of the previous revelation found their perfect fulfillment. And the subject of their conversation with Him there was the whole theme of which the Old Testament had spoken in veiled form: the law given on Sinai, the cult of sacrifice and the perpetual smoke ascending from the altar, the glorious Temple in Jerusalem, and the impassioned exhortation of the seers in the wilderness, all were for one end and purpose, to lead up to the surpassing glory of the divine revelation: the great Sacrifice, the "Lamb of God who takes away the sins of the world".

The presence there of Moses and Elijah offered also a tantalizing glimpse of the life beyond the present mundane dimensions of time and place, suggesting that the entire focus of the world above was centered and concentrated upon the events transpiring on this lowly ground. All that other realm awaited with anxious yearning and longing expectation the promised atonement, and for the return to their midst of the Lord of heaven and earth, baptized in the white fire of His suffering, and crowned with the incomparable luster of His victory. Yet these two also vanished away, and Jesus alone was left standing there, the perfect and final Revealer of the love of God, to take by the hand and raise His awe-struck disciples.

There is only one other place in the New Testament where the word *exodus* is used: the Second Letter of Peter, traditionally thought to have been written during the first fierce persecution of Christians, after Emperor Nero blamed them for the fire that burned Rome in 64 AD. In his letter it is clear that Peter knew he would soon have to "put off his tent", as Jesus had told him, and he therefore had an urgent desire to teach and encourage the Christians. "*Moreover,*" he wrote to them, "*I will be careful to ensure that you always have a reminder of these things after my exodus*" (2 Peter 1:15). That Peter chose to describe his imminent death as an "exodus" suggests he had thought long and hard about the Transfiguration scene and the words he had heard spoken there; in fact he immediately passed on to speak about that event, and the voice He had heard in the "holy mount". The conclusion seems inescapable that this meditation had brought a new understanding of his final destiny: Peter felt that in some way his "exodus" was to be conformed to that of his Master.

Through using this word, the Apostle was also exhorting the Christians to whom he wrote to view their own deaths as being patterned on that of Jesus: not something to be feared or avoided, but simply as a departure, a passage to a fuller life. The dread subject of death, the final irrevocable fate to which humanity had been appointed and which seemed to bring all mortal flesh to dust and oblivion, was in this one word robbed of its sting; more than that, the experience was transformed into a passage from bondage to entrance upon a more exalted state. In the first Exodus, the Children of Israel were delivered from the weary days of servitude under the lash of their Egyptian overseers to gather around the banqueting table, no longer slaves but free men and women. In the same way, after the brief moment of death, the Christians would find their chains falling off, old limitations vanquished, and they themselves raised up and ennobled, enabled to be partakers of the joy of God's eternal kingdom.

As another Church Father, Athanasius, wrote, "*Death has become like a tyrant who has been completely conquered by the legitimate monarch.*" On the cross Christ had borne all the bitter pangs and woe consequent upon human transgression and finitude; He then descended the deep abyss of death but rose again triumphant, achieving a victory so complete, signal and eternal that it forever robbed the grave of its terrors. It was therefore His exodus that made the final departure of those believing on Him a deliverance from captivity and an entrance upon a larger realm of existence. They were treading in the footsteps of the One who had gone before them, who through His death had conquered death and brought light and immortality to life. When they came to the iron gates of that *"undiscover'd country, from whose bourn no traveller returns"*, the bars would swing wide, ushering them into the presence of the Lord of Life and Love.

But it is not just the experience of death which needs to be reconsidered in the light of the exodus Jesus has accomplished through His cross and resurrection. The New Testament suggests that the whole of the Christian walk of faith, from conversion until final departure, is structured by that one redemptive event. And once again the figure of Peter is central to providing this understanding.

One of the last episodes featuring the Apostle in the Book of Acts is the account of his imprisonment appearing in Chapter 12, a narrative in which the language and historical details clearly evoke the story of the original Exodus. The spectacular events of the escape of the Children of Israel out of Egypt included a number of attendant miracles: the Passover meal eaten in haste as the blood of the lamb protected the houses of the Israelites, the triumphant departure with the silver and gold of their former slave-masters, the splitting of the Red Sea so they all passed through on dry land - all the complex narrative developments which formed the great type of Christ's redeeming work. The story in Acts 12 draws upon a number of these motifs.

It was during the Days of Unleavened Bread that Peter was seized and put in prison by King Herod, resembling here a tyrannical figure cast in the mold of Pharaoh. Herod was planning on handing Peter over "after Passover", and the Apostle was kept bound, guarded by four squads of soldiers night and day so that deliverance seemed impossible. But continual prayer was made for him by the church in Jerusalem, and an angel of the Lord came to him in the prison while he was sleeping, "struck" him on the side, saying: "Arise quickly." The chains fell off his hands and the angel continued: "Gird yourself and tie on your sandals…Put on your garment and follow me," again suggesting a parallel with the first Passover meal, which also involved readiness for action: "*Thus you shall eat it*," the Israelites were instructed, "*with a belt on your waist, your sandals on your feet, and your staff in your hand. So you shall eat it in haste*" (Exodus 12:11).

After the angel led him through the iron gates, which opened of their own accord before them, Peter rejoined his praying brethren, and there was a time of great rejoicing. The next scene shifted to Herod seated on his throne receiving the acclamation of his people; at that point he was "struck" by an angel of the Lord, and died - again intimating a connection with the Passover story, in which an angel of the Lord passed through the land of Egypt to "strike" all those not protected by the blood of the lamb. And then, when Peter was finally set free and told his fellow believers how the Lord had "brought him out" (cf Acts 7:36), his reflections on what had just transpired echo the language of the Exodus: "*Now I know for certain that the Lord has sent His angel, and has delivered me from the hand of Herod*" (Acts 12:11). It becomes clear that his miraculous escape from prison, just as much as his approaching death, is to be seen as an Exodus-like experience, bringing redemption and freedom.

Through these narrative links, the writer of Acts was encouraging the early Christians to understand that, when they were actively engaged in the work of the Kingdom, every deliverance from danger should be seen as recapitulating the experience of the first Exodus. As they came through various perils unscathed, as they were kept through fiery trials by the power of God, they were invited to see that same salvific power at work: the victory of the Cross which has won all things for the followers of Jesus, in this life as well as the next. And so, the account of the Transfiguration with its Exodus symbolism is ultimately calling Christians to a new understanding of their life of discipleship.

The great vision of the Transfiguration has significance not only for the present, but also has prophetic power: Jesus' metamorphosis was the pledge of the unveiling of the future glory of the human being - those men and women who will become entirely permeated with divine light as they gaze upon Christ. The rare word "transfigure" is used by Paul when he tells the Corinthians that: "*We all, with unveiled face, beholding as in a mirror the glory of the Lord, are being transformed into the same image from glory to glory, just as by the Spirit of the Lord*" (2 Corinthians 3:18). Not only that, but the Transfiguration points forward to the time when Jesus' glorified humanity shall be enthroned over the universe, and His *shekinah* glory revealed to all who dwell on earth.

The Secret of Power

A fter describing the Transfiguration, the Gospel writers lead their readers very abruptly out of that light-filled realm: the vision on the mountain top gives way immediately to a picture of human weakness, failure and suffering. After Jesus and His three companions descended from the mountain they were confronted with a scene of utter chaos. The nine disciples who remained behind had been given *"power over unclean spirits, to cast them out, and to heal all kinds of sickness"* (Matthew 10:1) and had initially exercised this authority with impressive results. On this occasion, however, they had been completely defeated. A father had brought to them his son, who was possessed with an evil spirit causing violent and shocking behavior – and they could *do nothing*. At that point a number of scribes had appeared, seizing the opportunity to noisily dispute with the disciples and disparage their actions. Something, it would seem, was greatly amiss.

But the most disturbing part of the story was still to come. The failure of the disciples drew from Jesus a strong rebuke, expressing both anger and frustration:

"O faithless and perverse generation! How long shall I be with you? How long shall I bear you?" (Matthew 17:17)

These were words which seemed in marked contrast to the many gracious pronouncements which fell from His lips. But there was another reason why His utterance would have shocked the disciples inexpressibly. They would have recognized His words as a quotation from the Hebrew Scriptures, from the Song of Moses in Deuteronomy 32:1-43.

The poem which Moses wrote and recited to the Children of Israel just prior to his death on Mount Nebo is one of the most remarkable passages in the Bible. The prophet looked down the vista of the long history of Israel, and saw everything that would befall the nation, not just in the immediate future but for a vastly extended period of time. Accordingly, the Song he delivered was a comprehensive prophecy which set forth all that would come to pass for God's people, from their wilderness wandering through their establishment in the land, to the very end of days. But it was with great heaviness of heart that Moses gazed into the distant epochs. He knew that, despite the manifestation of God's glory in their midst, there was an increasing tendency in the Israelite nation towards idolatry, and foresaw that this process of corruption would continue even through the days of kings and prophets, until the final breaking up of their nation and their consequent ruin and misery. Thus he delineates a story of great tragedy - but also one which, at its close, radiates with ultimate hope.

In this, his "swan song", Moses displays the creative power and genius of the poet, and the elevated themes and images which pervade and inspire the whole made an indelible impression on the people of Israel. He began his Song by summoning heaven and earth to hear his words, thus conveying a sense of the cosmic import of his message, and expressing the desire that his teaching would fall like gentle showers or the soft distillation of dew, life-giving essences sent from heaven. This introduction moved to a proclamation of the perfections of God's character, and the listeners to the song were called upon celebrate the divine justice and righteousness. Here for the first time God was given the epithet "Rock", the term later so beloved of David and the psalmists, suggesting the steadfastness of His character, His role as Refuge and Stronghold. But when Moses turned to address the people called to be especially God's own, the unlikeness between them and their God was brought out forcibly in two verses, contrasting the faithfulness and goodness of Yahweh with the disloyalty and apostasy of His people.

"They have corrupted themselves; they are not His children because of their blemish: a perverse and crooked generation. And He said, 'I will hide my face from them, I will see what their end will be, for they are a perverse generation, children in whom is no faith" (Deuteronomy 32:5, 20)

These were devastating pronouncements. Although originally formed in the divine image, their nature would become so marred that all marks of sonship to God would disappear; nevertheless, in order to stir their hearts to a fresh awareness of His goodness, Moses rehearsed for the people all that God had done for them in the days of old. In His love, He had chosen them to be His people, giving Israel precedence when the boundaries of the nations were set; it was through His Fatherly care they had been led through the "waste howling wilderness"; with the most tender kindness He had kept them "as the apple of his eye"; had borne them on eagles' wings and caused them "to ride on the high places of the earth". As they settled in their land, swift were their victories over their enemies, abundantly the earth yielded to them its riches: "honey from the rock, and oil from the flinty rock", the best of the flocks and fields, the "blood of grapes".

Here was incontrovertible evidence of God's all-encompassing care, yet with stunning ingratitude they became unmindful of Him: so that Israel, designated Jeshurun (from Hebrew *yashar* meaning "straight"), chosen to be a righteous nation, had forsaken its destiny and calling. Their rebellion led them to "lightly esteem" their Maker, but the impulse to worship which still resided in their hearts drove them to set up strange deities and sacrifice to demons. God had bound Israel to himself as by a marriage bond; therefore, in lines resonating with just indignation, He declared a commensurate punishment. They had lightly esteemed God, therefore He would spurn them; they had excited his jealousy by choosing another object of worship, so He would arouse their jealousy by choosing another nation to replace them. Those who had been exalted in privilege should suffer terrible calamities: the divine wrath would kindle a consuming fire, burning to the lowest depths, while arrows sent from above would rain down disaster.

"Oh, that they were wise, that they understood this, that they would consider their latter end!" (v 29): the sense of needless tragedy breathes through the lines with unbearable pathos. They had, as it were, set themselves against the moral course of the universe, and their conduct would lead to certain consequences as if by an inexorable law, one involving payment to the uttermost farthing. The inevitable results of their transgression would be full of poison and bitterness: when their Rock forsook them they would be put to flight before a handful of enemies, would taste "grapes of gall", fruit of "the vine of Sodom". Yet, notwithstanding the iniquity of Israel and the judgments that should come upon His people, when God saw their powerlessness and suffering He would have compassion upon them for his Name's sake, would whet His "glittering sword" and render vengeance to their enemies. Beyond the looming clouds of grief and disaster Moses could see on the far horizon gleams of light and hope. God would be merciful to His land and His people, and all nations would rejoice with them as a result of His saving actions.

Here then was set before Israel their whole history to the final consummation - and the events which came upon the nation in its long and frequently sorrowful history provide impressive confirmation of the truth of this poetic forecast. But Moses' prophecy concerns not just Israel: it is a delineation of the spiritual history of individuals and all humanity writ large. Perhaps the most powerful statement in the Song came in God's declaration: *"I kill and make alive"* (v 39). The God of Israel is the God of *resurrection power:* and when His people came to understand this truth they would forsake their idols, would recognize that there was no God beside Him. The Song closed with a final prophetic truth: that the Lord would *"provide atonement for His land and His people"*.

These are the words which tie the passage in with the New Testament writings and revelation, and which also help explain why Jesus chose to quote from the Song of Moses after His descent from the mountain-top experience. In fact this whole scene, comprising the events which transpired both at the top of the mountain and at its foot, has a certain air of divine mystery. It is only when both are interpreted parabolically that their meaning takes on a limpid clarity, and the overarching themes set forth in Moses' Song may be interpreted with new light and power.

First and foremost, this descent of Jesus from the mountain top may be seen as an illustration of what has been called His "kenosis". This was given its classic statement by the Apostle Paul in one of his most famous texts, Philippians 2:5-11, known as the Kenosis Hymn (from Greek *ekenosen,* "he emptied"). Every sentence in this matchless passage tells of a downward movement.

In His pre-incarnate state, equality with God was the indisputable possession of Jesus; but nevertheless, when the need arose in the world for a Saviour, He "emptied himself" in the infinite heights and took the form of a Servant. "How then did He 'empty' Himself?" asked Augustine, and answered, "By taking that which He was not, not by losing that which He was." To suggest that by becoming man Christ yielded up His divine attributes in any way is to suggest that the name "Immanuel" did not belong to Jesus Christ - yet He is "the same yesterday, today, and forever". During His earthly life Christ rather gave up the *independent* use of His divine attributes: everything He said and did was under the direction of the Father through the Holy Spirit, so that He could therefore attest: "I do nothing of myself, but as the Father taught me, I speak these things". As He thus spoke and acted, even as He set aside full knowledge of events, He was doing these things out of His human nature, in the room and stead of humanity, as Redeemer and Substitute. This conception allows for all those exhibitions of divine power and knowledge which appear during His earthly ministry - and at the Mount of Transfiguration, when the fullness of His divine glory shone briefly through the veil of His flesh.

Jesus' descent from the Mount of Transfiguration where His divine glory was revealed was a powerful symbol of His entire course as He stooped from the realms of heaven in order to descend to a world filled with darkness and pain. An unusual statement in Mark's Gospel describes what occurred when Jesus reached the foot of the mountain. *"When they saw Him, all the people were greatly amazed"* (Mark 9:15). What was the cause of their wonder? Perhaps, just as the face of Moses shone with the reflected glory of God's presence as he descended Sinai, so also the face of Jesus radiated a supernatural light, lingering gleams of His Transfiguration experience. Yet although the Children of Israel shrank back from Moses in fear, the glory of Jesus' countenance possessed a compelling attractiveness, so that the people, *"running to Him, greeted Him"*. He was welcomed to that scene of untrammeled misery and helplessness.

As the crowd gathered around Jesus, the father of the boy explained to Him that this, his only son, suffered a severe affliction which caused a diverse range of symptoms including a foaming mouth, a rigid body, convulsions and dumbness. This was not simply a physical problem; the boy possessed an evil spirit of tremendous malignancy, which caused him to "fall often into the fire and into the water". The mention of "fire" and "water" in connection with the boy's suffering has strong resonances in both Isaiah and the Psalms: *"When you pass through the waters I shall be with you; when you walk through the fire you shall not be burned"* (Isaiah 43:2). This suggests that in many ways the boy was a representative sufferer in the realm of fallen creation, completely under the sway of the ruler of that domain, and subject to his immense destructive powers.

It was then, when Jesus learned that His disciples had proved unable to effect any kind of deliverance for the boy, that He spoke the devastating words from the Song of Moses: *"O faithless and perverse generation"*. His use of the quotation moved the scene out of the temporal realm and tied it in with the cosmic significance alluded to in the poem. The condition of the people was no less dire than it was in Moses' day - still they were slow to learn, self-willed, faithless. Through His use of the term "generation" Jesus seemed to include in this denunciation all who were present - the father, scribes, people, disciples, especially the nine. Compounding this indictment, He added further words - *"How long am I to bear with you?"* - which echoed a phrase from the Book of Numbers, in which God Himself remonstrated with His people following the Sin of the Spies. The conclusion seems inescapable that Jesus was speaking out of the fullness of divine consciousness.

But it was also at that point that the divine mercy came into play. Jesus commanded the boy to be brought to Him, and at that very moment, according to Mark, the child experienced a fresh convulsion and appeared to be dead. However, in calm consciousness of His life-giving power Jesus raised him up and gave him back to his father, so that the crowd was astounded "at the greatness of God."

A further key to unlocking the meaning of this challenging text is the frequent appearance of the Greek word *dunamis* ("power") in the different Gospel accounts. This highlights the fact that the disciples were "unable" to bring deliverance to the boy; that is, that they lacked power. The disciples were deeply troubled by the incident, and afterwards came to Jesus privately, asking, *"Why could we not cast it out?"* The answer which He gave the disciples was extremely simple: *"Because of your unbelief."* It was not because of the difficult nature of the case, the length of demonic possession, nor the sheer power of the evil force which had gripped the child. Their failure was simply due to their lack of faith. The problem, moreover, was not the *size* of their faith. He said to them, *"For assuredly, I say to you, if you have faith as a mustard seed, you will say to this mountain, 'Move from here to there,' and it will move; and nothing will be impossible for you*" (Matthew 17:20). The problem, then, was the *quality* of their faith, which had seemingly become defective.

Jesus had just revealed to the disciples that His course was to be one of suffering and death; this was the second great step in Christ's humiliation as set forth in the Philippian text. In the first step, as God, He had emptied Himself, taking the form of a servant. Then, as man, He humbled Himself, becoming obedient unto death – *even the death of the cross*, when the whole penalty for human sin would fall upon the guiltless head of Yahweh's Servant. Jesus' words had provoked a silent crisis in the disciples' lives and their hearts had become hardened and resistant to this revelation; imperceptibly they had drawn away, were unable to see that their power to preach, to heal and cast out demons came only from Him and their identity with Him in His mission of mercy and sacrificial love.

This true faith is then attained in only one way: through faith in a crucified Messiah. Now, *now* had come the turning point of the ages. On the cross the true nature of sin was laid bare, as well as the remedy which was provided, which gives such incontrovertible evidence of the astounding depth and height of God's mercy and love for His wayward people.

> *Ye who think of sin but lightly*
> *Nor suppose the evil great*
> *Here may view its nature rightly,*
> *Here its guilt may estimate.*
> *Mark the Sacrifice appointed,*
> *See who bears the awful load;*
> *'Tis the Word, the Lord's Anointed,*
> *Son of Man and Son of God.*

This is the revelation which brings power - and how is it apprehended? Jesus' final words to the disciples in this situation give the answer: "*This kind*," He told them, "*does not go out except by prayer*". It is only in living communion with their Master that the disciples come to understand the mystery of His atoning death as well as the reality of His resurrection power - and in this way will be enabled to *dynamically* impact the lives of those to whom they are sent!

ROSH HASHANAH through to THE FEAST OF TABERNACLES

Yom Kippur and the Scapegoat

···

T he title of Israel's most popular modern folk song, *Jerusalem of Gold*, suggests the essence of the city's charm lies in the sunlight reflected from her walls and "palaces", where the proud and passionate past still seems to inhere in the stones which lie dreaming through the radiant days of high summer. This is especially true in the area of the Street of the Prophets (Rehov HaNevi'im), which meanders through several neighborhoods as it runs from Damascus Gate in the Old City until it reaches Davidka Square, close by the Mahane Yehuda market in the New City.

The road stretches across not only across Jerusalem's topography but also her history. It was one of the first thoroughfares built outside the Old City, as in the latter half of the 19th century Jewish and Christian groups began to move out beyond the walls and open up new neighborhoods. Prophets Street became a distinguished address, the location of hospitals, churches and many elegant homes. Fortunes changed somewhat in the mid-twentieth century after the British left the city in 1948; sections of Hanevi'im then served as the border between Israel and Jordan until Jerusalem was reunified in 1967. Now it is again possible to walk along the street without fear of sniper fire, and discover that memories of past events and personalities linger into the present.

In a picturesque garden setting at Hanevi'im 64 can be found a large and gracious home which was built by English artist William Holman Hunt. Along with Dante Gabriel Rossetti and John Everett Millais he was one of the founders of the Pre-Raphaelite Brotherhood, a group of nineteenth century painters who focused on recreating the attention to detail and pure, bright colors of medieval and early renaissance artists. Their idealistic program - to heighten the religious and moral sensibility of their viewers through portraying biblical and literary themes - was very much evident in Hunt's famous painting *Light of the World*. In 1854, after completing this, he traveled to the Holy Land to pursue his desire to paint biblical scenes in the land in which they took place.

The first subject Hunt wanted to depict was one of "the ceremonies of Jewish worship": the goat sent into the wilderness during the annual ritual of the Day of Atonement as described in the Book of Leviticus, an account which profoundly impacted his artistic imagination. Determined to find an authentic location for the painting, he made his way to a remote area of the Dead Sea known in Arabic as Oosdam (probably Sodom), a barren, scorched region which seemed to suit admirably his vision of an "accursed" landscape. Having purchased a rare white goat in Jerusalem, he tethered this hapless creature on the salt-encrusted shores of the lake, then proceeded to paint with a brush in one hand and a rifle in the other for protection against hostile Bedouin, much like a latter-day Nehemiah. The goat, unsurprisingly, proved a "fidgety" subject and after a number of days succumbed to the inhospitable environment; nothing daunted, the artist returned to Jerusalem and purchased another goat, then completed the work in his studio.

Holman Hunt's *Scapegoat*, exhibited at the Royal Academy in London in 1856, drew a mixed reaction from its very first unveiling. The animal abandoned to the wilderness stands mournfully on the desolate shore of the Sea, staggering beneath the weight of the accumulated sin of a nation, even as the band on its forehead marking its outcast state remains an ominous crimson. All around are the emblems of death, while in the background the bitter waters of the lake are framed by the purple mountains of Moab, gold-rimmed in the setting sun, colors which cast a lurid glow over the scene. In fact, the painting can only be described as *startling* - just as the ceremony it was intended to depict. Yet although the rituals surrounding the Old Testament feast of the Day of Atonement can seem today ancient and arcane, rich treasures of wisdom can be discovered when one delves into the fathomless ocean of their symbolism.

It was after the Children of Israel had been led out of Egypt, and constituted a nation at Sinai, that Moses had been given instructions concerning the building of the Tabernacle where God had promised to dwell in the midst of His people. The Book of Leviticus reveals more fully the nature of the Deity who was desiring to draw the people into relationship with Himself; above all, it focuses supremely on the holiness of God. The great problem with which the book then grapples is the formidable barrier to fellowship with this utterly pure and righteous Being caused by the existence of sin and transgression within the covenant people. Accordingly, it also details the ceremonies and rituals ordained for the Children of Israel which would enable them to draw near to God and appropriate the blessings He desired to bestow.

At the heart of this system was the idea of *substitutionary atonement*: the fundamental means of cleansing from sin came through the sacrifice of an innocent victim. The climax of the book is found in Chapter 16, the ritual for the great Day of Atonement (called "Yom Kippur" in Hebrew from the verb meaning "to cover"). Once in the year, on the tenth day of the seventh month, the High Priest was to enter the Holy of Holies in the Tabernacle and sprinkle the blood upon the mercy seat of the Ark of the Covenant to atone for the sins of the entire nation. It was here that the cloud of the divine glory, the Shekinah presence of God, rested between the cherubim.

The instructions for this culminating ceremony were delivered to Moses immediately after a tragic event had shaken the Israelite community: the two sons of Aaron, Nadab and Abihu, had ventured unbidden into the Most Holy Place and offered "strange fire" before the Lord and as a

183

consequence had died. The fate of his two sons gave Aaron a shattering awareness of the mortal danger involved in approaching the inmost sanctuary without proper preparation - and the rituals for Yom Kippur were elaborate indeed, requiring special festive sacrifices in addition to the regular daily offerings, a total of fifteen sacrificial animals in all. The whole ceremony, from beginning to end, involved a Herculean undertaking for the High Priest, and none but he was allowed to enter within the doors of the Tabernacle until the work of atonement was completed.

Laying aside his splendid priestly garments and dressing in simple robes of white linen, he was to take a censer full of burning coals from the altar, fill his hands with incense, then enter the Tabernacle and pass through the Holy Place, which on all other days was the limit of his approach. Conscious of his high privilege and with fast beating heart, he would lay his hand on the heavy veil woven with scarlet and blue which hung before the innermost sanctuary. With awe and trepidation he would draw this aside and enter the silent and mysterious space beyond, catching as he did so a radiant gleam of light from the Shekinah. Immediately, he was to cast the incense into the censer so that the cloud might cover the mercy-seat and hide God's presence. Then he was to depart, drawing the veil again.

Having re-emerged from the Tabernacle to the relief of the anxiously waiting crowd, the next task of the *Kohen HaGadol* was to make atonement for himself and the whole order of the priesthood, essential before his offerings for the people could be accepted. Accordingly, he took the blood of a bullock which he had previously killed, entered within the veil once again, and sprinkled it upon and before the mercy seat, then purified likewise the outer chamber of the tabernacle and the altar of burnt sacrifice. It was at this point that the most striking spectacle of the day was to commence.

Two goats were brought and presented at the door of the tabernacle, and by them was placed an urn containing two identical lots, consisting of two small tablets made of ebony or (later) of gold. On one was engraved the words "For Yahweh," and on the other "For Azazel," an expression signifying "to remove" or "separate", later translated as "scapegoat". These lots the High Priest drew out, placing one on the head of one goat, the other on the head of the other goat. The first was taken and sacrificed and its blood brought within the veil. The *Kohen HaGadol* then laid both his hands upon the head of the second goat and confessed over it all the transgressions of the children of Israel, thus transferring them symbolically to the animal. At the conclusion of the litany the goat was handed over to a man standing ready to send him away into the wilderness, into a land "cut off"; that is, completely isolated from the surrounding country by some natural barrier, which would make it impossible for the creature to return.

Why this strange ritual? The two goats were but a single offering, showing the completeness of the expiation provided for the Children of Israel through the sacrificial system given to them by God. The first goat offered in sacrifice represented the atonement and covering made by the shedding of blood, the second represented the utter removal of the sins of the people, which were conveyed far away and lost in the depths of the wilderness, a visible symbol of Psalm 103:12: "As far as the east is from the west, so far He has removed our transgressions from us". According to the Talmud a scarlet cord was tied around the neck of the scapegoat that was reported to turn white as the goat was led away; and this provided for many generations a miraculous confirmation of their cleansing.

The whole testimony of the Torah, Psalms and Prophets bears witness to the fact that the Israelites had a vivid consciousness of the reality of sin and their need for purification - but after the destruction of the Temple in 70 AD the priesthood could no longer fulfill the requirements of this supreme feast. Even before that time, according to the Talmud, there was a sad omen: for forty years, the scarlet cloth tied to the horns of the scapegoat no longer turned white. Since the first century, with rabbinic sanction, Jews have sought to observe Yom Kippur with the substitutes of prayer (*tefillah*), repentance (*teshuvah*) and charity (*tzedekah*). It is still the most solemn day in the Jewish calendar and a national holiday in the modern state of Israel. There is no radio or television, all businesses are closed, traffic is limited to emergency services and even the airports are shut down. Since the Yom Kippur War of 1973, when Israel came close to annihilation before achieving a stunning victory, strong new emotional associations have gathered around the holiday, intensifying the ancient theme of blood expiation.

Yom Kippur also marks the culmination of a ten day period of great intensity that begins with Rosh Hashanah, the Jewish New Year. According to tradition, it is on this day that the Book of Life, in which God records the names of the righteous, is opened. The following Days of Awe are a time of repentance and soul searching in hope of achieving a "good final sealing" on Yom Kippur, when the book is irrevocably closed. Five services are held at the synagogue during the feast day itself, with varying liturgies but all focusing on the confession of sins, leading up to the last service, *Ne'ilah*, with its ritual of the symbolic closing of the gates. For Jewish people seeking assurance of forgiveness, it is an uncertain time: will one's name be recorded once again in the Book of Life? Christians, despite also placing a strong emphasis on repentance, are spared a similar anxiety. For them, the pledge of sins forgiven is based on Jesus' atoning sacrifice and the understanding that those who belong to Him are inscribed in the Lamb's Book of Life.

In the New Testament, the book of Hebrews takes Jesus' death on the cross as its chief theme, as it seeks to demonstrate that all the elaborate rites of the Day of Atonement foreshadowed and found their fulfillment in this one perfect sacrifice. In fact, the very existence of the Yom Kippur ceremony was prophetic of the fact that another, more perfect method of atonement for sin was yet to come. The Book of Leviticus specified a myriad of sacrifices to be offered all the year round, but it was a striking mark of their insufficiency that the annual feast of Atonement was still needed to cleanse the Children of Israel, the very altar and tabernacle, from their impurities. And even within this supreme ritual there yet remained a glaring double imperfection: in both the officiating priest and in the victims sacrificed. The Levitical priests were themselves transgressors, as evidenced by the sin offering which the High Priest had first to offer for himself. As for the victims, it was impossible that the blood of animals such as bulls and goats could effectively and permanently wash away the stain of human sin; and for this reason the atonement had to be repeated annually.

Through its very shortcomings, therefore, the Feast pointed forward to a greater, more effectual atonement; moreover, as the Children of Israel witnessed their lone representative bearing the blood of expiation into the Most Holy Place it perhaps awakened within them a dawning hope that in some future day, they knew not how, all might have free access to the innermost sanctuary, there to pass into the very presence of God and find true communion made possible.

All these imperfections vanished when the one, all-availing sacrifice was offered at Calvary, when Jesus offered up His life for the sins of the world, since nothing but the blood of the incarnate Son of God could provide expiation for the accumulated mass of human transgression. Although the sin of God's people was great, the atonement which took it away was immeasurably greater, possessing a value beyond all estimation. Nor was it necessary that this atoning action should be repeated from year to year, for this single offering effected for all time the reconciliation between the infinite perfection of God and the imperfect humanity whom Jesus came to redeem. Through His sacrifice Jesus not only earned His people forgiveness of sins, but also gave them the assurance that their sins had been carried away for all time to the "land of forgetfulness". The profound drama of the Day of Atonement, the picture of the animal sent to the wilderness, evokes a vivid consciousness of the desolation which Jesus endured in order to provide this peace to their souls.

Jesus was the antitype not only of the sin offering made for the congregation, but also of the High Priest who sacrificed the offering. The simple white garments which Aaron wore when performing the highest act of expiation under the Law was a symbolical shadowing forth of the holiness and humility of the supreme and final High Priest, who put aside His heavenly glory when He effected the consummate cleansing away of sin. Again, there was much toil for the High Priest who did the work on that day: numerous beasts to be slaughtered, besides the lengthy prayers and oblations. Even so, for Jesus Christ, the work of atonement was a stupendous labor which He must complete alone: there was the Upper Room ministry, the agony in the Garden, the trial and scourging; then the cross itself, with all the weight of His people's transgressions resting upon His shoulders.

But when this true High Priest died on Calvary, the veil separating the Holy Place from the Holy of Holies was rent in two. The way was now open for all to come to God and commune with Him "between the cherubim", to experience the joy of lasting fellowship with God and receive all the heavenly benefits Christ came to bestow. In John 20:11-12, there is a moving pictorial symbol of this sacrifice: *"Now Mary stood outside the tomb weeping. As she wept, she bent over to look into the tomb and saw two angels in white, seated where Jesus' body had been, one at the head and the other at the foot."* It was an image of the mercy seat of the Ark of the Covenant, where Jesus made atonement for all, and fulfilled the sublime purpose of the feast of Yom Kippur.

Controversy! at the Feast

....

"*Ennion Made Me*" This is the inscription on an ancient glass jug found in the ruins of a palatial first-century home in Jerusalem, and presently on display at the Israel Museum. It is broken and marred by the conflagration that destroyed the city in 70 AD, after the Jewish Revolt against Roman rule had failed - yet remnants of its original beauty are still to be discerned in its lines and decoration. In fact, it could even be considered more arresting in its ruin than its original splendor, bearing as it does silent but eloquent testimony to one of the most dramatic times in Jewish history.

But who was Ennion? He was a glass artisan who worked during the period from 1 to 50 AD, and is reputed to have created the groundbreaking technique of blowing glass vessels into moulds, allowing the creation of delicate vessels adorned with complex patterns. His products, including drinking cups, jugs and flasks, were renowned for their beauty and highly sought after in the Roman world; so far 55 of his works have been uncovered in archaeological digs around the Mediterranean. Although Ennion signed his name in Greek letters his name was not common in that language and may have been Semitic in origin; a possible Jewish connection is also suggested by the fact that scholars believe he worked in Sidon in modern Lebanon, a major glassmaking center in the 1st century AD.

Another example of Ennion's work is located in the Metropolitan Museum of Art in New York, a glass amphora discovered in Cyprus in 1876; this is an exquisite piece which has, miraculously, survived virtually intact throughout two millennia. Of a translucent cobalt blue, it has a hexagonal body, with each of its six panels featuring different illustrations, including a bunch of grapes and ivy leaves, double flutes, a set of pipes, a flagon and a wine pitcher. Many of these festive symbols were associated with the Jewish Feast of Tabernacles and it is possible the amphora was purchased in Jerusalem by a pilgrim from Cyprus as a memento of his "going up" to the city. A further speculation is possible: if Ennion worked in Sidon during the years when Jesus lived in Galilee it is possible that he had heard the report of the charismatic Son of David as His fame spread throughout the region. It is also intriguing to think that Ennion may have annually attended the Feast of Tabernacles in Jerusalem as a Jewish pilgrim. If so, it is possible he participated in the most memorable but, at the same time, the most controversial of all the celebrations of the feast since Moses first gave it as an ordinance to the Children of Israel.

THE FEAST OF TABERNACLES

John's Gospel is in large measure structured around the Jewish festivals, and at the beginning of Chapter 7 he notes that Jesus was in Galilee as "the Jews' Feast of Tabernacles was at hand". This began on the fifteenth day of the seventh month, soon after the Day of Atonement, and was the most joyful of the convocations, a celebration of the final harvesting of grapes and olives. It was also the occasion when the time of Israel's wandering in the wilderness was remembered, so the people would construct small booths or "tabernacles" made from leafy branches and dwell in these during the eight days of the feast. Every court and housetop, every street and square would feature this verdant adornment, providing lodging for the vast multitude who came from Judea and Galilee as well as farther away. But as they thronged the narrow streets of the city, what drew every gaze was the goal of their pilgrimage, the Sanctuary of marble and gold crowning the summit of Mount Moriah, to which their footsteps would wend their way with song and in sacred procession. Then at night great candelabras burned in the Temple courts, illuminating the whole city and evoking memories of the pillar of fire by night which had served as a guide through the desert.

Despite the national significance of the feast, the first verses of John Chapter 7 record that Jesus did not plan to go up to Jerusalem to join the celebration. As He told His brothers, who were urging Him to attend, this was because His "time" had not fully come. Throughout John's Gospel it becomes apparent that Jesus' "time" was the hour of His full manifestation to the people of Israel, and also that Jesus understood the course of this program to be set in place by His heavenly Father. And yet, the Gospel account continues, after His brothers had gone up to the feast then Jesus Himself also went up, not openly but "in secret"; and it was only when the feast was halfway through that He revealed Himself to the crowds awaiting Him. Taking into account Peter's dictum that "one day with the Lord is as a thousand years", this feast of seven days, with an eighth day appended, may be regarded as representing the whole course of salvation history. The appearance of Jesus in the midst of the Feast of Tabernacles was therefore a symbol that He had come to dwell with His people in the midst of the ages; in fact, His coming was the very turning point of their epoch. But at this time He also came "incognito", secretly, hiding His divinity behind the veil of His flesh.

With Jesus' appearing came new revelations and understandings which would eventually shed their light over the whole human race. However, it was also at this time that a fierce debate sprang up over Jesus' mission and identity which has never yet died away. When He did not appear in the Temple during the first festive days all the pilgrims, from every part of the country and from abroad, were seeking Him and inquiring after Him. The question on everyone's lips concerned the true nature of the charismatic teacher from the north, and John recorded their confused discussions as they murmured in low voices for fear of identification with His cause. Their broken fragments of conversation distilled elements of eagerness and hope, suspicion and skepticism, perplexity and faith. In the fascinating Seventh Chapter of his Gospel, the Evangelist delineates with penetrating insight the nature of the controversies surrounding the Person and work of Christ.

FIRST CONTROVERSY

The chapter commences with the caviling of Jesus' closest brethren. Their reason for suggesting that He attend the Feast in Jerusalem was that He might perform there the miracles He was reputed to have done in Galilee and thus validate His claim to be the Messiah:

"No one does anything in secret while he himself seeks to be known openly. If You do these things, show Yourself to the world" (John 7:4)

Their rebuke carried an implicit suggestion that Jesus' motive for performing miracles was that He desired personal recognition and glory for Himself. According to the brothers' understanding the true spiritual leader was one who would win the acclaim of the people through spectacular deeds. If Jesus thought of Himself as Messiah, why did He not demonstrate His claims to this role openly before the people in a way that was irrefutable? It seemed logical to them that this should take place at the supreme feast and in Jerusalem, the city unparalleled in spiritual prestige, where affairs of great national moment should be decided.

Their words, however, demonstrated a fundamental misunderstanding concerning the true nature of Jesus' Messiahship. This cannot be recognized in His miracles, nor had He come in the way of political power, as a Warrior King who would lead Israel to military victory over Rome. The brothers had not yet comprehended the necessity for Christ's first coming in lowliness and hiddenness, nor the great purpose for which His divine glory had been laid aside - that He should be a Man of Sorrows as He fulfilled His great task of redeeming the world. Only in this way could He reveal the love of the Father who had sent Him and become victorious over all the forces of the Evil One. A leader who will seek glory and power for himself - or one who seeks to serve? This was the revolutionary understanding that Jesus of Nazareth brought into human consciousness.

SECOND CONTROVERSY

Then there was the argument among the multitudes over His essential nature:

"And there was much complaining among the people concerning Him. Some said, 'He is good'; others said, 'No, on the contrary, He deceives the people'" (John 7:12)

Just prior to the events recorded in John 7, Jesus had impressed the crowds in Galilee with His provision of abundant bread, but at that time He also made a declaration which scandalized many: "I am the Bread of Life". His words, and the divine title "I Am" on His lips, caused many disciples to turn away from Him and echoes of that controversy still lingered here in Jerusalem. A number of the Jews, with a distorted understanding of His teaching, believed He had come to do away with the Law of Moses and abolish the rules of purity and the Sabbath. Others, however, who had heard of or witnessed His deeds of compassion, perhaps even themselves received His healing touch, were vehement in insisting He was a "good man".

It is in the latter term that seekers after truth throughout the centuries have often evaluated the Person of Christ. Even adherents of different faiths are able to acknowledge that Jesus was a great teacher, with a sublime code of ethics which far transcended the systems of other wise men of antiquity. But it is not Jesus' lofty moral instruction alone which can explain the impact of His personality, not just on the people of His time, but on all subsequent generations. It was the claims He made concerning His own identity that ignited controversy and caused some to passionately devote their lives to following Him, others to turn away and reject Him.

THIRD CONTROVERSY

Then there were the quarrels over where He had come from, the nature of His conception and birth:

"We know where this Man is from; but when the Christ comes from, no one knows' ... Some said, 'Will the Christ come out of Galilee? Has not the Scripture said that the Christ comes from the seed of David and from the town of Bethlehem?'" (John 7:27,41-42)

It was a traditional expectation among the Jews that the Messiah, when he came, would make a sudden and spectacular appearance, perhaps on the clouds of heaven as in the vision of Daniel 7:13. But to the crowds in Jerusalem the prosaic facts of Jesus' background and family seemed obvious and unquestionable. This was the son of Joseph, born and raised in the region of Galilee. Was he not called "Jesus of Nazareth" and did He not carry out His ministry in the north? - there was none of the mystery about Him which they expected in the Messiah. For the Jewish leadership, moreover, it was unthinkable that God's Anointed One should appear from Galilee, an area they regarded with much disapprobation. The people were conscious also of the prophecy that the Messiah should emerge from Bethlehem and come from the royal line of David. It was unknown to them that the whole mystery of His Incarnation and birth would be dwelt on at length by the Gospel writers.

Strange it is that this same controversy should exist some 2000 years later, albeit in a more modern guise. The rise in historical criticism and developments in scientific knowledge have caused scholars of all disciplines to question the New Testament accounts of Jesus' supernatural conception. Yet the testimony of the church on this issue has remained unwavering throughout the centuries. On the one hand it was impossible that any being lesser than God Himself could redeem human beings from the consequences of their sin and thus bridge the infinite chasm which existed between humanity and the Creator. At the same time, however, the penalty ordained for human transgression, which was death, could only be suffered by one who was himself a human being. Therefore, it was God's purpose from eternity past that the only-begotten Son, God co-eternal with Himself, should become Man by taking on a human soul and flesh, and having thus become mortal that He should endure the pangs of death - a demonstration of the greatness of His love for fallen men and women.

WISDOM CRIES OUT

Then, in the middle of the Feast, Jesus Himself appeared in the Temple and taught. The effect of His words and teaching was to cause the people to marvel at the power and authority of His message which, they recognized, had not been drawn from any of the rabbinic schools. Jesus' response to their wondering statements was to disclaim all personal attainment of knowledge. His doctrine, He averred, was not His own, nor did it well up from the depths of His human consciousness, but was drawn from a far deeper source - from the very heart of God, the fount of divine wisdom, and bequeathed to Him through no intermediary but through His intimate fellowship with the Father. By way of contrast, the one who was not content to be merely a conduit for divine truth was seeking his own glory, aggrandizing self, and advancing his own cause and agenda. In this way Jesus answered those who suggested He should be seeking personal renown, and refuted the charge He was deceiving the people. He was utterly innocent of any desire to win honor for Himself: all glory was reflected back to God who had given Him these treasures of wisdom and understanding.

Jesus' words led to a further profound statement: He then "cried out", lifting up His voice in a proclamation which seemed to emerge from the fullness of an overflowing heart. The Eternal Wisdom of God at last had come to His people, clothed in human vesture, and had spoken to them - the same Voice which in the past had spoken to their fathers through the prophets. "You both know Me and you know where I am from," Jesus said to them (John 7:28). They had a deeper knowledge than they were aware: their Messiah had been set before them in the pages of their scriptures and it was Him for whom they had waited so long. Surely in the depths of their hearts would arise a recognition of the God-Man who stood before them, bone of their bone, flesh of their flesh, and at the same time the perfect image of the Father who had made human beings in His likeness.

But John records the sad verdict: "*So there was a division among the people because of Him*" (John 7:43). Yet the question "What think ye of Christ?" remains the inescapable query of the centuries and in this regard other words of Jesus ring out:

"*If anyone wills to do His will, he shall know concerning the doctrine, whether it is from God or whether I speak on My own authority*" (John 7:17)

Anyone – Jew or Gentile – who truly desires to do the will of God, who aspires after heavenly truth and hungers and thirsts for righteousness, can be assured that his or her heart will be opened to receive the divine revelation He has come to bring.

The Way to Soul Satisfaction

ccording to the rabbis, "Ten measures of beauty descended on the world - and nine of these were taken by Jerusalem". The city wears perhaps her most enchanting aspect in late September and early October when the first rains have come and washed the sky to a deep cerulean. An intoxicating scent of jasmine and lavender permeates the streets on a soft breeze, while magenta and white bougainvillea flowers blaze with special brilliance against the stone walls. The golden days of summer are imperceptibly withdrawing, hiding behind the gauzy skirts of autumn, but lingering seductively during the daytime hours and continuing to pour down their benison of sunlight and warmth. Yet during the early morning Jerusalemites reach for coats and scarves as a delicious breath of coolness steals in from the desert and wraps the city, then again as the sun descends over the western hills in a pageant of bright color and the velvety twilight draws in.

It is at this time the Feast of Tabernacles is celebrated and every small balcony features its "succah", some elaborate, others simple, but all adorned with the symbols of the season, palm branches, fruit and flowers. It is an acknowledgement of the bounty God has provided over the past year - but the people of Israel are ever-conscious of the need for rain, especially when the ground is parched after the long dry summer. At the Feast it is therefore considered essential to pray for rain to fill the wells and pools of the land during the coming winter months. In the first century, one of the most spectacular rituals at the Feast of Tabernacles was the water drawing ceremony. Each morning during the festival a white-robed priest led a procession of worshipers out through the Temple gates and descended by a steep stone pathway to the Pool of Siloam. Here he filled a golden pitcher with water and re-ascended to the Temple where a libation was poured out symbolizing the words of the prophet, "with joy you shall draw water from the wells of salvation" (Isaiah 12:3), while the great Hallel consisting of Psalms 113 to 118 was sung to the accompaniment of flutes.

On the year in which Jesus attended the Feast of Tabernacles, as recorded in John's Gospel, the symbolism of this ceremony was dramatically enhanced. On the "last great day" of the Feast, as the last notes of the psalm died away in the still air, He stood in the midst of the people and cried out in a loud voice, "If any man thirst, let him come unto Me and drink!" (John 7:37 KJV). So compelling was the cry that many gathered to Him and as they listened they marveled at His words, while the wondering recognition dawned in many souls that His discourse might be interpreted in the light of the ceremony they had just witnessed. The rite held a significance not simply related to agriculture and the seasons; rather, the link between water and the Spirit was implied by scriptures such as Isaiah 44:3 with its parallel structure: "I will pour water upon him that is thirsty, and floods upon the dry ground: I will pour my spirit upon your seed, and my blessing upon your offspring." It was therefore understood that the water drawing ritual pointed to that longed-for day when, according to the prophet Joel, God would lavish His Spirit (*Ruach*) upon all flesh (Joel 2:28-29).

The Holy Spirit was spoken of throughout the Hebrew Scriptures, introduced almost immediately in the creation account (Genesis 1:2) and thereafter revealed at work with life-giving, life-sustaining power in the nation of Israel as well as the lives of individual men and women. The *Ruach* was pictured as giving superhuman might to judges, wisdom to kings and rulers, knowledge of God's will and understanding of things to come to the prophets. It was the Holy Spirit which had given Bezalel his artistic vision, inspired David's songs, rested on the prophets like Elijah and gave them courageous words and power to call down fire from heaven. But other scriptures seemed to indicate a time would come when the Spirit would rest upon not just one or another highly-favored individual, but be poured out unstintingly on all God's handmaidens and servants, providing them with similar heavenly gifts.

In His words at the Feast Jesus laid His finger on the true malaise which afflicted the people of Israel, the deep hunger and thirst in their souls. This was a longing that no created thing on earth could satisfy, which could be met by nothing less than the overflowing beneficence of God and the gift of His Spirit. He understood that:

The thirst that from the soul doth rise
Doth ask a drink divine ...

It was the life-giving power of the Holy Spirit which alone could quicken within each person the desire for everything which was "noble, just, pure, lovely, of good report and worthy of praise" (Philippians 4:8), and bring streams of love, wisdom, power, and truth from the fountain of the Godhead. In this way, through the Divine *Ruach*, each one might be granted light for the understanding, sanctification for the spirit, power for the will, courage for the journey, joy for the heart and comfort in suffering, an infinite supply which would satisfy all individual yearnings.

Here, then, at the close of the most solemn ceremony of the feast, Jesus set Himself forth as the Bestower of the Spirit, possessing a singular ability to fulfill every aspiration and every true desire in the multifaceted hearts of the men and women standing before Him. In these wonderful and majestic words, "Let them come to *Me* and drink", was a claim that none who had gone before Him had made: it was a claim to be the Spirit-Anointed One sent from the Father, of the royal lineage of the house of David, the One for whom the people waited with such passionate longing. During Israel's long history the prophets had borne witness of his coming, and throughout this period many lofty attributes had become attached to the title of Messiah, as satellites cluster around the sun, but as He stood before them now in living vital color all the rapturous visions of the past were realized and also surpassed.

For if these words of Jesus to the people are rightly apprehended, only one logical conclusion can be drawn: He was making an offer that only a divine being had the power to make and also fulfill. It is a statement which reveals the unique strand in the teaching of Jesus which sets Him apart from other spiritual leaders who have appeared throughout history. He came not only to divulge splendid truths about the Father in heaven, nor simply to demonstrate His compassion and mercy through miraculous works, but in and through these words and deeds to reveal Himself as the very source of these blessings. Jesus' sweeping, stupendous claim at the Feast, in its calm assumption of divine prerogative and majesty, can be justified only on one assumption: that He who appeared before them was the Son of God manifest in the flesh.

So Jesus stood thus in their midst with the divine consciousness of power, calling to the sons of men with outstretched hands, bearing them a message from God's heart of love. He was offering an invitation, if they but knew it, of such breadth and magnitude that it transcended all the former hopes and imaginings as the light of the dawning sun eclipses the pale moon. The Divine *Ruach* would no longer rest on a few chosen individuals but was available to all the sons and daughters of Israel as an ever-flowing cascade of divine life. But the offer was greater yet: it was made to every person who was spiritually thirsting, to men and women of whatever time and age, to all generations and to the ends of the earth. And thus Jesus was not only the Messiah of Israel but also the Desire of all nations, for whom they unconsciously waited and longed.

Jesus' next words enlarged on this same theme: He promised that those who saw in Him the Anointed One of God and accepted the message He came to bring would not only receive the promised fullness of the Spirit, but give it forth also: *"He who believes on Me, as the scripture has said, out of his heart will flow rivers of living water"* (John 7:38). From the innermost depth of their being would spring up a veritable fountain to provide streams of refreshment and blessing for others, with power to transform the surrounding spiritual barrenness. Just as dry thirsty land saturated with rain would soften and fructify, so the divinely nurtured harvest thus created would blossom and bud and fill the face of the world with fruit. The verse looks forward to the outpouring of the Spirit at Pentecost, to the divine anointing on Peter as he preached his message with power and persuasion, to the courage of Paul as he bore his gospel of revelation throughout the Roman world, to the zeal of countless numbers of the early Christians who "turned the world upside down".

But after recording Jesus' words concerning the freely poured out Spirit, the Gospel writer then offered a theological aside concerning the tremendous cost involved in conferring this gift: the *Ruach* could not be given until Jesus had been "glorified" (John 7:39). In Johannine language the "glorification" of Jesus referred always to His lifting up on the cross where He bore the sins of the world and thus revealed the love of the Father to the uttermost. It is noteworthy also that in his account of Jesus' teaching at the feast John alludes to the fact that on two occasions Jesus "cried out" (Greek *krazo*). In an oblique fashion the Evangelist was suggesting this was a prophetic anticipation of the two cries He uttered from the cross (Matthew 27:46,50), where the way was opened for all to receive the gift of the Spirit. It was only when the work of atonement was completed, after Jesus had ascended to the Father and resumed His pre-incarnate glory, that He would send gifts for His people from the very throne of the universe, and streams of living water would begin to flow from every heart.

The glorious Messiah who was the whole theme and subject of the Old Testament writings, whom the seers and sages of Israel had foreseen in their most exalted moments of revelation, had come to His own. The Gentile world also, in its most noble aspirations, had yearned for such an ideal of goodness and virtue to appear on the earth. In the words of the Roman philosopher Cicero: *if they could fully discern Moral Worth itself in its absolute perfection and completeness, the one thing of all others most splendid and most glorious, how enraptured would they be.* But behold the sad contrast of history: when He, the embodiment of the hopes of humankind and the one perfect Man appeared on the worldly stage, it was not that He should receive the homage of the people but rather experience universal rejection.

And yet the strongest testimony to the truth of the words Jesus spoke at the Feast of Tabernacles came from an unexpected quarter, from some who could never have been expected to recognize His true mission and identity. John 7:32 relates that during this time the Pharisees and chief priests had sent officers to lay hands on the Nazarene and arrest Him - but eventually the troop had returned, unable to fulfill their task. As they watched Jesus while waiting for the opportunity to seize Him, as they listened to Him speak, they were held back from their course by a silent force, disarmed by the magnetic power which indwelt His presence and suffused His words. These seemed invested with a glamour and radiant truth which rendered impossible any action against Him and a strange awe fell upon them. They returned to the Pharisees empty-handed and in answer to the disgruntled queries of the religious leaders could give only one answer: "No man ever spoke as this man." It is a statement which has been attested by countless numbers since that time.

"As the Deer": David's Worship
and the Church

Jerusalem, wrote the psalmist, is "beautiful for situation" - but is nevertheless poised somewhat precariously on her mountain heights - to the east the land falls away precipitously to the Jordan Valley, part of the great gash in the earth's surface which extends all the way through Africa. Down at this staggering depth, the heat is intense – temperatures soar in summer to peaks of well over 50 degrees, creating a barren and desolate wilderness. On either side of the valley tower craggy, tortured mountain peaks, products of some ancient convulsion of the earth. Here at the world's lowest point lies the Dead Sea, named for the fact that in the scorching temperatures the moisture evaporates and leaves behind a concentrated mineral content, so although the lake is beautiful to behold - an expanse of shimmering turquoise – in its depths nothing can live. Here in this remorseless desert landscape the metaphor of death reigns supreme.

Dead Sea Vista

Yet hidden deep in the rocky fortresses surrounding the Dead Sea is found one of the most stunning natural wonders in Israel - a *wadi* or ravine called Ein Gedi, fed by year-round streams which originate in the Judean Mountains. Located within this rocky cleft one may discover a small paradise containing a myriad of waterfalls, sparkling pools of water and lush vegetation. The contrast between the arid landscape and this lovely oasis is so striking that many poets have extolled its secluded beauty; it is said that here King Solomon composed the Song of Songs with its enchanting metaphors drawn from nature: *"My beloved is to me as a cluster of camphire in the vineyards of Ein Gedi"* (Song 1:14). A rich animal and bird life thrives in the ravine including groups of ibex, and it is these gentle creatures resembling gazelle which have inspired the name Ein Gedi, meaning "Spring of the Kid". It is tempting to think that the poet who composed Psalm 42 was also inspired by this small Eden and the animals which live there, most especially as he wrote the opening line:

"As the deer pants for the water brooks, so my soul pants for You, O God. My soul thirsts for God, for the living God .."

The superscription of the Psalm notes that it was written "of" or "for" the sons of Korah — descendants of the Levite who led an insurrection against Moses and Aaron in the wilderness and as a result was swallowed up alive, together with all his company. During David's reign the Korahites were gatekeepers in the Temple, a role which showed how greatly they had distanced themselves from the spirit of rebellion which had motivated their ancestor. They were also celebrated musicians and singers (1 Chronicles 6:16-33) - and were warriors as well as poets. The story of the ascent of David to the throne of Israel recounted in the book of 1 Samuel tells of the vicissitudes of his early years, when he was forced to flee from the face of Saul, who desired in jealous anger to kill the young hero whom the people loved. The Korahites were mentioned as part of the band which accompanied the young son of Jesse into the wilderness, warriors *"whose faces were like the faces of lions, and who were for speed like gazelles upon the mountains*" (1 Chronicles 12:8). In that case they were undoubtedly with David when he camped in the stronghold of Ein Gedi as Saul drew near in hot pursuit with three thousand chosen men of Israel.

In their mountain hideout, the small group of exiles must have witnessed images from the natural world of great beauty which imprinted themselves indelibly on their minds - the graceful deer stepping by moonlight across the rock faces, or moving by day through the scattered trees with sunlight dappling their flanks, lowering their necks to drink of the streams that rushed through the ravine. Perhaps also they saw the stags hunted, as were David and his companions, parched with thirst and desperate for the water brooks - so that in a later time one of these men, a son of Korah or perhaps David himself, could compose this psalm with its exquisite opening picture of the soul's longing for God.

THE PSALM OF ISRAEL

Psalm 42 is a song of lament. The person who wrote it was sorrowing over the fact that he found himself far away from Jerusalem and its Temple, the place where he had been accustomed to worship his God. The psalm has often been thought to reflect the occasion when David was forced to flee the city as a result of Saul's murderous rage, or the time of Absalom's rebellion, and the centrality of Jerusalem and its sanctuary to the consciousness of the writer resounds throughout the text. A number of anguished questions dominate the psalm - "When? ...Where? ... Why?" - as it records an extended battle of faith, during which the psalmist moves from being overwhelmed by his adversities to an assertion of confident faith in God's deliverance. As a whole the psalm may also be seen as mirroring the later history of the children of Israel in their dispersion, far from the beloved "city of their solemnities".

The opening lines show that the circumstances in which the psalmist found himself, debarred from public worship and estranged from Jerusalem, had awakened in him an awareness of his fathomless need for God. He did not focus upon the malice of his enemies or the privations of his present dwelling place; rather, his whole being was caught up in the realization that in communion with God was found all the hidden springs of his life. This experience of worship was not for him merely one enjoyment among many, not simply a sweet idyllic pastime, but rather the deepest need of his soul, so that he became consumed with longing for a sense of the divine presence. And so, like a lover in absence, he yearned passionately for a renewed apprehension of "the beauty of holiness", just as in intense drought the fainting hind thirsted for the water streams.

But even as he languished in sorrow and loneliness of heart, the psalmist was forced to endure the taunts of enemies who derided his faith, a situation which caused him such grief that the tears gushed from his eyes. Nevertheless, the memory of past experiences of worshiping the Lord in the sanctuary which then came to him provided inspiration for a prayer of great intensity in which he "poured out his soul", a verbal expression of his sufferings in which his whole being - mind, heart and emotions - were involved. This strengthened him in so remarkable a way that the radiant wings of his faith began to unfurl, and he apostrophized himself with a resolute declaration: "*Why art thou cast down, O my soul? Hope thou in God*".

Yet the spiritual battle continued, and the poet next turned to remembering God's past deliverances, vowing to recall Him "from the land of Jordan and of Hermon, from Mount Mizar"; that is, from the great mountain range in the far north of Israel to the "little hill", and from thence to the lowest place on earth. The Jordan River which sprang from the melting snows of Hermon was a place of gushing streams and waterfalls and the memory of this scene brought another powerful image sweeping into his mind, causing him to make an amazed exclamation to the Lord: *"All your waves and billows have gone over me."* The psalmist and his company of fellow exiles were aware in their outcast state of their precarious futures, their closeness to death and the ascendancy of evil; in this situation David therefore felt engulfed by wave after wave of sorrow, and feared that the torrents of anguish would overwhelm his soul.

Yet in the midst of this vast calamity, encompassing the highest realms of his known world to the lowest depth, the thought of God's almighty creative power filled his imagination, and he arrived at a profound revelation: *"Deep calls unto deep at the noise of thy waterspouts"*. This noun occurring twice, "deep" (Hebrew *"tehom"* or "abyss") also occurs in the opening lines of Genesis: *"darkness lay upon the face of the deep"*, and in this present context suggested how fathomless was the depth of need in the psalmist's soul. From out of this depth, this abyss of need, he called to God, the One who was deeper than his distress, and waited for the Spirit of God to move over the chaos in his life, trusting that God who commanded the light to shine out of the darkness at the beginning would also intervene with power in his situation. It is this which evoked from him a statement of constant faith in God's goodness and love, and called forth from him a prayer to "the God of his life", who would help him sing in his darkest hour.

Still, however, his cruel enemies continued to reproach him, suggesting that his God had abandoned him or was unable to deliver him. This "oppression" of his foes, similar to that endured by the Children of Israel in their bondage in Egypt (Exodus 3:9), crushed his spirit and afflicted even his physical body. Under their relentless attack and apparently forsaken by God he was again cast down - but in this very predicament roused himself to take that powerful step which brought the turning point in the psalm: *"Hope thou in God"*, he once again exhorted his soul - and was able to then declare triumphantly that the Lord would "command His lovingkindness" - would not simply bestow His goodness but undertake a sovereign conferring of divine blessing in his life. And God's face would also shine upon him, transfiguring his own countenance with saving health — so that songs of praise and thanksgiving would well up in him. This was nothing less than a new creation through the power of God.

The psalm is ultimately the experience of all Israel writ large: the voices of Esther, Job, Joseph, Daniel and a thousand other heroes of faith who in their places of extremity and despair hoped in God against impossible odds. Within the compass of this small psalm can be heard also the voices of the Jewish people throughout their long history and dispersion, just as the sound of a vast ocean can echo within the tiny chamber of a sea shell. Beyond even these experiences, in and through the individual suffering and ardent longing of the psalmist, the voice of the whole universe is sounding.

THE PSALM OF THE CHURCH

The Book of Psalms - in Hebrew *Tehillim* or "Praises" - is often called "The Psalms of David" because almost half are attributed to the second king of Israel, the "man after God's own heart", known in the Old Testament as *"Israel's beloved singer of songs"* (2 Samuel 23:1 NET). The psalms which bear his name record the different phases of his life as a young shepherd, musician, warrior and king; many were said to be written in the days when he was fleeing from Saul, and a dominant theme was the determination to trust in God through manifold troubles - wars, temptations, failure and despair. But the psalms do not only chronicle the emotions and struggles of David through his wide and varied experiences; they also celebrate the promises God made to him: that a Messianic king would be raised up from one of his descendants, who would reign from Zion over the nations and set up an everlasting kingdom of peace and righteousness.

When the evangelists and apostles came to set down the writings of the New Testament they drew heavily from the psalms for their inspired testimony that Jesus was the long-expected "Anointed One" of David's line. Their accounts make clear that Jesus Himself meditated often on the psalms and believed that in their impassioned phrases was to be found a delineation of His own life. His reflections on the psalms recorded in the Gospels therefore provide precious glimpses into the interior life of the Son of man as He carried out His mission of love. The church fathers attributed the collection as a whole to David, but saw his compositions as a forecast of the experiences of David's Greater Son; for them the Psalter was a prolonged prophecy of the life, death and resurrection of Christ. Just as David endured many years of humiliation through the enmity of Saul, but was finally raised to the throne of Israel, so Jesus after His Passion was exalted to the place of supreme power and authority at the right hand of God.

The early church, like Jesus Himself, turned to the psalms for language in which to express their deepest emotions, and the Psalter became the hymn book of the Christians as it had been of the Temple. Above all, David was the quintessential lover of God who more than any other has inspired the worship of the church over the past 2000 years. There was always in David's soul a special apprehension of the "beauty of holiness", but his knowledge of God developed in the hard and difficult places of his journey and through his wilderness experiences. In these trials he came to learn his utter dependence on God's upholding hand, and to recognize Him as the complete and only source of blessing in his life, understandings which led him to worship God with an abandonment of self and degree of adoration that was unprecedented. The ancient Greeks and Romans had valued the classical ideal of an admirable character, one whose strength, intellect and personal attributes gained him personal glory and renown. Here was a radically different conception of spiritual reality: all good, honor and blessing streaming from the heart of God, bestowed by an infinite love, which then required the heart adoration of the subject of its care.

Thus it is from David and the Book of Psalms that Christians have discovered how to express the ecstatic praise to God that wells up in their hearts and souls, and to extol Him in the depth and measure that a spouse praises his lover. The King of Israel, his music touched with divinity, has furnished more lines that have been used as the foundation of exquisite songs, and more words which comfort the heart, than any other biblical writer. David's psalms were also to have a huge impact on one of the greatest thinkers in the Christian tradition, Augustine of Hippo, whose writings profoundly shaped the course of Western civilization.

Augustine on Psalm 42

The fourth-century African theologian known as St Augustine, who lived at a time when the Christian faith had girdled the Mediterranean world, is a towering figure in ecclesiastical history. Through his writings on original sin, grace, God's love and the Trinity he laid the foundation for the Western church, both Protestant and Catholic, but he is perhaps best known for his *Confessions*, the account he wrote of his conversion and subsequent devotion to God. In this work the reader is captivated by Augustine's immense intellect and filled with admiration for his beautiful rhetoric, but perhaps is even more carried away by the apprehension of Augustine's essential nature as consummate seeker of God and lover of God. Augustine viewed the desire for a relationship with God as a deep natural longing of the human soul which existed even in those far removed from Him, who were unconsciously seeking His presence in their lives with troubled and unsatisfied hearts: *"You have formed us for Yourself, and our hearts are restless till they find rest in You"* (*Confessions*, 1.1).

Augustine's biographical masterpiece takes the form of a series of ardently-voiced conversations to God, and on almost every page the voice of the psalms is heard, either in allusion or direct quotation.

The opening lines consist of two sentences praising God based on expressions from the Psalter: *"Great are You, O Lord, and greatly to be praised; great is Your power, and of Your wisdom there is no end"*. During the interval between his conversion and baptism Augustine went to stay in Cassiciacum in Italy with relatives and friends, and while there was "set on fire" through reading the psalms: *"O my God, how did I cry to You when I read the psalms of David, those hymns of faith, utterances of devotion which leave no room for swelling pride ...What cries I used to send up to You in those songs, and how I was enkindled toward You by them! I burned to sing them if possible, throughout the whole world, against the pride of the human race"* (*Confessions*, 9:4).

Throughout his long years as pastor of his flock Augustine continued to study the psalms, which assured him that God delighted in the emotional dimension of human love. He believed David to be their unique author, and as he studied the expressions and utterances of the passionate king he found therein a record of the feelings of Jesus. For Augustine, therefore, it was Christ's voice that was heard in the psalms, a voice "we should know intimately and make our own." The Psalms and Gospels were like one "seamless garment", relating the same story of the unfathomable love of God for His people, a love which had shone forth most brightly in the life and death of Jesus Christ, and which was like a magnet drawing the soul to God. In his *Commentary on the Psalms*, composed over a period of nearly thirty years, Augustine included a sermon on Psalm 42:

"What I am saying, that as the hart pants after the water-brooks, so longs my soul after You, O God, means this, My soul is thirsty for the living God. For what is it thirsty? This it is for which I am thirsty, to come and to appear before Him. I am thirsty in my pilgrimage, in my running; I shall be filled on my arrival. This too proceeds from that longing, of which in another place comes that cry, One thing have I desired of the Lord; that will I seek after; that I may dwell in the house of the Lord all the days of my life. Wherefore so? That I may behold (he says) the beauty of the Lord."

In the Songs of David, therefore, Augustine saw depicted above all the Son of God who was the beauty of the Father and the Spirit and who, in becoming human, desired to draw all men and women into the same Trinitarian life, the eternal love existing between the Father and the Son.

Augustine also had a profound understanding, not just of his own thirst, but also the thirst of Jesus. In his commentary on Psalm 68 he expressed the belief that the thirst of Christ was for the salvation of men and women, that they should come to faith in Him. The Passion account in John's Gospel records that one of the last words of Jesus on the cross was, *"I thirst"*. This was a cry which was the ultimate and illimitable instance of Deep calling out to Deep.

Wings Above Israel

....

There is another remarkable phenomenon which may be seen in the depths of the Jordan Valley when one lifts the gaze heavenward – the annual migration of birds, which is surpassed by no other in the world. Israel lies at the crossroads of three continents and an estimated 500 million birds pass through her skies each year on their annual migratory path. The vast flocks which can be seen winging their way north in spring from the lakes and jungles of Africa, then returning in fall with their young from as far away as Lapland, has made Israel a magnet for birdwatchers. Each year thousands of enthusiasts come to the land to watch the spectacular formations crossing the region and the endless variety of flight patterns - larger birds such as storks and pelicans gliding aloft on currents of thermal air, or smaller songbirds steadily beating their wings. Israel maintains a number of bird sanctuaries along the migration route, starting with Lake Hula in the Upper Galilee, through the Jordan Valley, Jerusalem and the desert north of Eilat on the Red Sea.

These journeys along the aerial highways were observed by dwellers in the land long ago: *"The stork in the heaven also knows her appointed times; and the turtledove, swift and the crane observe their time of coming"* wrote the prophet Jeremiah (8:7), clearly denoting a matter of common knowledge. The remembrance of myriads of migrating birds must also have impressed itself upon the mind of Isaiah, and he used this image to suggest how swiftly God would come to aid the Holy City in time of danger: *"As birds flying, so will the Lord of Hosts defend Jerusalem"* (Isaiah 31:5).

And yet the way in which the winged creatures cover thousands of miles on their annual odysseys and arrive at precisely the same spot year after year remains a mysterious and amazing phenomenon. These "extraordinarily vital scraps of feathered energy are defiant of gravity, undaunted by arctic cold, tropical heat, or all the immensities of space. With infinite grace they fly serenely through the world with its thousand dangers." Birds are true internationalists, sometimes crossing many borders in a single day: well might travelers in our own day and age cast envying glances upwards from our queues and checkpoints at the freedom with which they negotiate the skies. Through the centuries they have continued to wing their way tranquilly above the skies of Israel, over migrating tribes, marching armies and merchants carrying their wares – and today share the skies with other manmade avian traffic, including Israeli fighter jets swooping along the Jordan Valley.

It is not only migrators that make Israel a prime destination for bird watchers: this tiny strip of country, only 140 miles in length and averaging from 60 to 100 miles in width, has for its size an unprecedented number of resident bird species. The topography within Israel's small compass is that of a whole world: a single day's journey leads from snow-capped mountains in the north to the southern wilderness, from Mediterranean coastline to the depths of the Jordan Valley, and between these extremes can be found streams gushing into valleys, wadis and canyons, sand dunes and oases. Over all the sun pours forth a beneficent warmth, while the gentle sea breezes which blow over the land alternate with the scorching hamsin wind from the desert. The different climatic regions in the land promote a rich variety of trees and vegetation, nurturing the growth of pine and oak forests and the cultivation of orchards and vineyards, while even in barren areas the graceful palm tree provides shade and fruit. Thus a wide range of habitats is created within which different species of birds may flourish, creatures which range in size from the tiny Sunbird with its beautiful iridescent feathers to the mighty Golden Eagle with its wingspan reaching six to eight feet.

There are masses of flowers also to attract the winged creatures, trees with brightly colored blooms and intoxicating scents, while in spring the wildflowers carpet the earth in a dazzling display. King Solomon was famed as the wisest man of antiquity, but he was also a poet and an ardent naturalist who composed 1005 songs and *"spoke of trees, from the cedar tree that is in Lebanon even unto the hyssop that springs out of the wall; he spoke also of beasts and of fowl, and of creeping things, and of fish"* (1 Kings 4:33). In his matchless poem known as the Song of Songs he captured the essence of spring in the land - the song of the birds, the flowers which perfumed the air, and the delight in the glory of color, fragrant spices and fruit trees:

> *"For, lo, the winter is past,*
> *The rain is over and gone,*
> *The flowers appear on the earth;*
> *The time of the singing of birds is come,*
> *And the voice of the turtledove*
> *Is heard in our land"* (Song 2:11-12)

There were many other keen naturalists among the ancient Hebrews, and the Bible contains approximately three hundred references to birds, scattered from beginning to end. The opening chapter of Genesis recounts that when the fifth day of creation dawned both land and sea had been prepared for living creatures; it was then that God made every winged bird "according to its kind" to fly above the earth in the open firmament of heaven. And this "majestical roof" became fretted with the flashing images of the birds, some with brightly jeweled plumage, others with more sedate coloring, and the overarching blue dome was filled with the sound of wingbeats and the music of birdsong as an astonishing range of notes and harmonies poured from their throats.

The ancient Israelites were clearly enchanted by the winged creatures who flew above them in the celestial pathways and stories about birds were thereafter woven into many of the Bible narratives. These in turn provided images which became imprinted on the minds and hearts of generations: a dove bringing a fresh plucked olive leaf to Noah in the Ark, a miraculous abundance of quails falling to feed the hungry Children of Israel, a raven bringing food to a starving prophet. When Solomon's great Temple in Jerusalem was reared up, the birds were allowed to nest and raise their young there unmolested, so that their song mingled with the praise of the Levites: *"Even the sparrow has found a home, and the swallow a nest for herself, where she may lay her young - even your altars, O Lord of hosts"* (Psalm 84:3). Other images of birds were more unhappy: owls hooting mournfully about ruined cities, or the grim picture in the final chapters of Revelation depicting the fowls which gathered to eat the flesh of God's defeated foes. But the saddest story involving a bird remains the crowing of a cock one fateful Passover morning in Jerusalem.

"CONSIDER THE BIRDS"

In the days when the scriptures were set down, men and women lived closely to the earth, and their apprehension of the wonder and beauty of the natural world unveiled to them new understandings of the power and wisdom of its Creator. Feathered creatures in particular appealed to the hearts and sympathy of the biblical writers: their beauty of form and motion, sweetness of melody, dedication to nest-building and fearlessness in defending their young, as well as their devotion to their mates. When Job was answering the reproaches his friends heaped upon him during his afflictions, he suggested that great truths could be gleaned from the creatures around them:

> *"But now ask the beasts, and they will teach you;*
> *And the birds of the air, and they will tell you"* (Job 12:7)

A number of biblical passages also referred to birds as symbols of God's tender protection and care for His people. When Moses stood atop Sinai, while the mountain shook and burned with fire, God spoke to him in an extraordinary passage which revealed the nature of His covenant love toward the Children of Israel: "*You have seen*," He said, "*what I did to the Egyptians, and how I bore you on eagles wings and brought you to Myself*" (Exodus 19:4). This vivid image encouraged the people to look upon their God not so much as a mighty king, but as a loving parent who had delivered them from bondage and yearned to draw them into relationship with Himself. This image was then taken up by later writers of the scriptures. As King David watched the parent bird brooding over her young in their nest he also saw a picture of God's tender compassion toward those who put their trust in Him: "*He shall cover you with His feathers, and under His wings you shall take refuge*" (Psalm 91:4). Malachi, whose prophetic writings close the Old Testament, was inspired to set down a similar image, displaying a marked poetic power:

"*But to you that fear My name,*
The Sun of Righteousness shall arise,
With healing in His wings" (Malachi 4:2)

The Gospel accounts of Jesus' life and ministry disclose that the Nazarene had an intense appreciation of the wonder and beauty of creation, for lying beyond the realm of nature He was able to perceive the holy and eternal realities to which its manifold glories pointed. This Master Teacher who preached from a small boat to the crowds gathered on the seashore, or addressed them in the midst of the harvest fields, many times used the simplest of illustrations, drawn from nature and easy to grasp and comprehend, but His words enthralled the multitudes who listened. Since the time that His sayings first fell upon the clear air of the Galilean hills and fields they have reached countless others, and impressed themselves with unequalled power upon their hearts and minds. Nor have His teachings ceased to yield new depths of meaning as each generation contemplates them anew.

During His "hidden years", Jesus must have observed the birds flying about or nesting in His native village, and gathered together a storehouse of observations about the winged creatures which would later supply inspiration for His parables and preaching. He noticed that they possessed a wondrous freedom from worry and anxiety, which gave Him a deeper insight into God's provision, enabling Him to assure His audience: *"Look at the birds of the air, for they neither sow nor reap nor gather into barns; yet your heavenly Father feeds them. Are you not of more value than they?"* (Matthew 6:25). Even the commonplace sparrows which swarmed about the villages of Galilee furnished a lesson concerning the fathomless extent of God's love: *"Are not five sparrows sold for two farthings? And not one of them is forgotten before God"* (Luke 12:6). But Jesus had also observed the hen's maternal love toward her chicks, and this was reflected in one of the saddest statements that fell from His lips, as He stretched His arms toward His beloved city and cried:

"O Jerusalem, Jerusalem, the one who kills the prophets and stones those who are sent to her! How often I wanted to gather your children together, as a hen gathers her chicks under her wings, but you were not willing!" (Matthew 23:37)

Thus did Jesus set His imprimatur upon Job's call to ask wisdom from the birds of the air. And when the Bible is considered as a whole, it appears that the eagle and the dove are the birds which are most often represented and supply the most profound lessons for human beings.

The Eagle and the Dove

The magnificent eagle which nests on the rocky summits of Hermon, Gilead and the ranges along the Jordan Valley seems to reign supreme in the air. With awe-inspiring grandeur and grace it mounts into the sky, sweeps on broad pinions among the clouds, or folds its wings and darts earthward like an arrow. Despite all his wisdom, King Solomon had to confess there were some things that remained too marvelous for him to comprehend, and one of these was "the way of an eagle in the air" (Proverbs 30:19). For millennia, people watched birds soaring into the sky and longed to emulate them, and even today, although flying machines have been invented, the mystery of their flight is not fully understood. Feathered wings are amongst the most beautiful and remarkable structures in the animal world, enabling birds to perform all the functions of modern aircraft and still surpass them. And so, the way of an eagle in the air retains its wonder.

From the day Moses descended Sinai with the message of the eagle, the people of Israel saw in these majestic birds a symbol of God's faithful love toward them, reinforced by the winged cherubim above the Ark of the Covenant which accompanied them through the wilderness. As they made their difficult way toward the Promised Land they may have seen these great birds soaring above them in the blue ether, and thrilled with the memory of God's promise to bring them safely to their journey's end. Thus the image of the eagle, imbued also with its suggestion of limitless freedom, became firmly etched upon the religious consciousness of Israel, and even after the bitterness of the Babylonian exile continued to provide them with hope. In an allusion to the belief that the eagle has the miraculous power to resume its youth, Isaiah gave the children of the captivity the comforting promise of national renewal:

> *"Those who wait on the Lord*
> *Shall renew their strength;*
> *They shall mount up with wings like eagles,*

They shall run and not be weary,
They shall walk and not faint" (Isaiah 40:31)

The overwhelming impression of power produced by the eagle meant that it could also be used to represent the heroes and warriors of Israel. After King Saul and his son Jonathan perished in the battle against the Philistines on Mount Gilboa, David sang a lament describing them as "swifter than eagles, stronger than lions". Other biblical prophets and writers noted the ferocity with which the eagle was endowed, and so used images of the bird's swift flight and downward plunge toward its prey in making pronunciations of disaster against the nations which oppressed Israel. Perhaps the greatest symbolic value of the eagle, however, lay in its ability to represent the heights of human spiritual aspiration. John's vision in the Book of Revelation of the four living creatures in the midst of the heavenly throne room revealed that one of these was like a flying eagle (Revelation 4:7; cf Ezekiel 1:10).

And yet it is not the mighty eagle which figures in the opening chapters of both Old and New Testaments, but rather the gentle dove. The first verses of Genesis describe how, in the beginning, even before the light shone forth in the darkness, the Spirit of God was hovering on the face of the waters. This prototypical image suggested the picture of a bird with outspread wings settling protectively over her nest, and the Jewish sages interpreted that as meaning that God's *Ruach* was brooding "like a dove", watching over and nurturing the new creation. Since the dawn of civilization doves have flourished in the neighborhood of humans and were admired for their snowy plumage, swiftness of flight and tender love for their mates. Their gentle cooing would have been heard in the dovecotes around the villages of the land and the rabbis also taught that the "still small voice" which spoke to the prophet Elijah was soft and low, like the voice of a dove.

Accordingly the dove is mentioned more frequently in the Bible than any other bird. Perhaps the most exquisite of these references occurs in the Song of Songs, where the image of the gentle bird was pressed into service by the Divine Lover to portray the delicate purity of the bride:

> *"O my dove, in the clefts of the rock,*
> *In the secret places of the cliff,*
> *Let me see your face,*
> *Let me hear your voice;*
> *For your voice is sweet,*
> *And your face is lovely"* (Song 2:14)

There is a yet greater tribute paid to this beautiful bird. All four Gospels describe what occurred at the baptism of Jesus, when the Spirit descended upon Him: *"When He had been baptized, Jesus came up immediately from the water; and behold, the heavens were opened to Him, and He saw the Spirit of God descending like a dove and alighting upon Him"* (Matthew 3:15). Why was it that the divine *Ruach* manifested Himself in the form of the innocent and tender dove? Undoubtedly there was the traditional connection between the Spirit of God and this bird; but there was more in it than that. The key is to be found in the fact that the dove was the poor person's sacrifice, and was reputed to be the only sacrificial victim that willingly offered its neck to the knife.

The Spirit which descended out of heaven as a dove upon Jesus and hovered over Him prefigured all the qualities which stamped His character continually: gentleness, purity, charity, holiness, and voluntary sacrifice; for, although He was the Son of God, His power was always in subordination to His love. Jesus' suffering and death at Calvary, when He laid down His life for the redemption of the whole world, was a supreme, unparalleled act of oblation – but that was not the final word – for the sacrifice and the humiliation became windows through which the essential nature of God was manifested. The unfolding revelation of the divine character throughout both Covenants is summed up most succinctly and directly toward the end of the New Testament: "God is love". If that be so, then His glory shines forth most completely in whatever most clearly and fully expresses love; and therefore the cross, the emblem of utmost shame and suffering, is in reality the all-surpassing unveiling of the eternal glory of the Godhead.

Fleeting Life, Eternal Significance

....

In his *Ecclesiastical History of the English People*, the Venerable Bede records a famous story from the early days of the Anglo Saxon monarchy. In seventh-century Northumbria, King Edwin was approached by a missionary, Paulinus, who desired to convert him to Christianity. When the King consulted his friends and advisors about what he should do, one offered the following reflection:

"The present life of man upon earth, O King, seems to me, in comparison with that time which is unknown to us, like the swift flight of a sparrow through the mead hall where you sit at supper in winter, with your thanes and counselors, while the fire blazes in the midst and the hall is warmed, but the wintry storms of rain or snow are raging outside. The sparrow, flying in at one door and immediately out at another, is safe from the wintry tempest whilst he is within, but after a short space of fair weather, he immediately vanishes out of your sight, passing from winter to winter again. So this life of man appears for a little while, but of what is to follow or what went before we know nothing at all. If, therefore, this new doctrine tells us something more certain, it seems justly to be followed in our kingdom."

This comparison of a man's life to that of a sparrow, who flies out of a stormy winter's night through a mead hall, and briefly experiences light, warmth and safety before vanishing back into darkness, proved effective in the King's conversion. Yet this theme of the brevity of life had already been explored in a text far more ancient than Bede's *History*.

THE BOOK OF ECCLESIASTES

The wealth and splendor of the reign of King Solomon during the golden age of the united monarchy in Israel became, even during his lifetime, the stuff of legend. Above all, the king was famed throughout the ancient world for his gift of wisdom, which surpassed that of all the other wise men of the age. Granted an era of unprecedented peace and prosperity throughout his reign, Solomon determined to turn the searchlight of his gaze upon one all-important subject, the discovery of the meaning of life. Into this quest he threw himself vigorously, that he might *"see what was good for the sons of men to do under heaven all the days of their lives"* (Ecclesiastes 2:3). All the activities he undertook - the search for wisdom, pursuit of pleasure, philanthropic works, and the amassing of material goods - were those which traditionally were held to confer significance upon human existence. Then he took up his pen and under the *nom de plume* "Kohelet" or "Preacher" set down his findings in a book, called Ecclesiastes. This, his *magnum opus*, he opened with a superlative. Not "heaven of heavens" nor "holy of holies". No, Kohelet thundered forth words with an extreme shock value, a statement of maximum negativity:

"'Vanity of vanities,' says the Preacher, 'Vanity of vanities! All is vanity'" (Ecclesiastes 1:1)

As Solomon had engaged in his search for meaning, it became borne in upon him inescapably that, no matter how splendid his achievements, they would eventually be forgotten by the generations that came after him, the material wealth for which he had labored would be dissipated, and his most noble and philanthropic deeds would vanish into the mists of time: *"Therefore," he said, "I hated life, because the work that was done under the sun was distressing to me, for all is vanity and grasping for the wind"* (Ecclesiastes 2:17). The bitter realization that, since the very dawn of history, every endeavor of the human being had finally been checkmated by death seemed to him to cast a dark pall over existence.

And the sense of futility produced in the depths of his psyche was reinforced by his observation of the natural world and its ceaseless round, together with his perception of the inherent restlessness of life. All human beings have an incessant desire for new experience which is constantly thwarted, for "there is nothing new under the sun."

After this negative opening Kohelet continued to enlarge upon his theme in the chapters that followed, in which the Hebrew word *hevel*, translated as "vanity, meaninglessness, a vapor", occurs no fewer than 38 times. Yet at the same time, there are many passages in Ecclesiastes that appear to contradict the assertion that "all is vanity" and rather urge the reader to embrace the pleasures that life has to offer: "*So I commended enjoyment, because a man has nothing better under the sun than to eat, drink, and be merry*" (Ecclesiastes 8:15). It therefore seems possible that joy can coexist with the awareness of mortality and this presents an enigma: how are such opposing attitudes to be reconciled? The answer may be found at the very beginning of the Hebrew Scriptures, in Genesis chapter 4, where the most important clue to the mystery of Ecclesiastes is found. For *Hevel* is also the Hebrew name of Abel, the son of Adam and Eve, Cain's brother, whose story provides the foundation for much of Ecclesiastes' message.

The early chapters of Genesis leading up to the story of the first fratricide describe God's creation of an orderly and beautiful world and the placing of the man and woman in the paradise in Eden. There, however, seduced by the serpent, they had transgressed God's commands and been cast out of the garden; the punishment pronounced against them included the man's future need to toil for food, pain in childbirth for the woman, and ultimately the experience of death, the return to dust. Enmity between the seed of the woman and the seed of the serpent would be the enduring determinant of post-Eden life; nevertheless, ultimate victory would be given to the woman's seed. In the outside world, under these new conditions, Eve bore her first son and named him Cain, meaning *acquiring*, but her second son she named *Hevel*, a surprising, negative name, perhaps suggesting that the sentence passed upon the human race was becoming a fixed reality in her understanding: that human existence was brief and evanescent.

Genesis 4 then provided a portrait of life outside the garden. Cain and Abel were both able to labor and provide food from the earth and in the course of time each brought an offering to God. Although Abel's offering was accepted, Cain's was not, and this eventually led him to rise up and kill his brother. In many ways, Abel's name seemed appropriate for one whose life was so cruelly cut short: with seemingly no material achievement, no spectacular success, no children. His life appeared written like footprints upon sand, the brief flare of a shooting star, a ripple across a placid lake which soon vanishes away. His only recorded deed, the offering of the firstlings of his flock to God, ultimately led to his death. Nor did he speak any word which is recalled in the text; and at the end it was only his blood which cried out.

Yet Abel's short life and untimely death were not the whole of his story: the scriptures suggest there was one fact of overriding significance to be found in his existence, that *"the Lord respected Abel and his offering"* (Genesis 4:4). He was the first human being to offer a sacrifice accepted by God, and the significance of this can only be fully comprehended in the whole context of the story. The early chapters of Genesis show a picture of consistent human inadequacy and failure, as Adam and Eve transgressed God's commands and Cain then compounded their error. But as the words of divine approbation were given to Abel, a new luster begins to suffuse the ongoing human story with hope. Abel brings a profound message: that the significance of one's life does not depend on the attainment of outward accomplishments or material goals. Abel's life was evanescent as mist - yet his life's calling was nonetheless fulfilled.

Moreover, the verb "respect," *vayisha*, is related to the Hebrew *yeshua*, suggesting that God was not simply accepting his offering, but conferring salvation upon Abel himself. In the final analysis, his story reveals that it is the relationship with the divine established and maintained within the brief span of a person's existence which provides that life with eternal significance.

In Ecclesiastes, the preacher looks at the world through the lens of these archetypal events. He recognizes in a profound way that pain, toil and sorrow characterize the post-garden world; in fact, that the whole creation has been subjected to vanity and groans. The transitory nature of man is part of the common human existence; and in this world, where oppression and injustice appear to flourish unchecked, the seed of the serpent will continue to persecute the seed of the woman. Yet in the midst of judgment God also remembered and demonstrated mercy. Although grief and disappointment may be experienced in life, there are also many good gifts - food and drink, meaningful work, and marriages which bring delight - and these, even though they eventually pass away, are a cause for celebration. And in the end it will be well with those who are righteous and their offerings to God will be respected: "*Go, eat your bread with joy and drink your wine with a merry heart for God already accepts your works*" (Ecclesiastes 9:7).

Therefore the word *hevel* which appears so many times in Ecclesiastes should be interpreted not as "vanity", suggesting emptiness and folly, but rather as "fleeting", referring to the swift and transitory nature of life. Nor does this understanding of the transience of human existence nullify the possibility of achieving meaning and significance within our individual lives. The many moments of fleeting beauty that come to us all and imprint themselves on our souls - a sunset, a star trembling in the dark, a child's laugh - grant glimpses of the eternity that lies beyond. And this realization of the fleeting and uncertain nature of our existence gives a great impetus to live our days as fully as possible in the light of the divine vision which has been granted, days in which, by acts of loving kindness, we allow God's presence to flow through us into the lives of others. In turn, we are set free from the dread of death and our nihilistic fears and discover that God has put "eternity in our hearts". Kohelet's ultimate vision is that of *fleeting life yielding eternal significance*. And there is a further hope expressed in his book found in the allusion to Seth, the replacement seed for Abel: the mysterious statement in Ecclesiastes 4:15 that "the second one replaces the first", which looks forward to the coming of a Second Adam.

Life had posed to Solomon its great riddle as it does to every man and woman "under the sun". With much anguish of soul he eventually worked his way to a peaceful conclusion, was enabled to find the key to life that yielded its treasures of wisdom and opened the path to joy. And the end of his searching, the conclusion of the whole matter, was utterly simple and at the same time utterly demanding: *"Fear God, and keep His commandments: for this is the whole duty of man"* (Ecclesiastes 12:13).

It is in the light of the New Testament revelation that this conclusion unfolds its fullest meaning, as all the teaching of the Tanach is gathered up in a sublime summary: *"The end of the commandment is love out of a pure heart"* (1 Timothy 1:5). And the Book of Hebrews illuminates a further truth concerning Abel's sacrifice, disclosing the great reason why Abel's offering to God was accepted while Cain's was not: Abel's gift was offered through faith – faith working through love, so that *"he, being dead, yet speaks"* (Hebrews 11:4; Galatians 5:6). Abel's influence lives beyond his brief sojourn upon the earth and reverberates across the centuries to the present day.

A TWENTIETH CENTURY QUEST

Three thousand years after the King set down his *opus*, another writer took up the same quest, yet whereas Solomon undertook his search from a position of supreme privilege, this seeker after truth experienced life stripped to its bare minimum and was plunged into the most profound depths of personal anguish. Viktor Frankl spent the World War II years between 1942 and 1945 in the concentration camps of Nazi Germany, first in Auschwitz then in Dachau. Here he endured extreme hunger, cold, and hard labor as well as the constant threat of the gas ovens; here also his parents, brother, and pregnant wife all perished. In his later memoir he gave an account of those experiences, and of the quest he undertook to discover a meaning in life which sprang directly out of his being subjected to such hardships. This search became so intensely concentrated in the fires of suffering that he was able to offer reasons for purpose and significance in human existence, even whilst experiencing "man's inhumanity to man" to the utmost extent imaginable.

Frankl therefore emerged from the death camps to affirm the incalculable value of the gift of life in one of the twentieth century's most influential works, *Man's Search for Meaning*:

"Our generation is realistic, for we have come to know man as he really is. After all, man is that being who invented the gas chambers of Auschwitz; however, he is also that being who entered those gas chambers upright, with the Lord's Prayer or the Shema Yisrael on his lips"

According to Frankl, the classic sources of meaning in life are the opportunities it provides to engage in creative work, or to find fulfillment in experiencing beauty, art, or nature. However, if one is debarred from pursuing such experiences for various external reasons, there is a further source of significance. Suffering, he noted, is an inescapable part of life, just as fate and death; so that if there is a meaning to be found in life at all there must be also be a meaning to be discovered in suffering. He reflected on the men he had observed in the death camps who walked through the huts comforting others, even giving away their last pieces of bread; and it seemed to him that, though they may have been few in number, yet they were sufficient proof that a person may choose to retain his or her human dignity even in the worst of circumstances. It is this spiritual freedom — which cannot be taken away — that for him made life meaningful.

What is really needed, he went on to assert, is a fundamental change in our attitude toward life. It does not really matter what we expect from life, but rather *what life expects from us*. Ultimately, therefore, a person should not ask concerning the meaning of his or her life, but rather must recognize that it is he or she who is *being asked*. Frankl came to perceive that every person is continually being questioned by existence, and that the only response possible is that of being responsible, and thus becoming raised above outward fate through inner strength. And this philosophy is not just for those confined in concentration camps, but rather men and women everywhere are confronted with the circumstances that fate presents to them. In every such situation, they have the possibility of aspiring after exalted values and ideals which provide endurance in the midst of great tribulation.

The most poignant sections of this profound memoir are Frankl's recollection of the personal understandings that came to him while in the death camps and gave him the will to live on. One of these revelations was received while he was working in the harsh conditions of Auschwitz, when the image of his wife appeared to him with great vividness:

Real or not, her look was then more luminous than the sun which was beginning to rise. A thought transfixed me: for the first time in my life I saw the truth as it is set into song by so many poets, proclaimed as the final wisdom by so many thinkers. The truth — that love is the ultimate and the highest goal to which man can aspire. Then I grasped the meaning of the greatest secret that human poetry and human thought and belief have to impart: The salvation of man is through love and in love. I understood how a man who has nothing left in this world still may know bliss, be it only for a brief moment, in the contemplation of his beloved.

Frankl did not know, when these understandings flooded into his mind, that his wife had died. Nevertheless, the emotion he experienced went far beyond a yearning after the physical presence of the beloved. Just like Kohelet, he had discovered the power of love that transcended time and mortality.

CONCLUSION

It is time to turn again to the New Testament. Solomon had noted in the Book of Ecclesiastes that the world continued in its ceaseless round, but that the generations of men and women were swiftly passing away. Those assertions, however, seem to be directly challenged by a verse found in the First Letter of John: "*The world is passing away, and the lust of it: but he who does the will of God abides for ever*" (1 John 2: 17).

Yet a deeper examination proves this to be a complementary rather than a contradictory text. It is commonly acknowledged that John, the Apostle of Jesus, was granted the highest spiritual vision, soaring heavenward like an eagle to gaze into the heart of divine truth. In the understandings he was granted concerning time and existence, he saw therein an ineluctable spiritual process set in motion, by which the world system, seemingly so solid and secure, was being continually overturned and melted away. But the true antithesis which John discerned was not so much that of the vanishing material order and the endurance of the spiritual, as "the essential transiency of everything which is antagonism to the will of God, and the essential eternity of everything which is in conformity with that will."

And so, in the midst of all this change and dissolution, there are those who remain steadfast and unchanging, the men and women who do God's will. How, then, is His will to be obeyed, and this greatly desirable end, this permanence, to be attained? John tells us that it is through knowing and believing the love that God has to us, which is revealed in Jesus Christ and His great act of propitiation which took away the sins of the world. It is through faith in Him that a person's own love is kindled and issues forth in deeds of charity and goodness. As he continues to mold his will to the divine will in loving trust, the fleeting shadows of the outward life cease to impinge upon his soul, he lays hold upon immortality and comes to participate in God's eternal nature. And then, when all things opposed to the divine will shall vanish into oblivion, his own deeds shall last forever.

Meanwhile, in this interim period, the meaninglessness brought into the world through the Fall has forever been vanquished by the death of Jesus, the second Adam. This is a victory which shall be manifested to its full extent at the consummation of the ages, when the whole creation subject to vanity will be delivered from corruption into *the glorious liberty of the sons of God.*

What Did Jesus Write?

....

The Feast of Tabernacles in which Jesus made His dramatic appearance had drawn to a close and the time of sojourning in booths came to an end; and so, according to the continuing account in John's Gospel, "everyone returned to their home". Jesus, however, withdrew to the Mount of Olives where He was accustomed to go for prayer and communion with God. One could conjecture that a theme of His meditation on this occasion was a passage from the Book of Zechariah associated with the feast that had just been celebrated. The 6th century prophet had spoken of the time when God's Messianic Kingdom would be established in Jerusalem; this new reign would be ushered in after a battle raged around the Holy City and an ensuing earthquake caused the Mount of Olives to split in half. It was then that "living waters" would flow out to restore the earth, and after that all the nations of the earth would ascend to Jerusalem each year to worship the Lord and keep the Feast of Tabernacles (Zechariah 14:16).

The 8th chapter of John's Gospel commences by relating that Jesus then returned to Jerusalem and began to teach in the Temple "early in the morning" - as the breaking light of dawn over the horizon illumined the new day. On this occasion He chose to deliver His message to the people in the Treasury, located in the Court of the Women, and this became the setting for a new narrative which John then proceeded to unfold, one which is only 12 verses in length but has become one of the best known and loved stories from the Gospels. The story of the Woman Taken in Adultery is one of the gems of world literature. Within its small compass it is entirely flawless, and its revelation of God's mercy toward sinners as demonstrated through the words and actions of Jesus has captivated generations of readers. However, this singular narrative, and most especially Jesus' words, "He who is without sin among you, let him be the first to throw a stone at her", have been misunderstood in various ways, most particularly in order to demonstrate that it was Jesus' intention to overthrow the Law.

In fact there are a number of problems which may be found in many traditional explanations of the text. These frequently take a moralistic approach, arguing that because all have sinned it is therefore hypocritical for any Christian to presume to pass sentence on another. As it is only a completely righteous person who can make a decision concerning sin and guilt, such an interpretation leaves open one possibility: that God alone can act as judge. However, this conclusion flies directly in the face of a great number of New Testament scriptures concerned with disciplining erring Christians. It also demonstrates a fundamental misunderstanding of the Old Testament Law mediated through Moses. This great prophet never stated that a man needed to be perfect to judge adultery or any other crime – obviously, those existing under the Old Covenant had personal sin, yet were still held capable of making crucial decisions concerning civil justice.

Such interpretations have the further effect of "casting stones" at the Old Testament law itself, implying that the rules and regulations found therein were burdensome and administered by men who were harsh and judgmental. Although the Law mandated the death of the adulteress (Leviticus 20:10), Jesus is presented as granting her unconditional freedom and forgiveness, and so demonstrating that with His coming a new age of grace had dawned. And while that was true, it was never Jesus' intention to set aside the clear requirements of Mosaic legislation in order to demonstrate mercy. Jesus was not arguing on this occasion that adultery was not a punishable sin, nor that one needed to be perfect in order to judge anyone guilty of a transgression. In fact, in this episode of the Adulterous Woman, it can be demonstrated that Jesus not only obeyed the Mosaic Law as those present understood it, but also endorsed it completely.

After Jesus' proclamation at the Feast that He was the Giver of Living Water, many of the people had concluded that this was the Prophet for whom they waited. It seems likely that, as a result, the religious leaders in the city decided to present the controversial Galilean with a legal dilemma which would entrap Him into contradicting a clear Mosaic statue. As Jesus was thus teaching in the Temple the scribes and Pharisees brought a woman and set her in the center of the court, after which they pronounced the words, "Teacher, this woman has been caught in adultery, in the very act …". They were accusing her of having broken the seventh commandment, "Thou shalt not commit adultery", one of the foundational rules which God had given to Moses on Mount Sinai. Having enunciated the charge they continued, "Now in the Law Moses commanded us to stone such women"; by using the pronoun "us" they were also attesting they were the very witnesses whom the Law proclaimed should be the first to do the stoning (Deuteronomy 17:6-7).

It was a most cunningly contrived situation, in which, as John explains, the Pharisees were testing Jesus so "they might have grounds for accusing Him" (John 8:6). They assumed they had now firmly ensnared the Nazarene, for if He were truly from God then He must follow Moses' Law and condemn the woman – but if on the other hand He refused to confirm the judgment He would be violating the Law and thus exposed as a false prophet.

It is a dramatic picture John presents, full of the most intense human interest and pathos: the Pharisees and scribes standing on one side, their faces hard and accusing, Jesus seated over against them, and the woman in the midst. *"But,"* the narrative continues, *"Jesus stooped down, and with His finger wrote on the ground … And again He stooped down, and wrote on the ground"* (8:6b-8). Was this action of His simply an indication that He, who knew so well what was in the hearts of men, was unwilling to continue looking upon the display of arrogance and hypocrisy on the part of the religious leaders? Or was there some particular significance in the words which He had written?

The suggestions as to what Jesus might have written in the dust are numerous and full of ingenuity – some say He wrote the sins of the witnesses, or a pardon, others suggest it was the name of the man involved in the adultery who was noticeably absent from the scene. However, perhaps it is not so much *what* He wrote that was significant; rather, the important thing is *that* He wrote, for by this action He was surely alluding to the fact that the Ten Commandments given to Moses were inscribed on two stone tablets "written with the finger of God" (Exodus 31:18). Regardless of what Jesus actually set down, John was indicating that He was claiming to be the actual Writer of the Law. This view is reinforced by the fact that He wrote a second time, bringing to mind God's creation of the second tablets of stone after the first had been destroyed.

Nevertheless, there is an Old Testament scripture which has good claim to be the subject of Jesus' inscription in the dust. In light of Jesus' pronouncement at the just-concluded feast, it is possible to imagine that what He wrote upon the earth was the message of Jeremiah 17:12-13:

"O Lord the Hope of Israel, all that forsake You shall be ashamed. Those who depart from Me shall be written in the dust, because they have forsaken the Lord, the fountain of living waters."

According to this scripture, those "written in the dust" stand in profound contrast to those who have the honor of being written in the book of life (Exodus 32:32; Daniel 12:1). This powerful metaphor is also reminiscent of God's pronouncement to Adam and Eve in the Garden of Eden, "Dust you are, and unto dust you shall return" (Genesis 3:19).

It indicates with great finality the fate of those who turn away from the Source of All Life.

Yet Jesus not only knew the hearts of those making the accusation against the woman, He also knew the Law of Moses and was presently fulfilling it, in their hearing and in their seeing. He then raised Himself up and made His famous pronouncement, *"He who is without sin among you, let him be the first to throw a stone at her"* (John 8:7). With these words, He acknowledged the valid application of the Law of Moses to the situation before Him and ratified the punishment as given in the statutes. However, He did not leave the matter there. In calling for those who carried out the sentence to be "without sin" He was identifying another Mosaic requirement for the proposed action, namely that witnesses to a crime should have pure and dispassionate hearts:

"If a malicious witness rises up against a man to accuse him of wrongdoing then both the men who have the dispute shall stand before the Lord ... and if the witness is a false witness you shall do to him just as he had intended to do to his brother" (Deuteronomy 19:16-19)

The Law made very clear that only an objective, non-malevolent witness could testify in a legal matter and Jesus, through His enunciation of the "without sin" principle, was questioning the validity of the scribes and Pharisees as witnesses to this particular transgression. He knew they were testifying against the woman not out of a blameless heart of concern for justice in Israel, nor out of zeal for the holy Name of God; rather their intentions were so malignant that they were prepared to sacrifice another individual, one made in the image of God, in order to attain their purposes. Moreover, the Law was clear that if the witnesses were indeed motivated by evil inclinations they were subject to the very punishment they had proposed for the adulteress. It is noticeable also that, throughout the scene, Jesus never stood up but rather was sitting: the position of *Judge*.

As the saying of Jesus fell upon their ears, the accusers of the woman, who until that point had been so vocal, were silenced. Deeply, sharply, pierced His words into each conscience, bringing a stunned realization of the veracity of His judgment. One by one the Pharisees walked out of the Temple area, the oldest going first, suggesting that those who were most familiar with the scriptures recognized more quickly their guilt under the very Mosaic Law by which they had proposed to judge the woman.

Jesus remained on the scene, still bent over and writing, with the woman standing before him. In Augustine's words, "The two were left alone, *misera et misericordia*" - "a wretched woman and Mercy". Then Jesus straightened up and said to the adulteress, "Woman, where are those accusers of yours? Has no one condemned you?" This was a technical legal question, for witnesses were required before guilt could be established and a sentence passed. She answered, "No one Lord." And Jesus spoke to her the words which overflowed with His forgiving mercy and love, and have comforted generations of believers: *"Neither do I condemn you; go and sin no more"* (John 8:11).

As Jesus had already stated, He had not come to condemn the world (John 3:17), for the world stood already condemned by the Law of Moses; rather, He had come to save the world from the judgment that it merited: Moses had given the Law, but He had brought grace and truth. Furthermore, He had come not merely to forgive, but to lift up and exalt. One of the overriding concerns of the Apostle John in the Fourth Gospel was to present Jesus as the One who provided a new beginning for the people of God, so that many parallels may be discerned between this book and Genesis. In this particular episode of the Woman Taken in Adultery a clear comparison is drawn between Jesus as Second Adam and the first man in the Garden of Eden who so quickly placed the blame for his transgression upon the woman, Eve: "The woman you gave me," he said to God in desperate self-justification, *"she* gave me of the tree, and I ate" (Genesis 3:12).

But now, in this incomparable Gospel story, Jesus spoke gently and tenderly to this one to whom He gave the title "Woman", just as Eve and Mary were also called "Woman." In using this address, Jesus was raising up this former sinner as an image of the whole church, whom He will present to Himself "without spot or wrinkle or any such thing, that she might be holy and without blame before Him in love" (Ephesians 5:27;1:5) – the ultimate purpose of God's plan of redemption. The woman was, in this instant, translated from adulteress to bride, washed through the forgiving word of Christ, restored and renewed through His matchless love. The writer of the famous medieval hymn "Dies Irae" extols this mercy:

King of Majesty tremendous,
Who does free salvation send us,
Fount of pity, then befriend us!
Think, kind Jesu! - my salvation
Caused thy wondrous Incarnation,
Leave me not to reprobation!
Fain and weary, thou hast sought me,
On the Cross of suffering bought me.
Shall such grace be mainly brought me?
Through the sinful woman shriven,
Through the dying thief forgiven,
Thou to me a hope hast given.
Lord, all-pitying, Jesus blest,
Grant them thine eternal rest. Amen.

THE WINTER FEASTS: HANUKKAH, CHRISTMAS and PURIM

The Beautiful Shepherd

. . . .

One of Jesus' greatest discourses, gleaming with a wealth of wisdom and spiritual revelation, is recorded in the 10th Chapter of John's Gospel. He delivered this message during the Feast of Dedication (Hanukkah), the annual celebration of the victory of the Maccabees over the pagan forces which sought the assimilation and eventual annihilation of the Jewish people. It was the season of winter and Jesus was walking in Solomon's porch, the area adjacent to the large hall attached to the original Temple. It was here that the king of Israel had delivered his famous judgments and according to Josephus the porch was still standing in Jesus' day. But now a greater than Solomon had come, and in His discourse included the following words:

"Truly I say to you, I am the door of the sheep. All who came before Me are thieves and robbers, but the sheep did not hear them. I am the door. If anyone enters by Me, he will be saved, and will go in and out and find pasture. The thief does not come except to steal, and to kill, and to destroy. I come so that they may have life, and that they may have it more abundantly" (John 10:9-10)

The statement, *"All who came before me are thieves and robbers"*, has caused considerable perplexity: to whom was Jesus referring in this devastating critique? He was most surely not alluding to Moses and the prophets, the great succession of teachers and spiritual leaders in Israel who came before Him. Their number included John the Baptist, whom He had described in this Gospel as "the greatest of those born among women". The emphasis in His statement must rather be on the word "come", referring to those who "come" in their own strength or wisdom when not sent or authorized by God. In fact, Jesus' words can be illuminated greatly when the confluence of historical events leading up to His own era is considered.

With the Babylonian exile in 586 BC, Israel had ceased to be an independent nation. The Persian king Cyrus the Great, who took Babylon from Belshazzar while he was drinking wine from the priceless Temple vessels, permitted the Jews to return to their land - yet they remained under Persian domination until Alexander the Great defeated Darius. But at that point a new and insidious threat to Israel emerged: Alexander was committed to the creation of a world united by Greek language and culture, a policy followed by his successors. After his death (323 BC) the empire he won was divided among his generals, two of whom founded dynasties - the Ptolemies of Egypt and the Seleucids in Syria - which contended for control of Judea for over a century.

In 198 BC the Seleucids gained ascendancy in the Levant, paving the way for one of the most illustrious episodes in Jewish history. Antiochus IV Epiphanes ("God made manifest") adopted a policy of radical Hellenization and in pursuit of this aim brought his army to Jerusalem, slaughtered 40,000 people and sent an equal number into slavery. His system of tyranny and torture culminated in an ultimate outrage - the setting up of a statue of Zeus in the Temple and the sacrificing of a pig upon the holy altar. Mattathias, an aged priest of Modein and father of five noble sons, raised the cry of war and freedom and instigated the Maccabean revolt, in which the third son Judas Maccabee ("Hammer") took command of an irregular army of insurgents, overthrew the Syrians, and rededicated the Temple (167 BC). After a lapse of nearly three centuries the political independence of Judea had finally been restored, and it was this miraculous victory that came to be celebrated as the Festival of Hanukkah.

In the aftermath of the episode in which the "abomination of desolation" had been set up in the Temple, a large assembly of Jewish citizens met and, in gratitude for the courage and inspiring leadership of the family, nominated the last living son of Mattathias, Simon, as their perpetual leader. He became the founder of the Hasmonean dynasty, and under the rule of his descendants Jewish life flourished for a time, whilst the kingdom regained boundaries not far short of Solomon's realm. But this state of affairs was not to last: the new government soon began to evolve into an aristocratic, Hellenistic regime, sometimes hard to distinguish from that of the Seleucids - and there was a further cause for disquiet. The Hasmoneans not only assigned to themselves royal status, but also arraigned the power of the Temple priesthood, a dual role without precedent in Jewish history. Rabbinic commentary noted that the Hasmoneans were "saints of the most high, without whom the Torah would have been forgotten from Israel"; however, when they contravened the traditional expectation that the kings of Israel should be descended from the House of David, their fate became sealed.

Signs of decline and widespread corruption within the ruling family soon began to show themselves, as the Hasmonean kings (and queens) began to expand their power by means of conquest, forced Judaization, and mass executions of their opponents. The people became torn by bitter partisan controversies and the political situation reached a nadir with the emergence of Alexander Jannaeus around 100 BC, when as many as 50,000 died in a civil war in which the Pharisees sided against him and his Hellenized party of Sadducees. Josephus reports in his *Antiquities* that Jannaeus brought 800 rebels to Jerusalem and: *"As he was feasting with his concubines, in the sight of all the city, he ordered about eight hundred of them to be crucified."* The original legendary exploits of the Maccabees had set in motion a train of events leading inexorably to a tragic and inglorious ending.

Rome meanwhile was strengthening herself by lengthy wars for the great task of world conquest that lay before her, extending her territorial power and inspiring dread throughout the known world. Italy and Africa, Greece, Asia Minor and the northern barbarians were conquered in turn: the kingdom of iron was emerging with invincible might. Then in 63 BC a dynastic clash between the two sons of Janneus, Aristobulus II and Hyrcanus II, gave Rome the opportunity to intervene in the affairs of Judea. The Roman general Pompey took Jerusalem after a three-month siege of the Temple area, massacring priests in the performance of their duties, entering the Most Holy Place, and forever alienating the citizens of the land. The Jews once again were conquered and oppressed, and Roman rule would be a fact of Jewish life for centuries to come.

Pompey was assassinated in 48 BC and shortly after Julius Caesar played a critical role in the events that led to the demise of the Roman Republic and the rise of the Empire. One of the greatest military commanders in history, he conquered Gaul and extended Rome's rule as far as Britain in less than a decade. During this time, according to Plutarch, his army fought against three million men of whom one million died and another million were enslaved. With the Gallic Wars concluded, the Senate ordered Caesar to lay down his military command and return to Rome. Caesar marked his defiance by crossing the Rubicon with a legion in 49 BC, and illegally entering Roman territory under arms. The ensuing civil war resulted in the deaths of untold numbers, and Caesar emerged as the unrivaled leader of Rome. Yet although he had secured his own position and glory the underlying conflicts had not been resolved, and in 44 BC Caesar too was assassinated, and his heir Octavian, later known as Augustus, rose to sole power.

As the period between the Testaments drew to a close, Rome had become the undisputed mistress of the world: the era of the great *Pax Romana* had begun. At that point the Romans gave the Jews a show of independence by making Judea a client kingdom. Onto its throne, they put an Idumean collaborator named Herod, who gained a show of legitimacy by marrying a Hasmonean princess, Mariamne.

These are the momentous events which shed a clarifying light upon the words of Jesus which He spoke at the Feast of Hanukkah. His statement exposed the true nature of those who seized power over the nations by force of arms and superior military strength: they are cruel plunderers of the people, and because their hearts are corrupted by power their actions inevitably result in violence, class warfare and destruction. But Jesus' words go further than this: they included not only those who came to wield political might but all those who came claiming to possess the spiritual keys to the hidden wisdom which would bring benefaction to humanity - for neither did these have the true welfare of the flock at heart; nor have the myriad ideologies swaying the hearts of men and women since time began brought true freedom and blessing. When Jesus spoke of those coming "before Him", He also said they "are" (present tense) thieves and robbers, a sweeping statement which subsumed not only those of His own day who came seeking personal ascendancy and power, but all who would come in succeeding centuries.

"I am the door," said Jesus, another assertion vast in its import. It is He alone who is able to open or shut the door of heaven; He and no other is the One through whom access to God becomes possible - and according to the message He brought the only way that leads to the Father above is the way of service and love. Nevertheless, Jesus assured all those who heard His words and received His message that they would experience fullness of life and blessing on earth, they would experience the *summum bonum* He had come to bestow. He then uttered another phrase which has brought indescribable comfort to so many of His followers since that long-ago day in the Temple. *"I am the good shepherd,"* He said - simple words with an enormous depth of meaning, which paint one of the great portraits of His true role and identity.

The picture of the shepherd has been intricately woven into the language and imagery of the Bible. The main part of Judea is a central plateau, stretching from Bethel to Hebron for a distance of about 35 miles with ground mostly rough and stony, so that Judea was much more a pastoral than an agricultural country. It was inevitable, therefore, that the most familiar figure of the region was the shepherd. George Adam Smith in his *Historical Geography of the Holy Land* offered some reflections on the grandeur of this singular character: *" On some high moor, across which at night hyenas howl, when you meet him, sleepless, far-sighted, armed, leaning on his staff, and looking out over his scattered sheep, every one on his heart, you understand why the shepherd of Judea sprang to the front in his people's history; why they gave his name to their king, and made him the symbol of Providence; why Christ took him as the type of self-sacrifice ..."*

The earliest patriarchs of the nation were all keepers of flocks - these were the most regal shepherds of all time. Dwelling in tents under sun and stars, often wandering from nation to nation, they yet brought down from heaven truths holy and sublime which they passed on to succeeding generations. Moses, the great prophet of the Exodus, adopted this role, and the founder of Israel's first kingly dynasty, David, was "taken from following the flocks" (2 Samuel 7:8). Yet although many of the leaders of Israel were called shepherds, the prophet Ezekiel understood that God was the supreme Shepherd of His people, who would search for his scattered flock, gather them from the nations and lead them to rich pasture on the mountains of Israel, who would bind up the weak and injured but would judge those sheep who tended only themselves (Ezekiel 34:11-22). When Jesus called Himself the Good Shepherd He was declaring that, in Him, God had come to shepherd His people and demonstrate these divine actions of compassionate care.

But Jesus also passed beyond Old Testament conceptions as He continued His discourse and further defined that role: the Good Shepherd is the one who "gives His life for the sheep". Jesus as Shepherd does not merely risk his life for His flock; He will undergo a voluntary and vicarious death for them, for only in this way will His sheep receive the abundant life He has come to bring - a fullness of existence which transcended anything ever before available. In Greek, there are two words for good: *agathos,* which describes the moral quality of a person or thing, and *kalos*, which describes that which is not only good, but also noble, honorable and beautiful. When Jesus named Himself as the Good Shepherd, the word He used was *kalos*: Christ is *ho poimein ho kalos*. In this way He gave an image which referenced not only His inherent goodness and righteousness, but revealed that in such characteristics may be discerned an all-surpassing loveliness.

As Jesus fulfilled His task as a shepherd to the utmost extent possible, as He lay down His life for the sheep, there would be made visible in Him something so full of winsome appeal and heroic splendor that it would draw all people (John 12:32). The perfection of the Lord's character will attract all those whose hearts are able to perceive and respond to divine beauty - for in this death is revealed the heart of God Himself, since God is love, and love is the laying down of one's life (1 John 3:16). In Jesus is seen the grace and glory of the divine character, which impresses itself upon the heart with incomparable and radiant magnetism. Therefore Jesus may be described not just as the Good Shepherd; He is also the Beautiful Shepherd of the beautiful flock (Jeremiah 13:20) which God has given Him.

The Heroes of Israel -
A Personal Account

··

December is a wonderful month here in Israel, for first of all Christians may join with the Jewish people in celebrating the Feast of Hanukkah, occurring on 25 Kislev according to the Hebrew calendar. This is the memorial of the bravery of the Maccabeean brothers who, in the face of tremendous odds, delivered their country out of the hands of their Gentile oppressors and restored the true worship of God in the land. How inspiring were their exploits as they took up arms against their Syrian overlords and defeated them; and how miraculous the recapture of the desecrated Temple, the setting up of the great altar of burnt offering and relighting of the sacred flame! Yet it is not only Hanukkah, but also Christmas, which followers of Jesus may celebrate during this month.

The two festivals actually share much in common. The events they commemorate are separated by a comparatively small number of years - the story of the Maccabeean revolt in 167 BC was the final attempt of the Jewish people to seek deliverance from domination before the birth of Jesus and many of the heroes of that story even bear the same names as New Testament characters – the father Mattathias (Matthew), the five brothers Judah (Jude), Simon (Simon Peter), Yochanan (John), Eleazar (Lazarus) and Jonathan. Above all, however, both festivals are focused upon the themes of salvation and deliverance.

From the beginning, the Children of Israel were told of a coming Messiah who would emerge from their midst and usher in a great age of redemption and blessing. As the people of promise, they became subject throughout their long history to many threats of annihilation, from Pharaoh in Egypt, through the Babylonians, Persians, the Greeks under Alexander, then finally, before the might of Rome overpowered all, the Ptolemies and Seleucids. Had the Jewish people been destroyed or assimilated, the Messianic prophecies would never have come to pass, yet the scriptures record that the sovereignty and faithfulness of God preserved them through all their vicissitudes. With the Maccabeean victory, God once again intervened on behalf of His ancient people, but it can then be seen in the Christmas narrative that these same forces of destruction were turned upon the newborn Child. Miraculously, however, He was sheltered and kept by the determinate counsel and foreknowledge of God.

A Modern Hero

It was during Hanukkah that my husband and I learned of another more recent feat of heroism, and were reminded that this is still the season of miracles. On the last day of the feast we were scheduled to travel with other members of Christ Church Jerusalem for a congregational weekend in the north of the country. At this point the land was desperately in need of rain - and lo, a great storm, an unparalleled storm, was forecast - for the very weekend of our trip! About 40 of us arrived at Beit Bracha (House of Blessing) on the beautiful shores of the Sea of Galilee on the Friday evening. The next morning, just as we set out for the tour, thunder rumbled overhead, lightning rent the skies, and the rain came down in great sheets. And so it was to the sound of an abundance of rain that we made our way into the heart of the Golan Heights.

As we traveled further north, leaving far behind the Sea of Galilee with its calm turquoise waters sheltered peacefully in the encompassing hills, we noted the striking alteration in the landscape. Ahead were the tangled precipices of Mount Hermon, towering and snow-covered. Black basalt stone everywhere littered the ground, evidence of the formerly volcanic nature of the region; the terrain seemed ancient and convoluted, hills folding over ravines and tumbling into valleys. Nevertheless, agricultural and kibbutz enterprises have established thriving communities throughout the area, making it one of the most productive in the country. We also noted the strategic importance of the area: the Golan Heights as the "defensive wall" for the State of Israel. But above all, we were aware of *"old unhappy far-off things, and battles long ago"*. So many campaigns fought in this area, so many monuments to amazing valor, from the time of Josephus and the battle at Gamla in the first century, to the twentieth century struggles for Israel's survival.

David Pileggi, Rector of Christ Church and tour guide *par excellence*, is acquainted with some of the most intriguing and out-of-the-way places in Israel. One of our stops on that memorable day made a particular impact on the members of our group. We arrived at a kibbutz on the lower slopes of Mt Hermon, very close to the Syrian border, and dashed through the torrential downpour to the shelter of the kibbutz dining room and gift shop. Attached to this reception area was a small theater, where we were shown a film about the events which transpired close to the kibbutz during the Yom Kippur War of 1973, the battle over the Valley of Tears, *Emek HaBacha*. This remarkable short movie, called "Oz 77" (*oz* is the Hebrew word for "strength"), immerses the viewer in the experience of the Israeli soldiers during that crisis.

On October 6th 1973, the Day of Atonement, four Syrian Sukhoi airplanes suddenly appeared in the sky over the Golan Heights and bombed the Israeli military headquarters. The volcanic heights were completely covered with deadly fire and pillars of black smoke: it was clear a new war had begun. Israeli intelligence estimated that Syria had more than 900 tanks and 140 batteries of artillery immediately behind the Syrian line. Israel was unprepared, and hopelessly outnumbered in terms of fighting men and equipment. Over the following days, Syria launched a formidable attack from a valley north of Kuneitra, a primary penetration axis for their men and tanks. They planned to take control of the central

Golan Heights, a point from which they could move easily into Israel. The engagement with enemy tanks that ensued there on the fields of Kibbutz El Rom on the threshold of the valley was a battle of life or death.

On the fourth day of the war, October 9th, the conflict reached its climax. A bloody day-long battle took place between massive Syrian armored forces belonging to the Assad Republican Guard, and a handful of Israeli tanks, holding exhausted reservists led by battalion commander Avigdor Kahalani who commanded the 77th "Oz" Regiment belonging to the 7th Brigade, commanded by Avigdor Ben-Gal. Early on the day, the Syrians hit the Israeli positions with a massive barrage of accurate artillery and rocket fire. As the fighting ground on, the 7th Armored Brigade was down to only 7 of the 105 tanks with which it had started the battle; each tank had only about four rounds remaining. The remnants of the Brigade were completely surrounded and fighting at 360 degrees. A small number of reinforcements arrived, and Ben-Gal ordered Kahalani to hold back the Syrian forces. With a total of only 15 tanks, and almost zero ammunition, Kahalani made the decision to advance. It was a heart-stopping moment, and also an amazing demonstration of leadership, recorded live in the film we watched.

Kahalani was not sure at this point in the battle which of his men could hear him; he knew also how seemingly hopeless their position was. He could not bring himself to order his men to advance to almost certain death. "I am moving forward," he broadcast to them. "If anyone wants to follow me, you may do so." The other tanks followed his lead. Crashing into the Syrian left flank, the tiny force knocked out 30 Syrian tanks in short order. The unexpected attack stunned the Syrians, who assumed it was the point element of a large Israeli reserve that had finally reached the battlefield. Just on the verge of punching through into northern Galilee, the Syrians broke contact and started to withdraw along the line; their advance was effectively halted. Behind them they left over 500 tanks and anti-personnel carriers in the battleground which is known today as the Valley of Tears. The surviving members of the 7th Armored Brigade had been in combat for more than 50 straight hours and Kahalani was later awarded the Medal of Valor, Israel's highest combat decoration. Ben Gal told Kahalani, "You are the true savior of Israel".

Afterwards we stood together on a low mound overlooking *Emek HaBacha* and gazed over its desolate fields stretching away to the north-east, where lay Syria and Damascus, with a knife-like wind whipping through our layers of clothing. It seemed a fitting setting for meditation upon the story of dauntless courage we had just heard. As we did so, it seemed that other narratives of heroism made their presence felt insistently in our minds and imaginations; and naturally these included the story of one of the great figures of the Hebrew Scriptures - Samson.

Samson, the Archetypal Hero

The Book of Judges tells the story of the children of Israel during the centuries which elapsed between the time of their conquering the Promised Land under Joshua and the beginning of the monarchy. It is structured in a series of seven cycles, each repeating the same story: the nation of Israel would sin and begin to worship idols, God would place them under the dominion of one of the neighboring nations, they would then repent of their sin and call out to Him for deliverance and He would raise up for them a savior in the person of one of the judges. For a while there would be peace and prosperity – but as soon as the judge died the children of Israel would apostatize again, and the cycle would recommence. The story of Samson occurs in the seventh and final of these cycles.

As the last and ultimate deliverer, Samson - "splendor of the sun" - has more attention devoted to him than to any other judge. His birth was foretold by the Angel of the Lord, who informed his parents of the child's wondrous future: that he would be a Nazirite from the womb, totally consecrated to God, and would also *"begin"* to deliver Israel from the Philistines. Samson was born and grew up at a time when Israel was greatly menaced by these implacable foes and the overriding desire of his life was to do the work of the promised seed (Genesis 3:15), who would save Israel from their enemies.

As he grew to manhood the Spirit of the Lord began to stir him, equipping him with extraordinary strength and enabling him to carry out his legendary exploits. One of these occurred as he made his way to Timnah in Philistine territory: a young lion rushed toward him, but the Spirit of the Lord likewise rushed upon the hero, empowering him to tear the beast limb from limb. Later, he took honey from the carcass of the lion and composed his famous riddle *"Out of the one who eats came something to eat; Out of the strong one came something sweet"* (Judges 14:14). On another occasion he went to the Philistine city of Gaza and visited a harlot; when the Gazans heard that Samson had come, they lay in wait for him all night at the gate of the city. There was Samson, compassed in by his enemies, but at midnight he arose, took hold of the gates of the city as well as the two gateposts, pulled them up "bar and all", put them on his shoulders, and carried them to the top of the hill that faces Hebron – 38 miles from Gaza. The Hebrew used for Samson "taking away" the gates is that translated "possess" in the promises made to Abraham: *"Your descendants shall possess the gate of their enemies"* (Genesis 22:17).

Samson's mission came to its climax in his tragic but magnificent death, the story of which is justly famous. He loved a woman in the Valley of Sorek whose name was Delilah, but when the Philistines offered her eleven hundred pieces of silver to find the secret of his great strength she agreed. Samson at first resisted her enticements, but when she vexed his soul "almost to death", he finally revealed to her the significance of his Nazirite vow: "If I am shaven, then my strength will leave me, and I will become weak as any other man" (Judges 16:16). When Delilah saw that he had told her all his heart, she lulled him to sleep on her knees, called for a man and had him shave off the seven locks of Samson's head.

Then she cried out as before: "The Philistines are upon you Samson". And his strength went from him because God had departed from him, so he was unable to shake himself free from his antagonists.

In the final heartbreaking scene, this great hero is pictured in his utter betrayal and humiliation, his eyes gouged out by the Philistines, his feet bound with fetters, forced to grind the mill and subjected to the derision of his captors - and yet his hair began to grow again. Then came a day when the Philistines called for him to perform for them in their temple, where 3000 men and women were gathered on the roof to watch. And Samson in unparalleled intensity of prayer called upon the name of his Lord: "Remember me O God... strengthen me, I pray". And he took hold of the two middle pillars which supported the temple, braced himself against them, and said, *"Let me die with the Philistines. And he bowed himself with all his might; and the house fell upon the lords, and upon all the people that were therein. So the dead which he slew at his death were more than they which he slew in his life"* (Judges 16:30). Samson, made weak by a woman, out of weakness was made strong by pure faith (Hebrews 11:34).

All these things suggest that Samson was a striking type of Christ, as were the other judges whom God raised up to rescue His weak and failing people. Samson's words and actions indicate that he was a man dedicated to God, yet despite this he made some sad errors. When he first traveled to Timnah to take a wife from the land of the Philistines, he ordered his parents: "Get her for me, because she is the right one for me." A better translation would be "because she is *right in my eyes*". Samson thus pictured the spiritual condition of the Israelites at that time: "In those days, there was no king in Israel; every man did what was right in his own eyes" (Judges 17:6). So it was that Samson could only "begin" to deliver Israel, as was foretold. And yet the "great deliverance" wrought by him (Judges 15:18) foreshadowed one which was even greater.

THE GREATEST DELIVERER

When the Angel Gabriel appeared to Mary in Nazareth to make his announcement of the birth of a Son, he told her that the Child would be called Jesus - *Saviour*. The Angel next appeared to Joseph in a dream and revealed the reason for that name: "He will save His people" - not from the Midianites or the Moabites, the Philistines or the Romans, not from political bondage - but "from their sins". He would deliver "those who through fear of death were all their lifetime subject to bondage" (Hebrews 2:15). And the manner in which He would accomplish such salvation? - "Through death He would destroy him who had the power of death, that is, the devil" (Hebrews 2:14). And so with the birth of Jesus the great conflict of the ages reached its climax.

From the very beginning of the story of Jesus, from His nativity, there were intimations of this conflict. See the Babe wrapped in His swaddling clothes, lying in the manger! The Angel who appeared to the shepherds in the field, keeping watch over their flocks by night, informed them it was by this sign that they would know the Savior had been born. It was a sign of His birth, but also of His death: the swaddling clothes spoke of the graveclothes which would be wrapped about His body, while the stone trough of the manger prefigured the rocky tomb in which He would be laid. And the conflict unleashed with the birth of this Child was set in motion by the visit of Wise Men – Gentiles – who came to Jerusalem to enquire concerning the newborn King of the Jews. Herod, exceedingly angry, learned of the birthplace of the Messiah and slaughtered all the male children in Bethlehem who were two years old and under, according to the time he had determined from the Magi.

When Mary and Joseph brought the Infant Jesus to the Temple to present Him to the Lord as required by the Law, the just and devout Simeon, who was awaiting the consolation of Israel, took Jesus into his arms and proclaimed his readiness to die in peace: "My eyes have seen Your salvation, which You have prepared before the face of all peoples"

(Luke 2:30-31). Simeon's peace was not because he had an expectation that the Messiah would bring only joy and prosperity to His people; rather, he knew that Jesus would be a sign spoken against and that many would fall because of Him. Simeon's peace was in the assurance that God keeps his word and somehow, beyond all the conflict to come, salvation would prevail. Simeon also understood that the beneficiaries of God's deliverance were not Jews only but also Gentiles, that the mercy shown to Israel would overflow to bring the light of revelation to all the nations.

And when that Child was full-grown and about His Father's business - as He went about doing good and healing all who were oppressed – He made a conscious allusion to Samson's wordplay over the dead lion with the sweet honey in it. He Himself was the One who had come to bind the strong man and plunder his house (Matthew 12:29) and through His victory the roaring lion of the devil was defeated. The story of Samson's shameful final days also prefigured the humiliation suffered by Jesus as He undertook the payment for the sins of all humanity, while Samson's final great effort, bowing himself (in Hebrew *natah*, "stretching himself out to his full extension") with all his spiritual and physical energy foreshadowed the tremendous cost to the Savior of His atoning death on the cross. It was through this great feat of deliverance Jesus has brought "many sons to glory" - and there are yet further blessings to come as His kingdom continues to be extended throughout the earth.

The splendor and glory that godly Israelites longed for with the coming of their Messiah was pictured in this way by Zechariah, the father of John the Baptist (Luke 1:71-75): they were to be delivered from the oppression of their enemies, all the covenant promises would be fulfilled, and they would be enabled to serve God in holiness and righteousness all the days of their life. That did not happen at Jesus' first coming, for Israel as a nation rejected her Messiah - and yet through this very rejection a tidal wave of grace was released in the world so that salvation came to the Gentiles. But God is not done with Israel yet. Paul explains in Romans 11 that, *"A hardening has come in part upon Israel until the full number of the Gentiles comes in and so all Israel will be saved; as it is written: 'The Deliverer will come from Zion and He will banish ungodliness from Jacob'."* And thus will be fulfilled Simeon's prophecy that Jesus will also be a light "for glory to Your people Israel."

And what is our response to all these things? As he showed us the film "Oz 77" in Kibbutz El Rom, the young kibbutznik made the following remark: "Every day we remember and are grateful for everything that the 7th Brigade has done for us in saving the land and keeping our freedom". How much more should we be remembering the great atoning death and sacrifice of Jesus - all for love! The seventeenth century Bishop Lancelot Andrewes made this point in a sermon before the King in Whitehall one Christmas, referring to the song of the angels at Jesus' birth. Part of that address is as follows:

"They emptied heaven, this multitude of angels, to sing glory in honor of the One laid in the manger. Now to have Angels come by one and by two as at the birth of Samson and others is notable; but the grand Savior of all must be lauded by His troops of them, the Lord of Hosts Himself must be attended by the whole army. For at His birth was fulfilled that which the Apostle speaks of in Hebrews 1.6: 'When He brings His only-begotten Son into the world He saith, Let all the Angels of God worship Him' - let the whole host of Heaven do Him honor.

And thus this heavenly host comes, wearing the habit of war, but singing the song of peace - by virtue of Christ's Nativity, there is peace to earth from heaven, good-will to men from God. The blessed Angels rejoice and sing at the good of others, but those whom it concerns are to do it with far greater reason, and that is ourselves, to whom solely and wholly this birth and the benefit of this birth redounds. The choir of heaven did but take it up this song; we are to keep it up, and never to let it go down or die on our hands, but from year to year still to renew it."

The Shepherds Visit the Newborn Child

Esther - Revealing the Hidden

....

"If winter comes can spring be far behind?" In late February and March, the harbingers of spring in Jerusalem are the almond trees which line the streets, as they begin to blossom and send myriads of petals falling in drifts upon the sidewalks. The Holy City appears to don bridal attire for the season and one viewing this scene is reminded of God's declaration to the prophet Jeremiah as he saw the branch of an almond tree blossoming: *"I am watching over My word to perform it"* (Jeremiah 1:12). The linguistic connection between the Hebrew words "almond" (*shaqed*) and "watching" (*shaqad*) indicates that, just as the almond tree is the first to blossom in the spring, so it is certain that God will bring to pass the other promises He has made.

Other scriptures are also brought to remembrance in Israel during this time; in fact, a whole book is recalled, the *Megillah* or Scroll of Esther. This small jewel, only 12 chapters long, is read in the synagogues at Purim, the feast which celebrates the deliverance of the Jewish people from the plot to annihilate them while they were dwelling in the Kingdom of Persia. The Book of Esther is the only text set entirely in a place of exile; every other book in the Hebrew Scriptures is either based on events that happened *in* Israel or on the journey *toward* Israel. In this place far from the land, the place of *hester panim* ("the concealed face"), it is perhaps more challenging for the Jewish people to sense the presence of God. This is also suggested by the surprising fact that there is no mention of the name of the Hebrew Deity to be found anywhere in the scroll.

This omission of the name of God from the text has prompted various theological explanations, which include the following: that in this way the narrative suggests the presence of a providential Deity who, while not seen to be overtly directing the outcome of the plot, is nevertheless powerfully working "behind the scenes" to ensure that His benevolent designs are eventually brought to pass. The sacred name "YHWH" may be discovered woven into the text in acrostic fashion in several places, while the title of the book, *Megillah Esther*, also indicates that the book offers a depth of concealed wisdom which must be sought out. The word *megillah* comes from the root Hebrew word *galah,* meaning "to reveal", based on *galal* ("to roll"), in the sense of rolling away a covering. Hence the contents of a *megillah* or scroll unveil something which previously had been hidden from view, or "rolled up". This theme of concealment is underscored by the name of the heroine, Esther, which consists of three consonants "s-t-r", which designate the word "hidden" in Hebrew; in Deuteronomy 31:18 God says to Israel, "I will surely hide (*hastir astir*) My face from you." Thus *Megillah Esther* may be translated to mean "Revealing the Hidden".

So it is that one has to probe a little more deeply to uncover the spiritual dimension of the plot. Outwardly, all is glamour and opulence: the story is set in the courts and palaces of Shushan, capital of the mightiest empire upon earth at the time, while the characters themselves – the princes and rulers, the eunuchs and officials of the King's household, the nobles and courtiers - function at the highest levels of government. However, the lavish banquets and rich surroundings, the revelry and royal protocol which dominate the opening scenes at first provide a seemingly impassable barrier to understanding the fundamental game of life and death being played out at the highest levels of state. Only briefly are glimpses given in these glittering court scenes of the rivalry and plotting which dominate the inner workings of the King's palace, for the corridors of power in the ancient world were as rife with intrigue and power struggles as in the present day. At the same time the protagonists themselves seem to wear masks and disguise their true identities, so that only gradually the motives and passions which govern their hearts and direct their actions are divulged.

As a whole the book evokes the danger that so often has confronted the Jewish people when they live in exile, away from their land. Jews were a minority in the vast Persian Empire, and *Megillah Esther* depicts the threat that suddenly arose for them in the person of Haman, chief minister of King Ahasuerus. Offended by the fact that Mordechai, a Jew, refused to bow or pay homage to him, he went to the King and made the following allegation: *"There is a certain people scattered and dispersed among the other peoples in all the provinces of your kingdom; their laws are different from all other people's and they do not obey the king's laws. Therefore it is not fitting for the king to let them remain"* (Esther 3:8). His insinuation was that the Jews were a subversive fifth column in the midst of the land and this, together with the considerable sum paid into the royal treasuries, persuaded the King to act swiftly against these suspicious foreigners. A decree signed by him on the 13th day of the first month and sealed with his signet was dispatched to each of the provinces, instructing that all Jews, young and old, children and women, should be "destroyed, killed and annihilated" on the 14th day of the twelfth month, Adar. The couriers went out in haste and the King and Haman sat down to drink.

It was a catastrophic situation for the Jewish people - but a light arose in the darkness as a hero came upon the scene. The beautiful Jewish maiden Esther who had been adopted and raised by her uncle Mordecai had entered the royal palace after the King decided to select a new queen from amongst the loveliest young women in the land. Esther concealed her Jewish identity at Mordecai's behest and eventually the King, unaware of her family and heritage, placed the royal crown upon her head. And so it came to pass that this man to whom she had joined herself in marriage set his seal upon a decree to annihilate her people. When Mordechai learned of the fate assigned to the Jews, he appealed to Esther to go before the King and plead their cause, but she felt at first an understandable reluctance. She had not been called to go in to the King for many days, and the penalty for appearing unsummoned in his presence was death - unless the King should extend clemency to her by holding out his golden scepter. But when Esther expressed her fears, Mordechai responded with the famous words:

"If you remain completely silent at this time, relief and deliverance will arise for the Jews from another place, but you and your father's house will perish. Yet who knows whether you have come to the kingdom for such a time as this?" (Esther 4:14)

With that, Esther rose to the full height of her calling, and revealed herself as a true daughter of Israel who trod steadfastly in the steps of the men and women of faith who had gone before her. A mantle of royal authority appeared to descend upon her as she announced her plan of preparation to go before the King, then uttered a statement of sublime resolution - *"And if I perish, I perish"* (Esther 4:16). Her program succeeded beyond all imagining: she found grace and favor in the sight of the King, and the wicked Haman was unmasked and hung on the same gallows he had prepared for Mordechai. Although the King's decree concerning the annihilation of the Jews could not be revoked, he wrote a further edict giving the Jews authority to defend themselves against their adversaries on the same day which Haman had appointed for their destruction. And so, on the 13th day of the month of Adar, the day on which the enemies of the Jews had expected to get them in their power, the opposite happened and the Jews of Persia vanquished their enemies. It was Esther's ingenuity and courage which had saved her people and this great deliverance was decreed to be remembered each year at the Feast of Purim.

The tension between human freewill and God's purposes had played out to its fullest extent in the text. Both the King and Haman, who wielded the most earthly power in the story, acted in accordance with their own wishes and desires, seemingly taking no cognizance of the will of God. At the same time, Esther embarked on her course to bring deliverance to her people while denying her natural human impulses of fear and self-protection, and casting herself on the mercy and help of God. Yet as the plot unfolded the schemes of wickedness became exposed, a stunning reversal was effected, and God's overriding purposes of redemption and blessing become apparent. But although it was God's intention to save His people from annihilation, He did not accomplish this without the intercession and courage of this young Jewish woman. And as the Scroll of Esther is read more than two thousand years later, it becomes apparent that it is also a book "for such a time as this" – that is, for this very present moment in history.

The Rabbis were intrigued by the fact that in the Book of Esther the main action seemed to be completed by the seventh chapter with the downfall of Haman – and yet the storyline continues for another three chapters. However, this fact provides a key to unlocking the hidden symbolism of the timelines occurring in the narrative. A large part of the action of the plot – from the third chapter through the tenth chapter - takes place in the twelfth year of King Ahasuerus. It was during Nisan, the first month of the Hebrew sacred calendar that Haman cast lots (*purim*) to determine an auspicious day for the destruction of the Jewish people, and the decree for their annihilation was actually promulgated on 13th Nisan, the eve of Passover. Yet as it happened, the lot fell on 13th Adar – the twelfth or last month of the Jewish year. This suggests that the events which occurred in the twelfth year of the Persian king are also emblematic of the whole of redemption history, involving both Israel and the church.

By the end of the third month of this year, the wicked Haman had been unmasked and hanged, and the death of this Antichrist figure may be seen as representing the defeat of Satan and the powers of evil through Christ's cross and resurrection. Yet there remained still the ten sons of Haman as well as his servants to be dealt with, and the edict for the final destruction of all the enemies of the Jews authorized this to take place on the 13th Adar - the last month, which also represents the end of the church age, when the great battle and final judgement will occur. And so the era of the church is set to continue between First and Second Advents of the Messiah, during which time her members continue to look to Jesus, confident in the victory He has already won and sustained in their struggles by their faith in Him.

And Esther herself is key to victory for the church in her warfare against the principalities and powers of darkness which still appear to dominate the earth. Her story tells us that we too have been called "for such a time as this", to take part in a spiritual struggle of great intensity for which we have already been equipped with gifts and wisdom. It impels us to recognize the fact that God has known beforehand of the dangers we face and impresses upon us the need, wherever we are, to step out in faith and so deliver not just ourselves but others as well. Even though He may hide His face from us for a time, we may hear His voice sounding in the deep places of our heart: *"It is for this time you were called, for this particular purpose, and for this particular challenge."* When He does so, may each of us have the courage to answer "Here I am, send me"; to offer ourselves in sacrifice and love for His cause, and become channels of blessing to the world.

We can also recognize that the Jewish Queen has acted in a way which brought to pass, prophetically, one of the great promises of God. "Beauty" is a keyword in the Book of Esther, and in the 61st Chapter of the Prophet Isaiah, God promised His people that He would bring *"beauty for ashes"* – a fundamental wordplay in Hebrew, for ashes, *"epher"*, is an anagram of *"pa'ar"*, meaning beauty. And the word for "lot", *"pur"*, which lends its name to the festival which celebrates the Jewish deliverance on this occasion and contains similar consonants, bears an affinity with both these words. The connection is made apparent in the words of Israeli Rabbi Shlomo Riskin, writing in the *Jerusalem Post*. "In the final analysis," he writes:

"I believe that Purim legitimately celebrates Jewish survival in exile, a necessary survival since exile was the universal Jewish condition for 2,000 of the close to 4,000 years of Jewish history. And we survived despite the powerful forces of assimilation and anti-Semitism; we survived because of the image of God and the Jewish spirit-spark within each of us that refused to die, even if it had to go underground during the Spanish Inquisition, even if it had to blaze more brightly than the flames of the crematoria ..."

EASTER - REPRISE

The Cross for the World

Each Easter at Christ Church in Jerusalem's Old City, Rector David Pileggi displays behind the altar a copy of a painting by Marc Chagall entitled "White Crucifixion". Chagall, called "the quintessential Jewish artist of the twentieth century", is famed for his pictures of the Hassidic world and the Jewish *shtetl* or village, which blend elements from folklore and biblical themes in a dreamlike milieu of bright colors and joyous simplicity. Less familiar is his series of works which, unusually for a Jewish artist, portrays the death of Jesus; and his "White Crucifixion" evidences the profound spirituality of its creator, who once averred, *"When I paint, I pray"*.

Chagall was compelled to create the painting after the events of *Kristallnacht* or "Night of Broken Glass" which took place in Germany in November 1938, when Nazi pogroms were unleashed against the Jewish people, their synagogues burned and their homes and shops ransacked. The night of terror culminated in the arrest of thousands of Jews and their transportation to concentration camps, and as the events of the *Shoah* unfolded it seemed to Chagall that the image of the crucifixion alone could serve to demonstrate to an uncaring world the plight of European Jewry.

In the center of his picture is the figure of Jesus nailed to the cross, against a background of pure white light which streams from above. His head is surrounded by the traditional halo, but his Jewish identity is also very much emphasized. He is wrapped in a *tallith*, the Jewish prayer shawl, and above his head he bears the Hebrew inscription *"Jesus*

271

of Nazareth, King of the Jews". At his feet burns a menorah, while a Torah scroll below the cross emits a further supply of light which then moves up an unmoored ladder. This recalls the promises made to Jacob when he was forced into exile from his land, and the Lord God appeared to him above the ladder "whose top reached to heaven", on which the angels ascended and descended (Genesis 28:12).

But it is the scenes that surround the cross which cause Chagall's painting to depart most dramatically from other depictions of Jesus' death. Instead of the usual figures from the Gospels, a kaleidoscope of images shows the deadly contemporary attacks taking place upon the Jews: a Nazi plundering an ark from a flaming synagogue, Jewish refugees desperately attempting to flee by boat as their *shtetl* is set ablaze, soldiers of the Soviet Army waving flags. In the lower left an elderly man staggers imploringly towards the viewer, a placard fastened to his chest reading "*Ich bin Jude*", while at the bottom right of the picture is the figure of Elijah, dressed as the eternal Wandering Jew.

Above all, it is the image of the gentle, unresisting figure of Jesus on the cross which conveys the essential message of the painting. Chagall's Jesus is innocent, devout and holy, he is being punished without cause, crucified precisely because he is a Jew, while the biblical patriarchs Abraham, Isaac, Jacob, and the matriarch Rachel gaze down on the scene with unutterable sadness. Moreover, the burning menorah at the foot of the cross, with five of its six candles still flickering, lies toppled and the white light which suffuses the canvas also recalls the *kittel*, the shroud in which Jews are buried. It appears that this soft radiance illuminates not so much the hope of redemption, but rather the complete abandonment of that suffering figure on the cross.

Yet the painting was meant not only to pierce Christian indifference to the anguish of their Hebrew brethren – it called upon the Jewish people themselves to recognize that Jesus' hanging upon the cross represents the suffering of all Jews, not just in World War II, but throughout their stormy history. The Romans had used the cross extensively as a method of execution during the first centuries of the era, and in Judea tens of thousands had perished upon it. At the height of the Jewish War against Rome as many as 500 were crucified each day before the walls of Jerusalem, so that Josephus reported: *"Their number was so great that there was not enough room for the crosses and not enough crosses for the bodies."* It was in and through His cross, therefore, that Jesus became irrevocably identified with His people, and shared their anguish as His own.

But Marc Chagall saw his work as "not the dream of one people only but of all humanity". The execution of one particular condemned man by crucifixion almost twenty centuries ago, in a small province of the Roman Empire, is an event that has gripped the imaginations of men and women more than anything else which has occurred in history. And this stark emblem, the cross, this feared and loathed symbol of suffering, came eventually to be set up at the heart of the Christian religion, so that the Apostle Paul, in the letters that helped shape the faith of the early church, could speak of "glorying in the cross". How did the understanding of this instrument of execution become so transformed in Christian theology?

One answer is suggested by an important detail given in each of the Gospel accounts of the death of Jesus: *"Then two robbers were crucified with Him, one on the right and another on the left"* (Matthew 27:38). The cross of Christ did not appear in lonely isolation or solitary prominence, but was set between two other crosses in a terrible tableau which has etched itself upon human consciousness. It had been forecast long ago by the prophet Isaiah that Jesus would be "numbered with the transgressors" (Isaiah 53:12); that is, the Servant of the Lord, although himself sinless, would be punished along with malefactors. On the stakes on the right and left hand of Jesus were hanging two criminals who were dying unspeakably painful and shameful deaths - and their crosses may be understood symbolically as the crosses of all humanity. As such they explain graphically why Jesus had to die.

The cross was not introduced by the Christian religion to cast a dark shadow over the human situation and to plunge men and women into existential gloom and despair. Rather, the cross had always been present in the world, displaying its tortured shape in the manifold and varied tragedies which have beset human beings from the beginning, in every nation, clime and era. According to the biblical understanding, there is one overriding cause for this calamitous state of affairs - the whole complex situation of sin, guilt and shame in which all human beings are enmeshed. It is these intermingling factors denoted by the term "The Fall" which have created all the calvaries of history and brought untold suffering to millions, these inescapable realities which have caused this beautiful world to so often appear as a Golgotha. This was the world into which Christ came, the world He was sent to save.

The cross in the middle of the tableau, that of Jesus, appears just the same as the others except for the strange superscription - yet Christian artists have invariably portrayed that cross as lifted above the others – the focal point of a chaotic world. The cross of Christ is regarded by His followers as the central fact in the history of our race, and one which casts a whole new light on the other crosses. For burning in the heart of the One who hung on it and embraced the terrible ordeal, the climax of failure and tragedy, was the eternal love of God which caused Him to undertake the task of bearing the sin of the world. It was for this reason that when the Apostle Paul preached the gospel to the Corinthians, as he wrote:

"I determined not to know anything among you, save Jesus Christ, and Him crucified," (1 Corinthians 2:2).

Paul's statement is arresting and dramatic: that he, the brilliant and learned Jewish rabbi, was fixed in his resolve to *know nothing* apart from the crucified Jesus. It is true that, for him, Christ's atonement was the central sun and radiant pivot of Christian doctrine, without which the new faith would cease to exist - but there was more to it than that. Paul was asserting that all the treasures of wisdom and spiritual understanding which could be sought for and obtained were summed up in this one fact - *Jesus, and Him crucified.* Here was the Alpha and Omega of human knowledge, in which all other understandings were comprehended, here the lofty summit to which all learning led; and therefore to fix the gaze on Jesus and His cross was the all-surpassing way to the acquisition of spiritual truth. Yet Paul was also aware that in the figure of the crucified Savior there was nothing to attract the natural man, no beauty that He should be desired, but rather that the spectacle of such suffering would cause others to draw back. Accordingly, he added a corollary to his statement:

"Eye has not seen nor ear heard, neither has entered into the heart of man the things that God has prepared for those who love him" (1 Corinthians 2:9)

The Apostle was enumerating three different sources of human knowledge: the eye which can behold the created world, the ear which may hear theories propounding the meaning of existence, and the heart which seeks an even higher knowledge, one which appeals to the human imagination and is nourished on art and poetry. Nevertheless, he avers, all of these are insufficient to the attainment of the true knowledge of which he is speaking: Jesus Christ and Him crucified. The things that God has prepared for those who love Him cannot be comprehended through the power of natural reason; it is only when the Spirit of God opens human eyes and hearts that they may behold the power and wisdom of this crucified Lord and the glory inherent in the cross, its necessity and its benefits.

The first understanding which the Spirit must bring to an individual - Jew or Gentile - is the fact of the lost, guilty and helpless condition of humanity - a situation which no striving after holiness, no mere human endeavor, could rectify. The world in its wisdom had offered various means of blotting out the stains of sin, but none of these could raise the individual to a state of perfect righteousness. The classical world promulgated the idea of the true, the good and the beautiful as a lodestar, but these abstract concepts, although sublime, lacked power in themselves to render a transformation within the psyche. The Old Testament provided a pure and holy law which was God-given, but also proved unable to bring unshakeable peace to the heart and overflowing life to the soul. The ultimate purpose of the laws and institutions of Israel was to reveal that true life could only be given from the source of life, the living God, and through the coming of a personal Messiah. Therefore Paul preached, not the crucifixion, not the cross, but *Jesus crucified*, a living Savior.

This, then, was the great mystery that Paul expounded, that God Himself had come down to earth and become manifest in the flesh, that the Everlasting Lord has joined Himself irrevocably to the finite existence of the human being and for this purpose above all: that the Incarnation should led to the Crucifixion. In the life of Jesus there was a continuous revelation of divine love and holiness and yet throughout the whole course of His ministry He was continually looking ahead to see the cross which lay in His pathway, testifying of the great purpose of His mission and the necessity for His sacrifice. For Him, this was the great and overriding theme of the whole of the Old Testament prophecy: that the Servant of the Lord should be led as a lamb to the slaughter and give His life as a ransom for many.

And so it came to pass that the One who was perfectly holy and righteous entered into the darkness of human pain, shame, suffering and death. There upon the cross God gave His only Son for the life of the world; there Jesus bore the weight of human transgression and paid the whole of the just penalty required, there with unshakeable strength of purpose He suffered all the waves and billows of God's wrath to go over Him. Even in that terrible moment of abandonment when the Father turned

His face away from the Son, He affirmed His commitment to the task He had undertaken, completed to the utmost His mission to rescue and save those He loved as His own. It was on Calvary that Jesus' meekness, obedience and sacrifice shone forth most gloriously, at Golgotha that the infinite extent of the mercy and grace of God was set forth in the most illustrious light, so that our sin became the occasion for the greatest revelation of God's true nature - that He is *love*.

On the cross of Christ human transgression was not merely atoned for but was destroyed; it was there that the record of our sin, the handwriting of ordinances against us, was blotted out completely. Yet the benefits of Jesus' atoning death extend even further than the expiation of sin, as the radiance of the noonday sun outstrips the glimmering stars of night. In the crucified Savior, God the Father sees us perfectly acquitted and justified, but also regards us as dressed in Christ's own righteousness and clothed in His perfect purity, a state far exceeding the innocence possessed by Adam before the Fall. Through Jesus' death on Calvary all obstacles which separate sinners from divine favor have also been removed, and it is the Exalted Lord who is now at the right hand of God who Himself dispenses the blessings which He purchased for us through His Passion. It is not the cross to which we look for these heavenly gifts, but to Jesus our merciful High Priest, and from His hand receive all things that pertain to life and godliness.

As we survey "the wondrous cross" thought staggers. We may behold in the redemption Jesus won for us there both the magnitude of our fall, which required so inconceivably grand a remedy, and the greatness of the height to which we have been raised by the love of God. In this beholding, we understand that the cross stretches from the lowest depth - the abyss of human guilt and misery - and reaches into the highest heaven, where abundant measures of grace and glory have been bestowed upon us. These are mysteries which could never have been discovered by human intellect, for the hidden wisdom revealed in the cross transcends all thought and imagination. It is the Spirit alone who fathoms the "deep things" of God and can make known the fullness of love which proceeds toward us out of the divine heart - this love which is infinitely out of proportion to the objects of its affection, and seeks not merely to deliver them but to bring them into everlasting union with itself.

It is the Holy Spirit who also draws us continually back to gaze upon the cross of Christ, the radiant center of God's universe of love. It is there that the Spirit sheds abroad this same love in our hearts and fills us with overflowing gratitude and joy; it is there that Jesus, who commanded us to "love one another as I have loved you", provides the power of His resurrection. And just as the High Priest in Israel bore the twelve jewels representing the tribes upon his breastplate, shining with light and beauty, so those He has redeemed will forever sparkle like gems upon the breastplate of Jesus.

NOTES

In the short notes that follow I have endeavored to identify the sources and quotations I have used in composing the articles that have appeared in this book, as well as acknowledge the writers and thinkers who have provided particular inspiration. Any errors which have appeared in the previous text are, of course, all mine.

PREFACE

I have also, throughout this text, attributed the biblical books including the Gospels to their traditional authors, and made the dictum of German theologian Jurgen Moltmann my own: "It is an inadmissible assumption that on the basis of its experience with the risen and present Christ the Christian community projected anything into the history of Jesus which was inconsistent with the remembrance of him as he was during his lifetime" (from *The Way of Jesus Christ*, 1990).

The folk song "Jerusalem of Gold" (*Yerushalayim Shel Zahav*), which describes the 2000-year longing of the Jews to return to their land and city, was completed by Naomi Shemer after the reunification of Jerusalem which followed the Six Day War in 1967.

THE SONG OF THE EXILES

In this introductory article, I have sought to weave the exegesis of Psalm 137 into a short overview of the history of Israel, its land and its people. In the following articles I attempt to present perspectives on the biblical narratives which come from both Israel and the church.

THE KING COMES TO HIS CITY

In this article, as in many, I have drawn upon the rich theological insights offered by Alexander MacLaren in his series of sermons covering all the books of the Bible, entitled *Expositions of Holy Scripture*, and first published in England in 1904. Called the "prince of expositors," MacLaren became a renowned preacher during his fifty-plus years of ministry through the second half of the 19th and the early 20th centuries.

THE RUNNERS TO THE KING

The Christian pilgrimage itself is also often likened to running a marathon - the writer to the Hebrews exhorted his readers to run with patience the race set before them (Hebrews 12:1). The life-and-death nature of this venture is vividly illustrated in the words of Roger Bannister, the first four-minute miler:

"Every morning in Africa, a gazelle wakes up. It knows it must outrun the fastest lion or it will be killed. Every morning in Africa, a lion wakes up. It knows it must run faster than the slowest gazelle, or it will starve. It doesn't matter whether you're a lion or a gazelle--when the sun comes up, you'd better be running."

THE RUNNERS TO THE TOMB

The objections made to the authenticity of the Garden Tomb as the site of the death and burial of Christ usually focus on archaeological data which suggests the tomb is typical of those constructed in 8th-7th centuries BC, and thus is far too early to fit in with the Gospel accounts. However, even if the Garden Tomb features an unusual design for a first-century tomb, this may be explained by the fact that the wealthy Joseph of Arimathea had this unique design constructed in a style which reflected that of earlier tombs nearby.

PHARAOH'S HARD HEART AND THE MYSTERY OF FREE WILL

I was originally inspired to write this article by the wonderful online teachings of Rabbi David Fohrman from the Aleph Beta Academy and in particular his video entitled "Va'era: Did God Take Away Pharaoh's Free Will?" Fohrman's brilliant insights into the Hebrew text are presented in an engaging, witty and accessible manner.

The 20 scriptures which describe the hardness of Pharaoh's heart (and in some cases the Egyptians') are found in : Exodus 4:21; 7:13; 7:14; 7:22; 8:15; 8:19; 8:32; 9:2; 9:7; 9:12; 9:34; 9:35; 10:1; 10:20; 10:27; 11:10; 12:33; 14:4; 14:8; 14:17. Beside the Hebrew terms *kavod* and *hazak* there is another verb used to describe this effect in Exodus 7:3: *qashah*, signifying "to be hard, fierce or severe". The plagues on Egypt described as "heavy" are those of insects, pestilence, hail and locusts.

A further comment on the "impossible commingling of divine powers" which takes place in the seventh plague: the medieval commentator Rashi remarks (on Genesis 1:8) that the Hebrew word for heaven, *shamayim*, comes from the Hebrew words *esh* (fire) and *mayim* (water), as the two came together in harmony to make up the heavens. This is referenced in the daily Jewish prayer service: *"May He Who makes peace in His heights (between fire and water) make peace upon us and upon all Israel."*

Pharaoh's story sheds light also on the nature of the freewill we have been granted as part of our human estate, and the wonder of our choosing to be able to love. English writer C.S. Lewis explains the theological importance of the concept in the following way: *"God created things which had free will ...Because free will, though it makes evil possible, is also the only thing that makes possible any love or goodness or joy worth having. A world of automata - of creatures that worked like machines - would hardly be worth creating. The happiness which God designs for His higher creatures is the happiness of being freely, voluntarily united to Him and to each other in an ecstasy of love and delight .."* The Case for Christianity, originally published 1943.

THE PSALM OF THE SHOAH

The opening quotation in this chapter appeared in an article in the *Jerusalem Post* of April 2013 called "Needed, Israeli Dialogue of Mutual Gratitude" by Yossi Klein Halevi, who is a senior fellow at the Shalom Hartman Institute in Jerusalem and a noted author. The Christian visitor to Yad Vashem was the Episcopalian priest Malcolm Boyd, who wrote a 1975 article entitled "The Crucifixion and the Holocaust", subsequently quoted in *Faith and Fulfilment: Christians and the Return to the Promised Land* by Michael J. Pragai, 1985, Vallentine, Mitchell & Co, London, p 247. The further reflections on the church and the Holocaust have been influenced by Michel Renaud's book *Israel, Servant of God*, 2003, T & T Clark, London.

THE PSALM OF THE LORD'S APPEARING

Judah HaLevi's poems appear in numerous anthologies including the *Penguin Book of Hebrew Verse*, edited by T. Carmi, 1981.

The Branch of Jesse

A further more lengthy discussion of Jesus' Messianic role as the "Branch" may be discovered in David Baron's *Rays of Messiah's Glory: Christ in the Old Testament*, originally published in 1886. Baron was a Jewish convert to Christianity who subsequently devoted himself to explaining the Christian faith to the Jewish people, as well as helping Christians understand prophecy and the future restoration of Israel. The famous description of Nazareth as "a handful of pearls in a goblet of emerald" comes originally from *Philochristus: Memoirs Of A Disciple Of The Lord* (1878) by Edwin Abbott.

The Intertwined Miracles

The quotation in the first paragraph concerning the roads of Galilee is taken from George Adam Smith's *The Historical Geography of the Holy Land*, 1894, Fontana Library Edition, Ariel Publishing House, Jerusalem, p 280.

The famous 19th century preacher Charles Haddon Spurgeon sees a devotional significance in the intertwined miracles: "Our Lord worked this miracle while moving on to work another—like the sun, He shines while He pursues His course and every beam is full of grace. Not only what He does with full purpose is glorious, but He is so full of power and grace that even what He does *incidentally* by the way is marvelous!" (from a sermon entitled "The Touch", delivered in 1877).

Many commentators also see a significance in the fact that the woman with the issue of blood probably touched one of the tassels - *tzitziyoth* - of Jesus' prayer shawl, His *tallith*. According to Numbers 15:37-39 every Hebrew male was bound by the Law to make four tassels on the corners of his garment and to put in them a blue thread, to designate his identity as one of the elected people of God. Further reflections in this chapter concerning the intertwined history of Israel and the church were enriched by Adolph Saphir's *Christ and the Church: Thoughts on the Apostolic Commission (Matthew Xxviii. 18-20)*, originally published 1874, Keren Ahvah Meshihit, Jerusalem, 2001.

Universal Dominion and a Universal Task

Saphir's description of the Risen Christ and His commission to the disciples which appeared in *Christ and the Church* also provided invaluable inspiration for this chapter.

Girded with Divine Strength

My understanding of the metamorphosis which took place in Peter's soul, as described in this article, was contributed to greatly by the sermons on John 21 which appeared in the massive 19th century *Pulpit Commentary*, created under the direction of Rev. Joseph S. Exell and Henry Donald Maurice Spence-Jones. G. Campbell Morgan's articles on the Epistles of Peter, which appeared in *Living Messages of the Bible* (1912), also provided much insight.

Fire in the Heart

For the theological insights concerning the transformative power of fire which appear in this chapter I am indebted to Aviva Gottlieb Zornberg's profound commentary on Exodus, *The Particulars of Rapture*, Schocken Press, 2001. Ms Zornberg lives in Jerusalem, and her fascinating commentaries on the biblical texts combine classical Jewish interpretations and Midrashic sources with a range of ideas from literature, philosophy and psychology.

The Upper Room and The Ultimate Petition

The article by Isaac Gottlieb of Israel's Bar Ilan University entitled "Law, Love and Redemption in Exodus: Legal Connotations in the Language of Exodus 6:6-8" which appeared in a 1998 Journal of the Near Eastern Society provided the valuable understanding expressed in this chapter concerning the fourth promise of the "Four Redemptions". Gottlieb suggested that the construction of the verb used in this promise, the Hebrew verb *laqah* meaning "to take", denotes a marriage relationship. This insight is foundational to the argument I have developed in this chapter.

THE WAY OF THE MESSIAH

Where did the events of Acts 2 take place? Luke tells us in Acts 1:13 that after the Ascension the disciples were staying in an upper room – "*hyperion*". This is a word which differs from that which he used to describe the Room of the Last Supper, which was *anagaion* (Luke 22:12). In his Latin translation of the New Testament, the Vulgate, Jerome rendered both these Greek words by the single Latin word *coenaculum*, meaning "dining room" (customarily located on a second floor), subsequently rendered in English as "cenacle", and Christian tradition has considered ever since that these two places were one and the same. However, when the events of the Day of Pentecost occurred (Acts 2), Luke tells us simply that the 120 disciples were "together in one place" when the sound of the rushing mighty wind came from heaven and "filled the whole house where they were sitting." It could hardly be that 120 persons, especially if they were seated, could fit into an upper chamber of a residential building, no matter how spacious. It seems more probable that Luke's language reflects a manner of speaking within Judaism about the Temple of Jerusalem as the "House of the Lord", both in the Old Testament, and in Jewish prayer books down to the present day.

We read also that after Jesus' Ascension the disciples were continually in the Temple praising and blessing God, for the House of God with its vast corridors or "porches" was the regular gathering place of all the various parties and sects of the Jews. The Temple Court, a single structure about a quarter of a mile in circumference, was a massive complex with hundreds of rooms, while the Royal Stoa, the colonnade at the southern wall, was also a possible meeting place; in either location the apostles would have been immediately accessible to thousands of Jews and proselytes gathered for the festival. It seems certain, therefore, that the events of Acts 2 took place on the Temple Mount; it was here that Jews and proselytes alike would have heard the sound of the mighty rushing wind, have been drawn together to ascertain its source, and heard with wonder the Galileans speaking in their own tongues. It appears especially fitting that the proclamation of the Good News of the salvation through Israel's Messiah should go forth from the Temple, and that the beginning of the building of the *spiritual* House should have been on the site of the *physical* House.

THE TEACHER COME FROM GOD

Many of the thoughts in this chapter were inspired by Alfred Edersheim's classic and monumental text, *The Life and Times of Jesus the Messiah* (1990), Hendrickson

Publishing, (originally published 1883) which provides a perennial fountain of wisdom and insight into the Gospels. From his commentary on the story in John 3:

"And here lies the true interpretation of what Jesus taught: if the uplifted serpent, as symbol, brought life to the believing look which was fixed upon the giving, pardoning love of God, then so, in the truest sense, shall the uplifted Son of Man give true life to everyone that believes, looking up in Him to the giving and forgiving love of God, which His Son came to bring, to declare, and to manifest ... this final and highest teaching contains all that Nicodemus, or, indeed, the whole church, could require or be able to know" (p 763).

It is possible also that, during the final week of Jesus' ministry on earth, Nicodemus again played a major role in the Gospel story. A very good case is to be made for the Pharisee as the mysterious owner of the Upper Room in which the Last Supper was held. According to rabbinic literature, Nicodemus was one of the three wealthiest people in Jerusalem and was exceedingly generous, and the Talmud also referred to him as one who supplied water for the feasts in the city. If indeed he was providing the guest chamber for the use of Jesus and His disciples for their Passover meal, what more natural a pre-arranged sign than "a man carrying a pitcher of water" (Luke 22:10), who should lead the way to a house containing a large furnished upper room – and that there should be plentiful water available for Jesus' washing of the disciples' feet?

COMFORT IN DIRE STRAITS

Some of the well known disasters which befell the Jewish people on the 9th Av are as follows:

- *The first Crusade was declared in 1095*
- *King Edward I expelled all Jews from England in 1290*
- *All the Jews in Spain were expelled in 1492*
- *Pope Paul IV moved all the Jews in Rome into the first ghetto in 1555*
- *World War I began in 1914*
- *The Nazis made the decision on this day in 1942 to implement "the Final Solution", and destroy the Jews of Europe*
- *The latest event on this day was the expulsion of all Jews from Gaza in 2005 (technically postponed by Prime Minister Ariel Sharon until the day after 9th Av to avoid the comparison)*

THE WEEPING PROPHET

Josephus' description of the destruction of Jerusalem by the Roman legions under Titus appears in *The Jewish War,* first published in 75 AD. Josephus was the Jewish-Roman scholar and historian whose works have contributed so much to our understanding of first century Judaism and the background of early Christianity. The quotation given in this chapter continues as follows:

There was the war cry of the Roman legions as they converged; the yells of the partisans encircled with fire and sword, the panic flight of the people cut off above into the arms of the enemy, and their shrieks as the end approached. The cries from the hill were answered from the crowded streets, and now many who were wasted with hunger and beyond speech found strength to moan and wail when the saw the Sanctuary in flames. Back from Perea and the mountains round about came the echo in a thunderous bass. Yet more terrible than the din were the sights that met the eye. The Temple Hill, enveloped in flames from top to bottom, appeared to be boiling up from its very roots; yet the sea of flame was nothing to the ocean of blood, or the companies of killers to the armies of killed; nowhere could the ground be seen between the corpses and the soldiers climbed over heaps of bodies as they chased the fugitives.

Flavius Josephus, *The Works: Comprising the Antiquities of the Jews, A History of the Jewish Wars, and Life of Flavius Josephus,* 2015, Scholars Choice, p 283.

GLORY ON THE MOUNTAIN TOP

Another notable personage buried in the Church of Mary Magdalene is also a member of the British royal household: Princess Alice, mother of Prince Philip the Duke of Edinburgh, mother-in-law of Queen Elizabeth of England, and a fascinating character in her own right.

In icons, to show the gradation of spiritual receptivity on the part of the disciples, James is usually portrayed thrown backwards to the ground, with his hand covering his face; John is also on the ground, face down, covering the lower part of his face; and Peter, on his knees, is looking towards Christ but shielding his eyes.

The Theme of Exodus

The church fathers mentioned in this chapter are Gregory Nazianzus, c. 329 - 390 AD, who was a 4th century Bishop of Constantinople; his famous quotation comes from his Epistle 101. Athanasius, c. 296-8 - 373, was Patriarch of Alexandria, and the statement of Christ as the legitimate Monarch conquering death comes from *On the Incarnation of the Word*. The thematic connections between the Gospel of Luke and the Book of Acts, as suggested in the usage of the word "exodus", are finely drawn out by Robert C. Tannehill, in *The Narrative Unity of Luke-Acts, A Literary Interpretation*, Fortress Press, Philadelphia, first published 1986.

The Secret of Power

The thesis of this chapter is that the two Gospel scenes which take place at the top of the mountain and its foot - the Transfiguration and the Healing of the Demoniac Boy - should be interpreted together. This same understanding is encapsulated in one of Raphael's paintings, described by sixteenth century biographer Giorgio Vasari as his "most beautiful and divine work". The last masterpiece by this great Renaissance artist was his painting of the Transfiguration, which he was still working on when he died in 1520. Unusually, in this altarpiece, Raphael has departed from the traditional depiction of the Transfiguration in Christian art, for he combines both the image of the glorified Jesus, which dominates the upper half of the piece, with the heartbreaking scene surrounding the demon-possessed boy which appears in the lower half.

Augustine's comment on the "emptying" of Jesus is taken from Chapter 2 of *Sermons On Selected Lessons Of The New Testament,* while the verse at the end of the chapter is taken from the hymn "Stricken, Smitten, and Afflicted" by Thomas Kelly, 1769-1854.

The Way to Soul Satisfaction

The quote from the 1st century BC Roman orator and philosopher Cicero is taken from *De finibus bonorum et malorum* ("On the ends of good and evil").

WINGS ABOVE ISRAEL

Birds are *"extraordinarily vital scraps of feathered energy ..."* The quotation is taken from Alice Parmelee's *All the Birds of the Bible: Their Stories, Identification and Meaning* (1959), Keats Publishing, a charming and informative book which suggested many of the thoughts expressed in this chapter.

FLEETING LIFE, ETERNAL SIGNIFICANCE

The original inspiration for this chapter came from an insightful article written by Ethan Dor-Shav called "Ecclesiastes: Fleeting and Timeless". This appeared in a 2004 issue of *Azure: Ideas for the Jewish Nation*, a quarterly journal published by Shalem Press from 1996 to 2012. Whereas Mr Dor-Shav has focused on the importance of gaining wisdom in our fleeting life I have chosen to focus on the question of attaining significance.

The reflections from Viktor Frankl are taken from *Man's Search for Meaning*, Beacon Press, Boston, Massachussetts, 1959, pp 48, 136, published online. The quotation which appears in the final paragraphs - "the essential transiency of everything which is antagonism to the will of God, and the essential eternity of everything which is in conformity with that will" - comes from Alexander MacLaren's fine commentary on Ecclesiastes.

WHAT DID JESUS WRITE?

I have not entered into the vexed question of whether John actually wrote this short story of the Woman Taken in Adultery or if it was inserted later. The story's omission from the earliest Greek manuscripts may have been due to fear on the part of the early church fathers that the story could encourage sinfulness; my own feeling is that the exceptional narrative bears the ring of authenticity.

THE BEAUTIFUL SHEPHERD

George Adam Smith's quotation is taken from: *The Historical Geography of the Holy Land*, 1894, Fontana Library Edition, Ariel Publishing House, Jerusalem, p 210.

The final words are taken from Bishop Lancelot Andrewes' "Sermon of the Nativity", preached on Christmas Day 1618 before King James at Whitehall, which may be found in *Lancelot Andrewes Works, Sermons, Volume One* in the Library of Anglo-Catholic Theology of Project Canterbury.

Printed in the United States
By Bookmasters